THE STRANGE HISTORY OF
BUCKINGHAM
PALACE

PATRICIA WRIGHT

The History Press

First published in the United Kingdom in 1996 by Sutton Publishing Ltd.
This paperback edition first published in 2008 by
The History Press Ltd
Cirencester Road, Chalford,
Stroud, Gloucestershire, GL6 8PE
www.thehistorypress.co.uk

British Library Cataloguing in Publication Data.
A catalogue record for this book is available from the British Library.

ISBN 978 0 7509 4803 6

Typesetting and origination by The History Press Ltd.
Printed in Great Britain

Contents

List of Colour Plates

PROLOGUE

1838

Everyone said they had never seen London so crowded. On the day before Queen Victoria's coronation it was not just a case of a mob here or there, but a mob seething everywhere; jostling, staring, marvelling aloud at everything and nothing. Flags flew from makeshift poles on roofs, out of windows and above a vast encampment of tents in Hyde Park, where a firework display was planned for the following night, followed by a grand fair. The fashionable world, while just as excited as everyone else and determined not miss a single opportunity for showing off its jewels and robes of state, pretended that so much uproar was uncommonly tiresome, but the queen was not so hypocritical.

Nineteen-year-old Victoria was enjoying every moment of this most glittering of seasons. She had already attended three State balls, two levées, a drawing-room and a State concert, and only regretted that she had not been able to waltz, since there was no one whose arm was considered fit to encircle the royal waist. This in spite of guest lists being ruthlessly scoured for any scent of trade, which, among others, led to the Rothschilds being excluded. Now the time for her coronation had come.

Next day, Victoria woke early, when guns in the park fired salutes at four o'clock in the morning. Unable to get to sleep again for the bustle and blare of soldiers and military bands marching past, she was soon peeping at the crowds from behind her bedroom curtains.[1] No previous sovereign had ever looked out on this scene. In 1838 Buckingham Palace was new, the landscaping in St James's Park was new, the ceremonial arch outside the palace was new. Only at the last moment had someone thought to try whether the State coach would fit through its centre span, only to discover that it stuck ignominiously. There had not been time to demolish the offending object out of sight, although a pitch would eventually be found for it at the end of Oxford Street, where, with its name changed to Marble Arch, it continued its career of impeding the traffic for no particular reason; a monument to the fact that even eminent architects make silly mistakes.

The coronation route was also new, a roundabout way decided on by the cabinet in the hope that it would be to their political advantage if the young queen was seen by as many of her subjects as possible. Perhaps no institution is quite so finely tuned to public sentiment as an unpopular government, and Lord Melbourne's administration had seized gratefully on the chance to gain badly needed credit from a great national occasion. Generous sums were voted to make this coronation unusually splendid, squabbles over the scandalously insanitary condition of the queen's recently completed palace forgotten, and matched cream horses solicited as a gift from Hanover to draw her gold State coach, since Lord Melbourne declared that anything less would look like rats in harness.[2]

But contradictions still abounded and the day started badly for the aristocracy, who rose before dawn to dress in antique finery only to find Westminster Abbey still locked and dark. A growing throng of irascible nobility shivered in a drizzling wind for nearly an hour before the keys were found. A good few hip-flasks were probably swigged to keep out the cold and a picnic atmosphere soon developed inside the abbey, from which the decorum of the day never quite recovered. These were people whom inter-marriage had interlocked for generations and to them, coronations were tribal occasions.

Those who had endured the earlier rigours of the day made their own entertainment out of the later, official arrivals; clapping and shouting if a country or its representative was popular, preserving a daunting silence if not. When Prince Esterhazy appeared he was dressed in such oriental splendour he was said to look as if he had been caught in a shower of diamonds, while old Marshal Soult, special envoy from France and veteran of Napoleon's wars, was overcome by the cheers which followed him down the aisle, and burst into tears.

Queen Victoria leaving the palace for her coronation, but behind all the splendour the building was a domestic disaster. (Hulton-Deutsch Picture Library)

Life around the Court became much more ceremonial during Victoria's reign, and the surroundings of Buckingham Palace were improved to provide a backdrop to her empire. (Illustrated London News, 1856)

As the morning wore on, wind and rain gave way to bright sunshine. 'Queen's weather' these lucky changes would come to be called, because Victoria so often enjoyed them in the future, and the onlookers thronging the processional route revelled in it. 'The crowds of people exceeded anything I have ever seen,' Victoria wrote afterwards. 'Their good humour and loyalty was beyond everything, and I really cannot say <u>how</u> proud I am to be Queen of <u>such a nation</u>.'[3]

She was as gay as a lark, one observer commented, laughing like a girl on her birthday as she drove past him. Some of her entourage felt that a properly bred queen should not enjoy herself quite so obviously on a day of sacramental significance, and there were other ruffled sensibilities too. The Duke of Albemarle, for instance, had claimed the right as Master of the Horse to sit beside her on that triumphal drive, and was still smarting from a crushing snub administered by the Duke of Wellington. He had roundly told Albemarle to do as he was told, since the queen could if she pleased make him run behind her coach like a tinker's dog.[4] This, for a constitutional monarch, was certainly untrue and not language a fellow duke readily accepted.

But however sulky Albemarle felt, the crowds remained good-natured, enthusiastic and orderly, though it was less than five years since the previous king, William IV, had leaned out of his carriage to spit at a crowd which failed to cheer him. Victoria's youth and her feminity were both the cause of and served to underline this change in feeling. 'We have got a shabby kind of family to rule over us,' Boswell had once remarked about the Hanoverians,[5] and now quite visibly it was shabby no longer. Victoria on her coronation day was resplendent, joyful, girlishly innocent; a new age seemed to ride beside her in the golden coach.

Once she reached the abbey she became dignified and solemn, the scene sufficiently spectacular to make even a queen falter for a moment. The old grey building blazed with colour; from banners, clothes, and carpets. Stars glittered from precious plate on the altar and the copes worn by the bishops had been embroidered for the coronation of James I more than two hundred years before.

As she moved down the aisle, the sun struck through the windows high above Victoria's head to play with extraordinary effect on the quantities of jewellery worn by the packed congregation, splitting light into prisms and rainbows which broke like spray as the lines of people turned to bow and curtsy as she passed. The men wore more exotic colours than the women: scarlet, blue and gold for the military and crimson for the peers, while representatives from the Empire and the world appeared in every shade imaginable, studded by precious stones as large as eggs.

If the queen briefly trembled at such a sight, the effect she produced on a sceptical and hardened audience was astonishing. Her diminutive size and instinctive poise, when surrounded by such a vastness of worldly pomp, seemed to overwhelm them all. Attended by ten unmarried girls as train-bearers, she seemed to float down the aisle towards the altar in an ethereal, shining cloud. 'Everyone gasped for breath,' wrote one onlooker.[6] 'The rails of the gallery where I sat trembled from the grasp of a hundred trembling hands. I never saw anything like it. Tears would have been a relief.'

Only the passion aroused by the coronation of Charles II, when a congregation in this same abbey had celebrated the restored mystery of monarchy itself, may have exceeded it in intensity. Yet no one could subsequently describe exactly what it was they had felt. Not patriotism exactly, nor spiritual dedication; not poignant sorrow at the sight of a young girl faced by a crushing burden, nor awe for an ancient office. A mixture of all these and more besides; pure emotion, unforgettable in its impact.

Such intensity lasted only a few moments. Almost at once the queen needed to mind her feet, in danger of tripping as her unpractised trainbearers tangled her robe with theirs, while young Mr Disraeli unkindly noted that Lord Melbourne, prime minister and leader of the party Disraeli intended one day to oust from power, looked very uncouth with his coronet tipped over his nose and wrestling with the sword of state like a butcher wielding a cleaver.

So far as Melbourne was concerned, he found the sword so heavy he hardly knew how to keep hold of it, but apart from this the service remained for him a highly emotional drama. He had plunged into a relationship with the queen which alarmed and amused all social London, offering a hatful of opportunities for malice: part fatherly, partly the infatuation of an elderly roué grasping at a last chance to charm youth, and partly born of the very real need to educate a naive girl in the realities of power. Cynical and disillusioned old Whig that he was, Melbourne would struggle against tears for most of the five-hour service.

A new State Ballroom was added in the 1850s, and the kitchens were at last moved on to the ground floor from the basement, although working conditions for staff remained very bleak. (Illustrated London News, 1856)

Unfortunately, neither he nor anyone else had thought that a rehearsal of the highly complex ceremony might be desirable, and the clergy soon plunged into disarray. The Bishop of Durham thrust the orb at the queen at quite the wrong moment before disappearing entirely at a time when his presence was urgently required; the Archbishop of Canterbury became so confused that the queen could distinctly be heard asking what she should do next as none of the bishops knew, and when he brought forward the Ring of State, crushed it on the wrong finger despite her protests, making her nearly scream with pain.

The enthronement and homage followed, these most solemn moments spoiled by an undignified scramble in the congregation to snatch one of the commemorative medals thrown among them by the Lord Chamberlain. Even the queen's maids of honour abandoned their posts by her side to rush down into the nave. After the service Melbourne asked the queen whether it was true that her trainbearers had chattered throughout the ceremony, and if so did she hear them? With grim brevity Victoria inscribed her reply in her journal, 'I said they did, & I heard them'.[7]

She was even more distracted by the applause which again broke out as the peers came forward to offer their individual homage, and could not help noting who obtained enthusiastic claps and who did not. The greatest sensation was provided by Lord Rolle, who fell down the steps and whose efforts to recover were accompanied by the kind of encouragement more commonly reserved for the hunting field. Victoria gracefully resolved that particular difficulty by descending the steps to meet him herself, a gesture which again touched most people's sensibility, though one bitchy lady remarked that if *she* had helped an old man no one would think twice about it.

When the service resumed, the clergy, who might profitably have used the time to study the next section in their prayer books, were even more at a loss than before and the Bishop of Bath and Wells abruptly brought the proceedings to a close. The queen retired to Edward the Confessor's chapel, and in consternation the sub-dean went to enquire if her majesty was ill only to be told that everything was over. He remained convinced that it was not, and after a pause established that Bath and Wells had turned over two pages by mistake. Characteristically, Lord Melbourne considered that this did not matter;[8] he was worn out from carrying the Sword of State around and badly needed some of the refreshment laid out in the chapel. But the sub-dean was adamant: the service must be finished. So the queen returned and the ceremony proceeded to its finale; the choir sang the Hallelujah Chorus and she was able to withdraw again to the chapel. 'Although anything more unlike a chapel you never saw,' Melbourne remarked, in approbation rather than any spirit of criticism. 'The altar was quite covered with sandwiches and bottles of wine.'[9]

A considerable delay followed while the queen's hand was soaked in ice-water before the Ring of State could be pulled off, during which time those around her ate and drank heartily, although glasses appear to have been somewhat lacking. One peer was observed drinking champagne out of a pewter flowerpot.

About 4.30 p.m. the queen re-entered the State coach, holding the orb and sceptre and wearing the lighter-weight crown especially made for her. This included among its jewels the ruby worn by Henry V at Agincourt, a sapphire taken by James II when he fled to France but subsequently and acrimoniously repurchased by the British government, and another said to have been taken from the finger of Edward the Confessor when he was exhumed from his tomb in this same abbey some seven hundred years before. Since the exhumation was intended to prove that his flesh remained uncorrupted, a recognized first step to sainthood, the chroniclers are vague over the result of their diggings, but there was Edward's purported sapphire in Victoria's crown all those centuries later.

The queen took another hour and half to drive back to Buckingham Palace, while the bells of London pealed and guns fired. The crowds were even denser and more enthusiastic than before, the queen's response a flawless blend of dignity and warmth. Only an unrepentant radical like Harriet Martineau stood out against the tide of feeling, complaining that the coronation service had confused royalty with the Almighty, and attempted to endow a mere queen with divinity. The whole thing made her feel tired.[10]

Eventually the crowds dispersed, many of them to enjoy the firework display in Hyde Park, which was so spectacular that one small child later likened it to the destruction of Sodom and Gomorrah. The queen decided to give her dog a bath before watching such fireworks as she might see from her window; a guard came to lock the crown safely away, and Lord Melbourne took too large a dose of laudanum to help him through the State banquet shortly to follow, which violently disagreed with him. As for Buckingham Palace, that new centrepiece for royal pageantry, it soon settled back into slovenly discomfort.

Nevertheless, 28 June 1838 remained a day people remembered. Perhaps with that same nameless tingle of emotion, or nostalgic regret because the sunlit promise of a new age remained for so many a nightmare of squalor and despair. Perhaps with laughter, recalling absurdities, or anger because privilege, precedent and fantasy remained entrenched at the core of the nation at a time when confident innovation swept aside so much that people had previously taken for granted, good and bad together.

But in a strange way, many of the struggles and issues which would trouble Queen Victoria's subjects during her reign were already starkly mirrored within her own household of Buckingham Palace, where the chimneys were so badly designed that small girls – even frailer than the boys and better able to negotiate a lethally intricate labyrinth of flues – were said to be used to clean them.

This is the story of a site. A hexagonal stretch of swamp and forest which on the day of Victoria's coronation became the ceremonial heart of the largest empire the world had ever seen. Forty acres of prime development land which somehow had escaped London's sprawl and remained a single entity in private hands; only its most recent history was royal. A rural site protected by water, within strolling distance of the social, political and ecclesiastical centres of the nation, it is a site we think we know, but in reality do not know at all.

Its past owners and occupants are unexpected: soldiers in barracks, harlots in a garden, a witch in her hut, the many fraudsters who fought and schemed to build there.

This site shimmers with ghosts, and now nobody remembers them any more. Does it matter if they are forgotten? Probably not. But like Queen Victoria, in their time they too were often symbols, and reflected events with the same enjoyable twist of exaggeration which comes from living beside the axis of a nation. In this one central place they gather to form an image of all our pasts, sometimes starved or tragic, more often swaggering and deceitful, hilariously frivolous, light-hearted with love. Like dreams focused and refocused, those past scenes merge with the present and its ghosts exist again.

CHAPTER 1

A Frontier of Empire

The earliest glimpse of the palace site occurs in connection with the second Roman invasion of Britain, nearly two thousand years ago. In the first expedition Julius Caesar was forced to retreat after reaching the Thames, and once he had gone Britain was left to its own devices for nearly another hundred years. The palace land then was a secret place, caught between marsh and ancient forest, intersected by pools and springs and tiny trails. A single path emerged out of the trees, to curl through undergrowth until it reached a steep-sided stream at a point where its bank had been worn down to make the crossing easy. From there, a causeway probably led out across marshland, marked by driven poles because whenever the floods came it disappeared completely.[1] This causeway would have been a ramshackle affair, zig-zagging wherever gravel banks offered a foothold above the bog, and reached southwards to the Thames.

These long ages of isolation were abruptly shattered when, in AD 43, four Roman legions landed at Richborough in Kent, prepared for a full campaign. Their commander, Aulus Plautius, was tough. He was also angry. His men had mutinied rather than embark for Britain, a place, they said, renowned only for its evil; where magicians tore out the entrails of living men and drank their blood. To add to Plautius's humiliation, it had not been his threats which eventually forced the legionaries to march down to the boats, but the taunts of a Greek freedman called (of all things) Narcissus, a creature of the Emperor Claudius. And if Claudius was enough to turn any soldier's stomach, Narcissus was worse.

Now that his men had finally braved the passage and disembarked, Plautius was determined to drive them to success. Unfortunately, Claudius needed a glittering victory just as much as his general did, and had sent orders that once this was assured he personally would travel from Rome to lead his troops. It was up to Plautius to judge when this moment had arrived. If he followed his military instincts and routed the Britons as and when the chance arose, Claudius would revenge himself on a general who had stolen his glory; if he sent for the Emperor too early, a fool like Claudius was bound to foul up the whole campaign by taking command while there was real soldiering to be done.[2]

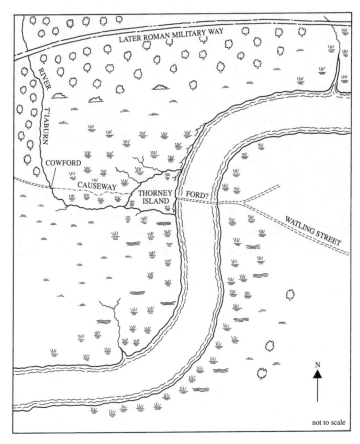

Sketch showing approximate topography around Thorney Island, later to become known as Westminster, first century AD.

When the legionaries eventually slithered off the North Downs and into the flood plain of the Thames, the river looked very different from today. Then it was neither embanked nor dredged, and spread over a much greater area; even in summer, marshland stretched widely on either side. A formidable barrier, where the Britons were certain to stand and fight. Aulus Plautius had collected all the intelligence he could about the Thames, the largest natural defence before he could march on the south-eastern tribal capital at Colchester, and he knew that a crossing place existed. A later Roman historian even mentioned a bridge, but no evidence has been found to support this and it is likely he misunderstood the evidence he handled.

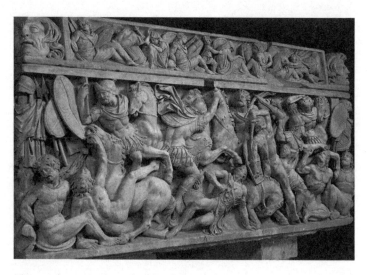

This scene from a sarcophagus shows how little mercy her enemies could initially expect from conquering Roman legions. (Mansell Collection)

Where was the ford that Plautius's men found? It used to be thought that the Romans crossed the Thames near where they would later build a bridge, at the north end of which Londinium, the City of London, grew. Modern archeology points to Westminster as the likelier site, where the pattern of early tracks suggests that a crossing predated the invasion. The earliest Roman roads, too, reinforce this evidence.

Probably somewhere in the region of the Elephant & Castle, Plautius's men squelched through pools making their preparations for assault, often glancing in fear or eagerness to where the enemy waited on the opposite bank. Among the legionaries were some Batavii from the Lower Rhine, a more hostile place than this; in their homeland, wetlands spread for hundreds of miles around what today is the centre of industrial Europe. Then, an infinity of fenland stretched from the Ruhr into modern Holland, and the native Batavii spent more of their lives on or under the water than they did on dry land.

These were the men Plautius sent forward under cover of darkness to find and measure and assess the ford he had to use, if he was to have any hope of clinching this campaign in a single season.

And while everyone else waited, even across such a width of water it was possible to see that the opposite bank was so cut up by rivulets that the ford emerged on to a triangular islet, perhaps half a mile wide and surrounded by swamp. Beyond that triangle, a single causeway wound away into the distance, the stakes marking its course just visible if gulls sat on top. On the Roman side, speculation must have centred on the advantages such a constricted battlefield offered, if only they could succeed in fighting their way ashore. The Britons were crammed together even before the battle started, shouting defiance and getting their chariots stuck on the boggy foreshore. They would not find it easy to launch their tactical speciality in such conditions: reckless charges which in the heat of action helped their warriors to disregard even mortal wounds. And if they were forced to retreat, that single exit offered the hope of turning victory into a slaughter which might destroy all further will to fight again.

The principal British chiefs were Caradoc and Togodumnus, and they led a mixed array of footmen and chariot-fighters. Their men were largely Celts who had absorbed an older culture still, and the Romans had learned to their cost elsewhere in Europe that Celts fought like rabid wolves. They loved to fight. If other enemies were lacking, they fought for the pleasure of it among themselves. While this may have honed their skills in battle, it also fuelled bitter hatreds between tribes, and the force the Romans faced was by no means disciplined or unified.

Nevertheless, they made a terrifying sight as the sunlight flashed on the gold ornaments their chieftains wore, on spears and the blades fixed to the wheels of their chariots. Defiant shouts and weird brayings floated across the water and all that restless, bold stir of colour left no doubt in anyone's mind that the British yearned to make the river run red with Roman blood.

The Celts were taller and fairer on average than the majority of men in the legions, and some warriors stiffened their hair into spikes with lime or dung to frighten their enemies more. They liked bright colours and display, but were said to strip naked for battle and paint themselves blue with magic able to turn the edge of a driven sword. Romans were superstitious at the best of times, and the mutiny before embarkation had a great deal to do with the soldiers' dread that Celts could control the supernatural.

In reality, most of the Britons awaiting battle on the far bank of Thames probably wore skin trousers, a tunic and cloak, often clasped with the curved brooches they were skilled in making. They looked forward to an exceptionally promising fight, but understood that they lacked the weaponry of the Romans. Body-armour was rare among them and their throwing spears and thin-bladed swords were unsuited to close combat with heavy infantry. To many, this genuinely may not have mattered much. They possessed significant advantage of position and fought for honour, lacking the concept of total conquest that the Romans cherished. Anything approaching national resistance would take time and other circumstances to develop.

As soon as the Batavii brought back the information Plautius needed, the battle began. There was no point in waiting, while his legionaries camped in such discomfort that each day a little of their courage leaked away. Besides, there remained the Emperor's order to send word for him to come and take command before the campaign ended. A pampered court might take weeks, if not months, to travel from Italy to Boulogne, and then on to Britain. There was even a rumour that Claudius intended to bring elephants with him, to terrify the Britons and act as a stage from which to acknowledge his triumph. Loading those on unseaworthy cross-channel barges in a gale did not bear thinking about, when a single drowned beast could cost Plautius his career.

The assault did not go well. Probably the Second Legion spearheaded it, a formation whose commander, Vespanianus (later the Emperor Vespasian), was known for his flair and steadiness in attack. Vespasian was the son of that first-century rarity, an honest tax collector. Much later, he was nearly executed for dozing off during one of Nero's stupefying bouts of self-glorification; contemporaries described him as deliberate, a good organizer, and, less flatteringly, looking as if he suffered from permanent constipation, with his face screwed up in folds.

Once he and his men started to cross the Thames, they confronted a nightmarish situation which gave all the advantages to the British. Plautius's staff must have found it extraordinarily difficult to keep the forward movement orderly; the troops would be tense, grumbling over inevitable snarl-ups as they shuffled slowly forward, held up by the narrowness of the ford. Centurions prowled up and down the lines, lashing out with their staffs if any man broke order, and water reached to their knees, lapped icily up their thighs, long before they reached the river proper. When they did, the legionaries slithered and slipped in the strengthening current and sometimes lost their footing, to bob screaming for a moment before they vanished, dragged down by their equipment.

As they reached closer to the northern bank, the unencumbered Britons darted in and out of the shallows, maiming, aiming slingshots and throwing spears, their chariots scything bloodily through the Roman ranks as these emerged in increasing disorganization on the foreshore. All the bellowings from centurions, the example of Vespasian and urgings from Aulus Plautius for the rest of his men to get across the river fast, were failing to stop escalating disaster from turning to bloody rout. Triumphant braying from the British horns, shouts of command, the desperate clash of metal on metal, the hiss of missiles, all began to betray an unmistakable whiff of panic.

In this extremity the Romans somehow held their nerve. Gradually small knots of men coalesced in the shallows, protecting their comrades as they waded to join them, stabbing the fearsome Roman short sword into their assailants' unprotected bodies. The auxiliary horse lost heavily in a British counter-attack, but perhaps distracted the Britons from the crucible of battle – the place where the ford reached dry land, which must be held at all costs. Because slowly, slowly, the Romans were fighting their way towards solid ground and even a handful of armoured men established there would make their weight and discipline tell. As rank after rank arrived and the legionaries began to widen and strengthen their line, the constricted battlefield became their ally, trapping the British against a delta of steep-sided streams, preventing their warriors from using agility to compensate for their lack of armour.

This nineteenth-century painting by Checa gives some idea of the terrifying impact of the barbarian war-bands which broke in successive waves over Roman Britain, and ultimately destroyed it. (Mansell Collection)

Then from among the British a cry went up that their chief, Togodumnus, was killed, and all his personal following wavered in dismay. Caradoc, his brother, survived, but almost immediately afterwards took the decision to withdraw. The Roman advance, although still contained, was gaining momentum and he probably realized that his men, however brave, could not now stand against it. He must save what he could before the entire fighting strength of his tribe was destroyed. In Germany not many years before, three legions had been annihilated by native warriors fighting as guerrillas in the forest; the tale of the lost legions had shaken the entire Roman world and probably Caradoc had heard it. In the English midlands the forest was as black and trackless as any beyond the Rhine; he could reasonably hope to wait, and win on a more auspicious day.

Now it was a question of trying to get his men away, down that single causeway which curled across the surrounding marsh until it reached the safety of the forest, in distance little more than a mile away. But if the Romans could reach where that causeway left the island before Caradoc's withdrawal was complete, everything was lost, because the legionaries would drive fast and hard down into the retreating Celts jammed inextricably along its length, and turn a rout into a massacre.

Yet the Romans never did quite reach it in time. Only those Britons who could not fight on because they were helpless in the crush seem to have retreated; the rest continued to fling themselves against armoured legionaries until they died. By the time Vespasian's men leant on their swords as victors, Caradoc had gone.

Once Plautius realized this, he knew it was time to send for Claudius, elephants and all. Possibly he was glad of an excuse to consolidate his victory, since other hostile tribes still threatened his army on every side. Better still, he could blame delay on the Emperor, while remaining sure that everyone in Rome understood whose triumph this really was.

Caradoc's retreat from the Thames must have been a fearful business, with everyone around him by now aware that this was not just another tribal battle to be revenged next season. It was something fearful, alien, as yet incomprehensible in its impact.

The causeway down which they retreated snaked from one foothold to the next until it reached a stream called Eia Burn, the first natural barrier since the Thames, but nothing, nothing at all compared to the defensive position they had lost: little more than a drain within a fenland wilderness, carrying clear water which was sweet to drink; a mercy for wounded and worn-out men. Beyond it, the Thames flood plain petered out in thickets and clearings where deer grazed off sufficient undergrowth for coarse grasses to grow. The causeway became a continuous path beyond Eia Burn and as soon as the ground dried out sufficiently, there was forest to offer sanctuary.[3]

Very likely Caradoc paused by the Eia and stood to offer encouragement at the place where steep stream banks dipped down to make his men's passage easier, and they could scoop up water to slake their thirst. All their proud colours of the dawn were splattered with blood and mud, sweat had dissolved the lime out of their hair and plastered it in streaks across their faces, a further agony on open wounds. Some glanced over their shoulders, ashamed because their deeds had not been as valorous as their dreams, but thankful all the same when they saw that the Romans were not yet at their heels. Once through Eia Burn the Britons scattered to walk home, except for Caradoc and his close following. When he looked back and in the distance saw the dust of battle begin to settle on men who had honoured him, and died while he escaped, an enduring hatred of Rome burned in his heart. He would not give up. Never, never. An oath he kept for eight long years and in the end only treachery defeated him.

With time, the name of the Eia Burn would be slurred into T'iaburn, or Tyburn, and it runs today beneath the courtyard and south wing of Buckingham Palace; quite swiftly still after heavy rain. The place where its banks dipped down to make a crossing would soon be called Cow Ford and also lies beneath the palace site. A small stream, and an insignificant crossing place; but Cow Ford would become crucial to the development of the palace site.

It would be surprising if Aulus Plautius did not push an outpost forward along the causeway to the Eia Burn crossing, with orders to keep watch on the forest, for a few brief weeks making the Buckingham Palace site the frontier of Imperial Rome. Whether, some twelve weeks later, Emperor Claudius and some rather unwell elephants also came this way on their triumphal route to Colchester is impossible to say, but very likely they did; elephants could easily wade the Thames in summer and be a tremendous spectacle. Nor is there archaeological evidence of downstream settlement for another seven years.

There are traces of occupation from around this time on the triangular island at the north end of the Thames ford, which for the next thousand years or so would be known as Thorney Island and only later as Westminster, but with the abbey and Houses of Parliament now occupying much of it, excavation has necessarily been very patchy.

Cow Ford became the place where Roman Watling Street crossed Eia Burn. As Londinium grew on the present site of the City a muddy lane began to follow the north bank of the river from there towards Thorney, wherever this strand (which eventually became The Strand) normally stood above flood level. Inland of this, a huge semi-tidal swampland stretched, where only the old staked causeway remained passable in all but the foulest weather.

Once over Eia Burn, where the Romans probably built a timber bridge, Watling Street struck through forest to cross the Military Road (Oxford Street), near modern Marble Arch. From there it drove north-westwards, an artery of Roman civilization and supply route for her armies. Any guardpost at Cow Ford would have vanished as pacification pushed into the Midlands, but the crossing became a place many travellers knew, and cursed perhaps for its mud and dubious causeway in the wet. Probably they could buy a drink there, or a woman to keep out the chills. Then they remembered it with more pleasure, as a good place to rest before tackling the long haul north, or the hazards of crossing Thorney's ford travelling south.

CHAPTER 2

Queen with Handbag

During the fourth century, the whole Roman world was threatened as barbarian peoples broke through its frontiers. Troops were withdrawn to defend
Rome, and outposts like Britain were left to fend for themselves. Watling
Street was still used but coinage was replaced by barter and towns decayed,
although the walled City of London probably retained an impoverished
population and fisher-families continued to exist on Thorney Island. The
causeway from Thorney to Cow Ford may have continued to be a useful
access to the fruits and game of the forest, but when travellers were few and
Thames marsh dwellers born light-footed, the hard work of shovelling mud
to keep it in repair probably seemed pointless. Nimble leaps between gravel
banks suited their needs well enough.

No contemporary source mentions an established religious community
on Thorney/Westminster before the early eleventh century, when William
of Malmesbury remarks that one existed, 'To whom the endowments of the
faithful provide no more than their daily bread'.[1] The sneer of a man who
belonged to an infinitely grander establishment is unmistakable. By then, six
hundred years had passed since the Romans left. Untroubled by the disasters
which so frequently afflicted the people crossing it, the Tyburn continued to
flow from its source in the Hampstead Hills, through trees encroaching on
the old Roman roads until it reached Cow Ford and curved to reach the
Thames, enclosing Thorney Island in its delta. A variety of wild animals used
the ford as a convenient drinking place: wolves, tree martens, bear, boar and
deer. The calls of marsh birds echoed across the fen country surrounding it,
which over this period increased in size as Eastern England continued to
tip infinitesimally downward.

Very slowly, quite different institutions were established in England from
those known to Rome, and London, too, was trading again by 730, when Bede
wrote that it was 'A mart for many peoples'.[2] The most recent excavations,
however, have proved that the London of this time centred on the Thames
foreshore west of the City. Only a few smallholders still lived inside the old
Roman walls and grew real corn on Cornhill; the modern name of Aldwych
('Old Trade Settlement') still remembers that distant Saxon past beneath what
is now a very different part of London. And bustling though it was, Bede's

A small part of the palace site was apparently cleared for agriculture in Saxon times, and a defensive stockade constructed at 'Eiaburgh', or modern Ebury Square. (Mansell Collection)

London had ceased to be an imperial city. Rather it became a frontier settlement, growing back to importance through all the excitements and casual violence which characterises pioneer outposts. Saxons, Mercians and Danes conquered it in turn. Then King Alfred of Wessex came and persuaded its citizens back inside the Roman walls, an ancient defence revitalized in desperate times. When Vikings came conquering in their turn, Londoners fought hard to hold these walls, decaying here and there. They defeated the first attack, but in 1012 the Vikings burned shipping, wharves and off-lying buildings, and murdered the Archbishop of Canterbury when they caught him outside the walls. Next time they came, they fastened grappling ropes to the old Roman timber bridge and rowed furiously downstream on the tide. One can imagine the people of London watching, horror-struck, as their link with the whole south country and main reason for their city's revival, wavered, creaked, and finally tumbled into the Thames.

London lived by trade, there was no other reason for its existence. Without it the city died, and when the Vikings settled to the task of destroying everything in reach, its citizens decided that they must make what peace they could. Cnut, the Dane, became king in England as well as Denmark and by force of character continued the consolidation begun by Alfred and his successors, but it was order of the most basic kind. Heroic carousings in his hall remained the staple relaxation, where minor disrespects were punished by pelting the offender with greasy bones. Major disrespect bloodily terminated a life.

When Cnut died the succession was again disputed, the situation exacerbated by his son's death at Lamb's Hythe (Lambeth) during a drinking bout. Nor did matters settle when the ancient line of Wessex kings was restored in the person of Edward the Confessor, although it was during these years that

English kings began occasionally to live on Thorney Island, and eddies from the current of their affairs were for the first time faintly felt in the wilderness around Cow Ford. The causeway was repaired, so that tired messengers could ride in haste to reach the king. Restless, volatile gatherings from the royal hall came this way to hunt, a pest to families beginning to settle on lands by then called Eia, or Eaia, after the burn or stream beside them, and which included the present palace grounds. Partly because the ground remained so wet, the settlers would have lived mostly on game and forest produce, eels and Thames fish, but during the ninth century a new name, Eiaburgh, suggests that enough people lived around the palace site for them to build a stockade, or burgh, in the hope of defending themselves, and with luck a few of their swine and cattle.

It is difficult to speak of a royal court at this time, since ruling was such a rudimentary art that in order to exercise it, kings needed only a string of baggage mules, some priests to act as scribes and confessors, and a collection of cronies whose advice they must consider, or whose persons they were wise to watch. This caravan administration ranged across the countryside, though it was sensible not to range so widely that the heartlands of a realm were tempted to forget their king's existence, or were unable to locate him in a hurry.

For these reasons, in normal times an English king began to follow a reasonably set itinerary, a pattern William the Conqueror would alter and update, but also establish more firmly. Part of this pattern included keeping Whitsun at Westminster, and once kings regularly held a formal court or crown-wearing on Thorney, they made sure that the island's only exit towards the forest belonged to them. Edward the Confessor is the first known owner of the palace site, but he probably inherited it with his crown.

Edward built his own fine hall on Thorney, and a sprawl of yards, huts and stables grew up around it. He also decided to build an abbey there, which could be described as Edward the Confessor's peace dividend, and for the next five hundred years its history and that of the palace site become inextricably intertwined. Edward was thrifty over money and this one major capital investment of his reign grew out of a decade when the country was mostly free from war. Building work began around 1063 and was pushed forward at a phenomenal rate for a project powered by muscle. Even so, a great deal remained to be done after his death, and during the centuries of its existence the community of Westminster would rarely be free of anxiety over how to pay for building works at the abbey.

But if Edward is the earliest identifiable ghost in the throng inhabiting the palace site, he is also the most difficult to reach across such a gulf of time. Contemporary opinions are contradictory, and coloured by nostalgia for an imagined golden age before conquest by Normans, which followed within months of his death. His later canonization as a saint confuses the picture further, since he does not shine out of the chronicles as a particularly saintly man. At the same time it is difficult not to accept Edward the Confessor as

An illustration from the Vita Edwardi *which shows Edward the Confessor beset by clamouring opinions and petitioners, but not on this occasion (unfortunately) by his wife.* (By permission of the Syndics of Cambridge University Library)

a symbol of something; most notably for transmitting continuity. For this reason alone, it seems appropriate that he should be the first recorded owner of the palace site.

Edward himself was culturally a Norman, in blood a descendant of Wessex kings. He faced enormous difficulties throughout his reign and yet by the end of it England was regarded as a prosperous realm, and he passed it on as a single whole. He lacked real power and was reduced to speaking belligerently while rarely fighting even a minor skirmish; habits which attracted contempt but helped him to weave a devious course past other more warlike men. He struggled to recover and then maintain his royal rights, but spent most of his life hen-pecked by women; he had no children, and rhymsters made sly jokes about his sex life. He was seriously religious and annoyed his followers by not allowing them to chatter during mass, but there is little evidence to suggest he was particularly ascetic. He loved hunting with a passion shared by most English kings, his court ate and drank its way through the countryside, and the miracles he is said to have performed come over as little more than minstrels' tales. He may even have possessed a sense of humour, a rare virtue among reigning monarchs. Above all, he was a survivor; one of the very few contemporary kings who died in bed. His abbey still lives, and halls on the site of the one he built at Westminster were inhabited by his successors until Henry VIII decided that someone else's home in Whitehall offered him more modern comforts. Then Henry generously gave Westminster's fire-damaged remnants to parliament as their permanent meeting place.

The strong-minded women who put Edward in the unenviable position of being an eleventh-century king visibly reliant on skirts behind the throne, were his mother, Emma of Normandy, and Edith, his wife. Edith was rich, beautiful and greedy, the daughter of Edward's most dangerous subject, Earl Godwin. Either as her dower or as a later gift from the king, she received the lands beyond T'Eiaburn,[3] called Eia or Eiaburgh, as her personal property, the first of several women to own the palace site. To be exact, she did not quite own it all. Because the Tyburn nowadays flows beneath the palace and Edith was only given land to the west of the stream, part remained in the king's possession until he gave it to Westminster Abbey.

Queen Edith was an interesting and combative personality. While much of her husband's character remains elusive and alien to modern minds, she fairly leaps out of records written nine hundred years ago. Some she probably commissioned, since Edith courted valuable publicity; more independent writers were doubtful about a woman with power in high places, but where all agree is on her intelligence and importance.

Her father, Earl Godwin, was a man of obscure origins only recently ennobled, probably as a reward for family treacheries, and whose ambitions remained limitless. Probably he had murdered King Edward's own brother, and one of his sons, Swein, had only recently been forgiven for raping an abbess and murdering his cousin. The bishops who consecrated Edith as queen must have had serious reservations about the ability of a woman with such blood in her veins to keep the oath they administered to her 'by the power of God to bring the barbarous to a knowledge of truth'.[4]

At the time of her marriage Edith was about twenty years old, half the age of her husband, and the chronicler is probably not lying when he describes her as fair and beautiful, since the Godwins were notable for physique. Like the rest of her kin, she seems to have been strongly acquisitive, but more skilled than they at dissembling her intentions. For her, soft words paid the best dividend.

The wedding feast was splendid, full of 'dance and frisk and leap', but as the drinking grew deeper she withdrew from the king's hall to eat with abbesses and nuns, and over the years people often remarked with surprise (or cynicism) on her modest behaviour. It was not a quality they expected in a Godwin, especially when many of her other actions suggested that she shared their fires only just beneath the skin. But Edith could afford gestures which cost her very little. At court she never sat beside the king each time he invited her to join him, sitting instead at his feet. She embroidered his clothes and at least in the early years was discreet over where and how she offered him advice. That she did offer advice which increasingly he took, gradually became clear.

It must have been a severe shock to a young woman raised among a lusty, violent and brawling family, whose father bred sons wholesale on his wife and mistresses, to discover on her wedding night that her husband was sexually cold. As one of the more pious commentators put it, 'She was delivered to the royal bridal chamber with ceremonial rejoicing, but Merciful God . . . kept the king all the days of his life in purity of flesh'.[5] There is no way of knowing whether Edward was clinically impotent at the commencement of his marriage. He may have hidden sexual malfunction behind a smokescreen of celibate piety; he may simply have been uninterested in sex, perhaps because he suspected himself of being sterile. On the other hand, he does not appear the kind of man who would be bullied into a marriage he knew he could not, or did not wish to, consummate. There is no reason to believe that Edith possessed a less passionate nature than the rest of her kin, and many reasons to believe that she did, and knowingly to embark on an insultingly unsatisfied relationship with a woman who possessed a gang of powerful and dangerously fierce relatives was to invite disaster.

What is certain is that there were no children from the marriage, and that rumours grew up around it. As the chronicler delicately says, 'She kept the secret of the king's chastity of which she had learned, and kept those counsels that she knew'.[6] This is hindsight, however. There is no evidence that Edward was actively homosexual, and his performance in bed could have been adequate during the early years of their marriage; only with childlessness and perhaps a further decline in his abilities over the years did apathy towards physical relations become sexual neglect. For King Edward, this same period of time was skilfully used to turn sneers into respect, since chastity once offered to God was regarded as a noteworthy sacrifice.

For Edith, life must often have seemed enormously hard, and after Edward's death, William of Malmesbury wrote a remarkably even-handed obituary of their relationship:

> The king's treatment of his wife had been neither to remove her from his bed nor to act the man with her. But whether he did this because of his hatred for her family (which he wisely dissembled at the time) or because of his love of chastity, I really do not know.[7]

One snapshot of Edward and Edith's married life exists, a remarkable survival which shows two people at apparent ease with each other, although Edith's skill in public relations is revealing. Sometime around 1045, they were visiting Abingdon Abbey together when Edith remarked that the children being fed there had only bread to eat. In reply, she was told that the abbey could rarely afford to give them anything else, and she called across to Edward, asking if he would assign some revenue so the children might occasionally eat better. He laughed and turned the request aside, saying he would be delighted, but only if someone offered him something to give. You can sense his irritation at being put at public disadvantage: people everywhere existed mostly on bread, and abbeys were rich enough to give out meat occasionally if they chose. As he had reason to know, since the Abbot of Abingdon doubled as his personal jeweller. Give to one specious mendicant and you would find yourself giving to them all.

But Edith's reply is sharp and instant. She has a village she would be delighted to offer, if the king will allow her. He will, and she does: who wins this particular encounter is left to the imagination. Edith lost a village, and she was a passionate collector of land. The king lost in the estimation of the monkly chronicler, but perhaps not with his hard-headed henchmen.[8]

In essence this story accords with an overall impression of both their characters. Edward may later have invested a great deal of money in building Westminster Abbey, but the provision he made for its future revenues by endowment was notably mean, causing endless headaches for future abbots there. Only a few years after the incident at Abingdon, Edith showed herself capable of fraudulently dispossessing Peterborough Abbey of an estate and eventually she owned lands, including Eia, which yielded rents amounting to a fifth of the king's own income. Yet she skilfully succeeded in retaining what one cannot help feeling was an unjustified reputation for generosity. Possibly she enjoyed the very real pleasures of giving relatively small sums. There must also be the suspicion that she did not grudge spending where she could gain credit for it. Her wish to acquire land might be unbounded, but what she actually wanted it for was as a stepping-stone to influence.

Her ostentatious servility before the king at court has similar psychological roots: she wanted people to remark on her behaviour, and saw no point in deferences which would pass unnoticed. Edward himself disliked showy gestures and grumbled about wearing the rich clothes she insisted on embroidering for him. Since on less formal occasions she may have behaved towards him almost with arrogance, as at Abingdon, he must have been unbearably irritated when people remarked on his wife's meek manners while the chroniclers were watching.

Storm clouds began to gather soon after that day at Abingdon. There was no open feud between the king and his father-in-law, Earl Godwin, rather a private trial of strength made more bitter by the unbridled conduct of Godwin's sons. Edward usually hid his anger, but his modern biographer considers that he was the kind of man who could have relieved his feelings on his wife, the only Godwin at his mercy. Around 1047 her name disappears as witness to his charters, previously a sign of her presence wherever the court travelled. By this time too, their childlessness must have worsened the relationship between them; the explanation that he was too saintly to copulate circulated later, during the years of increasing separation. As differences flared with the Godwin clan, Edward made more use of Norman advisers too, and may even have promised his throne to Duke William, as at least being preferable to the Godwins.

This section of the Bayeux Tapestry shows Edward the Confessor's body being carried from his hall at Westminster into the abbey for burial. A workman fixes a weathervane, possibly to show that construction is nearly complete, and the hand of God affirms consecration.

Matters limped along until 1051, when Earl Godwin refused a royal order to punish Dover for inhospitality to some visiting Flemings, and suddenly everyone's patience snapped in a way which shows how great had been the underlying strain. People galloped helter-skelter to gather up their followings, but Godwin soon discovered that his family was so heartily distrusted, and the prospect of civil war so much disliked, that the other great earls preferred to back the king and not worry too much about the rights or wrongs of Dover. At first Godwin did not believe it. He had chosen a popular cause on which to rebel; surely ordinary people would follow him even if the great earls did not? At one stage he was camped with his followers at Southwark while Edward waited with his at Westminster, offering an impartial judgement at his Court. Godwin hesitated, but with London showing no sign of actively supporting him, he felt unable to risk his person in the king's hands and fled the country with his sons.

This represented a stunning victory for Edward. He had tripped over arrogant Godwins ever since he became king and now he was free of them; he gained financially too, his wealth doubled overnight as their estates fell forfeit into his hand. There was only one small consequence of their downfall he regretted, and that was the expulsion soon afterwards of his jeweller, his old friend the Abbot of Abingdon, whom he had been in the process of conjuring into position as Bishop of London. The Normans Edward had gathered around him over the years to help him oppose the Godwins included clergy, and they had long been shocked by English unorthodoxy in religion; to be more precise, they considered the Bishopric of London should be held by a Norman. Quite definitely not by a man who designed gewgaws for the ladies of the Court, and traded on his own account. Unfortunately for Edward, this particular priest, whose splendidly pagan name of Spearhavoc suggests that the Normans had a point, took with him when he fled to safety not only all the money he could find within the London diocesan coffers, but also the jewels and precious metals entrusted to him by the king as raw materials from which to make a new crown for England.

In the general upheaval, Queen Edith was banished to a nunnery in Hampshire and her lands probably joined those of the rest of her relations, back in the king's hands. The Eia/Eiaburgh lands therefore briefly belonged again to Edward the Confessor.

For a few months Edward enjoyed the only time in his reign when he was free from masterful women, and then the Godwins were back, at the head of a strong force and determined to recoup their losses. The only brother missing was Swein, the most violent of them all, who had suddenly become alarmed by the state of his soul and decided to walk barefoot to Jerusalem. When last seen he was said to be walking fast, in order to be back and start caring for his earthly interests again.

The invasion force landed in Kent, where Earl Godwin found strong support. Edward's foreign friends were much disliked and the concept of murdering a few of them with impunity, as Dover had done, looked more attractive than ever, but rather surprisingly, considering the times and temperaments involved, there seems to have been a general disinclination to embark on civil war. When Edward realized the reluctance of his following, he was said to have been mad with anger over the necessity of making terms. His leading Norman counsellors fled in their turn and the Godwins received back most of their lands, a process eased all round by news that Swein had perished on his walk to Jerusalem.

Earl Godwin died only a few months later, leaving another son, Harold, to become earl in his place. Queen Edith returned to Court as part of the settlement, but some years passed before her name reappears regularly on charters. Nevertheless, her influence was soon remarked upon, whereas her grace and good deeds had been of more interest to chroniclers before. She recovered ownership of Eia and may have put in hand the first tentative drainage works there. It also became much clearer that she had inherited all of her father's light-fingered attitudes to church lands. At least two royal clerks obtained bishoprics by pledging her a slice of their prospective diocesan estate, and in 1060 came her brush with the Abbot of Peterborough, when she extorted payment of twenty gold marks and quantities of church plate as her price for abandoning a fairly spurious claim to property donated to his church. It is suggestive, too, that her dresser, Matilda, towards the end of Edward's reign married a rich thegn; as if anyone with the chance to whisper in the Queen's ear by then could market their personal value successfully.

In other ways Edith's influence was more positive. She was seen by many as a go-between, a courageous and cheerful peacemaker with her quarrelsome family in the king's interest, a role on which the future of the realm depended. 'By her advice, peace laps the kingdom on every side and warns the nations against breaking their bonds,' wrote one observer, and another adds the highest compliment of all in those pre-feminist days, 'She was as intelligent as a man, well able to distinguish good from evil'.[9]

The portrait of the first female owner of the Buckingham Palace lands which emerges from these accounts is complex. Edith is often shown beside or behind the throne, offering advice to the king, who by these last years was perhaps wearying of the burdens of his office. She is equal with his great earls, an exceptional position for a consort in any age, and truly extraordinary for a woman who had failed to produce the longed-for heir. She greeted guests in her own right, flew into a rage if she suspected a snub, interfered with plans and officiously set about teaching scholars their grammar. In spite of praise for her peacemaking, she often sided with her brothers in disputes, and one of the king's most awkward problems became how to satisfy his queen's greed on their behalf without instantly antagonizing everyone else.

In these latter years Edith became dangerously attached to her brother Tostig, an able, passionate and brutal man, but personable and decisive, characteristics which may have appealed to her frustrated sexuality. At her insistence he was given the Earldom of Northumbria, thereby significantly extending Godwin possessions, but his rule there was so tyrannical that it soon provoked revolt. The most serious allegation made against Edith is that during her time of greatest power at Court she connived with Tostig to murder a Northumbrian noble called Gospatric, who was attending the king's Christmas feast and therefore protected by his special peace. It is not clear whether Gospatric was a potential or active rebel hoping to gain Tostig's earldom for himself, or came to petition the king about the evils of Tostig's rule. Either way, Tostig was the beneficiary of his death.

In 1065 the Northumbrians rose in revolt while Tostig was away hunting with the king. Even more seriously for Edward, those of his earls who were not of Godwin blood flatly refused to fight in order to restore a man they detested. Eventually even Tostig's own brother, Harold, deserted him. Possibly he was already calculating his chances of becoming king when Edward died, which would be greatly improved if he could cut loose from his family's excesses. Tostig was forced into exile, and never forgave Harold for what he regarded as the worst treachery of all: abandoning blood-kin in their time of need. Away in Scandinavia he began to plot an invasion, and by his actions would eventually lose Harold his throne and the English their independence.

When Tostig fled, Edith was inconsolable. The change in her caused astonishment and dismay, and the charge that she had become deeply involved in Tostig's cause must be reinforced by her behaviour during the final months of her husband's rule. Precisely because she was by then acknowledged to be a power behind his throne, the chroniclers paid as much attention to her state of mind during this time as they did to Edward's. After all, he had several times reacted in the same way, first raging against fate and then making the best terms with it that he could. To the eleventh-century mind, such behaviour was both inglorious and not particularly interesting. Edith was different. She was renowned for her resilience and respected for her wiliness, known to be hungry for power and possessions. No one expected her simply to give up.

Edith by this time was aged just over forty, an unsatisfied, strong-minded, quick-tempered woman. Possibly a first-class bitch. If she had had lovers, they were snatched affairs the chroniclers failed to discover, which left her passions stronger than before. If the king had ever bedded her, it was long in the past; nowadays he lay beside her like an indifferent, taunting monk. The emotional void inside her had been eased by power, but nothing cured it until Tostig came to Court. Instead, she had become harder with the years, more grasping, soured by the struggle for influence. For Tostig's sake she may have connived at murder.

It is commonplace for a certain kind of criminal charisma to take advantage of starved emotions, and there are indications that this is what happened between Queen Edith and her young brother. When Tostig fled, Edith knew enough about ruling kingdoms to understand that it would not be easy for him ever to return; whether she realized that through their schemings the whole of England would be delivered up to an invader is uncertain. Perhaps she no longer cared. As for the Court, nearly everyone trembled for the future when they saw a woman they believed to be tougher than iron, shaken day after day by unheeding storms of grief.[10]

On the Christmas Day following Tostig's exile, Westminster Abbey was dedicated to St Peter, but the atmosphere at Court was filled with too many forebodings for even a great festival to be truly enjoyable. The king was ill and unable to attend the dedication; he lived to hear the first chants of his new Benedictine foundation sound softly across the wintry spaces separating his hall from the new abbey, but died a week later.

Queen Edith sat in her usual place at his feet during the vigil before and after his soul's passing, and perhaps genuinely mourned his death; they had, after all, been companions for a long time. Beyond her grief would have been fear, because all the life she knew and which mattered to her might now be lost with him.

Harold was crowned next day, almost certainly in Westminster Abbey, which made him the first king to be consecrated there, and Edith was left on one side even more quickly than she feared. From being watched, she was disregarded. As others have learned since, nothing disappears so completely or so rapidly as loss of political power.

A detail from the Bayeux Tapestry depicting Harold, son of Godwin, who was briefly crowned King of the English in 1066.

This seems to have jolted her into recovery from nervous collapse. It is not clear how she tried to help Tostig in his ambition to invade England and seize the crown, but during the year of 1066 'with prayers and stratagems'[11] that is what she tried to do. As soon as she heard that Tostig was gathering a fleet together, Edith is recorded as secretly opposing Harold, and the inference is that she tried to canvass support for Tostig, but unsuccessfully. Harold was more generally liked than the rest of his family and the great earls understood that unity was vital against possible attack on two fronts, from Tostig and from William of Normandy. Probably an otherwise male-dominated gathering of advisers was relieved to be rid of an interfering and bossy female from their counsels, notwithstanding that they had recently respected her judgement and authority. It is easy to reflect on a modern parallel.

During the dangerous, brooding summer of 1066, while a great comet blazed across the heavens at night and people felt their entire world poised on a sword-edge of uncertainty, the lands at Eia remained in Edith's ownership. There were still only three ways to ride out from Thorney island: south across Thames ford, and this had grown deeper and more dangerous in recent years; east by the Strand banks to the City, or north along the causeway to Cow Ford. This last would have been Edith's favourite, since her estate of Eia lay that way and she was the kind of woman who loved her own land with a fierce possessive passion. This northern route passed the clutter and chaos above which the abbey's new-cut surfaces glittered in the sun, before reaching across bright green marsh grass where birds rose from stagnant pools in a whirl of wings. A few jog-trot paces away from Westminster and everything changed into emptiness, solitude and space. Only some huts would have been distantly in sight ahead, on Eia Burn's – Tyburn's – further bank.

When Edward was alive he, too, often came this way to hunt; especially in recent years when he had stayed longer and more frequently at Westminster, while the abbey was being built. Grooms, kennellers and spearmen found Eia's fields a useful place to gather, laughing and cursing together under an early orange sun while great oaks close by stood black against the sky; hounds tangled with the horses as they yearned in circles to taste blood, all waiting until King Edward and Queen Edith rode to join them down the causeway. Then the rams' horns wailed and everyone swarmed into the forest, Edith following more decorously; she enjoyed hunting, but liked even better to drop a word here, encourage a supplicant there, reel in her delicate schemings with a smile, a frown, a turn of the head.

Edith's manor of Eia (the term 'manor' was just coming into use, and indicated a more or less independent unit of ownership with feudal undertones) stretched north into the trees as far as the old Roman Military Road (modern Oxford Street), and south to the Thames. The future palace site at Cow Ford was roughly equidistant between these boundaries, and also marked where flood plain became potentially cultivable. Any traveller standing there in 1066 and looking with narrowed eyes into flat September sunlight, would have seen only an occasional islet among the reeds between there and the river: a hut, an orchard, a few tiny closes of pasture on some of them. But around and beyond the palace site small fields were advancing into the undergrowth, gradually to be made richer by oxen and pigs: Westminster sucked in food now the abbey and Court provided work for a great part of the year.

All through that same summer of 1066 Edith's hopes had remained fixed on Tostig, but although she regained enough calm to try and help him to victory, she may have sensed that this time hope would be denied. The Court followed Harold out to muster men against both Tostig and Duke William: by September Westminster was empty, empty, waiting for whoever would return in triumph. Only the bulk of Edward's new abbey was left, sailing alone across a bleak horizon like some abandoned Noah's ark.

CHAPTER 3

The Conqueror and his Plutocrat

The Battle of Hastings, which took place in October 1066, put only a fraction of England into Duke William's possession, but it was decisive in winning him time to subdue the rest. Harold, two of his brothers and many of the natural leaders of English resistance were killed there; Tostig died in personal combat with Harold, his brother, at an earlier battle at Stamford Bridge.

William knew that he must capitalize fast on victory and force-marched his army to London, where the calamitous speed of events threw opinion into turmoil. When in spite of this he found London Bridge sealed against him, 'he thundered forth menaces, swearing that given time he would destroy the city's walls and raze its bastions to the ground'.[1]

Unlike his predecessor, William did not rely on static anger to achieve his purposes, and at once set out again on a threatening circuit through Surrey, Middlesex, Berkshire and beyond. By then it was November, a time when carts stacked with provisions would normally be moving along the river banks and tracks of England to stock the towns for winter. Starvation would come quickly once this trade was sent scuttling for cover, and Winchester capitulated first, on the advice of Queen Edith,[2] who owned it and had taken up residence there. The vital Thames crossing at Wallingford followed, and lacking any leadership, London submitted soon afterwards.

William's force immediately converged by various routes on the Thames, some coming directly down old Watling Street and across the palace site to wade the Tyburn and reach Westminster. As they approached, ahead of them they would have seen the abbey grow from a speck on empty flatness into a truncated, awesome block of stone still lacking towers, as well as most of the administrative buildings required by a community of monks. Like the Roman legionaries, William's followers came from all over Europe, hungry for the loot and land which victory would bring them. A few were magnates or lords with a following; most were adventurers, younger sons, landless knights for whom this madcap invasion represented the best opportunity of their age for personal aggrandizement, if by chance it should succeed. Now that it had, their greed was unbounded.

There cannot have been a man among William's followers who, as he crossed Edith's Manor of Eia in the early winter of 1066, did not cherish almost unlimited dreams of plunder and lawless, grasping pleasures. William was set in the same mould, except he did not intend his triumph to be diminished by the licence of others. England must remain in his gift, and violence be channelled into the overall purpose of consolidating his new kingdom. The process would be difficult and brutal, but by the time he died a few thousand invaders were firmly in control of perhaps half a million English, and his throne so solidly established that no subsequent conqueror ever came to seize it.

As the old year drew to a close after a tumultuous twelve months in which three kings reigned, William I was crowned in Westminster Abbey. The same monks who sang Edward's funeral rites and at Harold's coronation celebrated William's crowning, with the Norman addition that the new monarch was presented formally to his subjects, first in English and then in French. The unfamiliar shouts of acclamation that followed caused the Norman soldiers standing on guard to believe that the king was being attacked, and they retaliated on the crowd gathered by the abbey doors. Some huts were set on fire and the flames soon spread in an instant crackle of sticks, causing panic everywhere. Inside the abbey no one knew what was happening, and screams from a packed crowd trying to escape, the crackle of flames and stench of smoke acted like a tocsin of disaster. Ordericus Vitalis records that even the king began to tremble, before he grasped at his courage and indicated that his coronation must proceed.[3] An unknown number of people were killed in the tumult and the loss of shelter must have caused great hardship. William was soon off again on his travels, but he left behind the poorer inhabitants of Westminster camped wretchedly in snow wherever they could find a pitch above flood level. Some would have fled as far as Eia, and the xenophobic rage which smouldered in London against these new conquerors was further reinforced by bitter, personal grievance.

Queen Edith lived unmolested under the Conqueror. Her name was not linked to any of the conspiracies against him, nor is she recorded as involved in any official business. Life as she valued it indeed had ended and nothing could regain her a share in power. She seems to have divided her time between Winchester and Wilton, where she had built a fine abbey, and there were rumours that she lived unchastely during her widowhood, which she denied.[4] But if she did, it might be considered a pleasure she had earned. The evidence suggests that she kept the Manor of Eia for her lifetime and even slightly increased her wealth under the Conqueror, which only goes to show that real skill in acquisition will survive almost anything. When she died, the palace site and Eia reverted to the king.

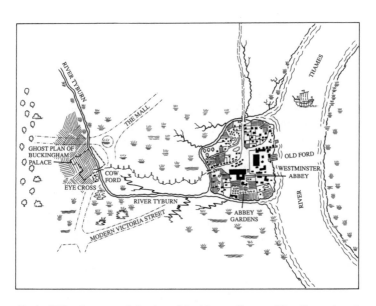

Sketch of Westminster around the time of the Norman Conquest. The abbey and royal establishment encouraged some settlement, but the whole area remained so wet that the king's servants were sometimes forced to use punts to move around inside his hall.

Part of William's strategy for ruling England was to display his person with calculated magnificence to his subjects. He continued to keep Whitsun feast at Westminster whenever he was in England, but set out to elevate his kingship more deliberately than his predecessors had done. Even stripped down for travel William's retinue radiated a sense of businesslike glamour, and extravagant displays were staged for such occasions as welcoming ambassadors to Court: sharp-eyed individuals forever on the lookout for weakness in a ruler.

William's Great Courts were council, government and legal arbiter in one, and at a time when few men of fighting rank expected to get through life without committing an occasional homicide, they contained the additional excitement of never knowing what would happen next. Since idleness bred quarrels, officials arranged a constant round of hunting, gluttony, prayer and combats, stiffened by ceremonial and underpinned by marriage bargainings. Personally, William regarded time spent sitting down as wasted, but on formal occasions feasting might begin at midday and last until after midnight. Even then, the king expected those with whom he wished to transact business to remain reasonably sober; a career was no longer improved if its possessor was drunk by noon.

At Westminster, William could also keep an eye on London. As the Bishop of Amiens austerely reported not long after the Conquest, 'London is a great city, overflowing with froward inhabitants and richer in treasure than the rest of the kingdom . . . it neither fears enemies or dreads being taken by storm'.[5] Its unruly aspirations were politically important before the Conquest, as was royal covetousness of London's wealth, and by holding court outside its walls kings avoided the uncomfortable reality that, inside them, he was either the guest of purse-proud traders and their mobs, or an occupying power. At Westminster, a strong king could extend his own peace and in an emergency block his island approaches quickly. A weak king found no hiding place, in Westminster or anywhere else.

William soon decided to tip the scales further in his favour by fortifying no fewer than three royal castles inside London's walls. Only one, the Tower, survives, but in his time Mountfitchet and Baynard's Castles were similar: mounds fortified by timber in the early years, soon to be replaced by stone. Ground was ruthlessly cleared, and the sudden appearance of white block walls where everything else was wood or wattle must have been deeply shocking: like waking up one morning to find the Berlin Wall across a familiar street. The City seethed with resentment, but so did towns and villages all over England, where five hundred castles were built in under twenty years, flattening graveyards, homes and markets. Everywhere, Normans took over English estates and offices.

One of William's most important followers who helped to carry through this enterprise was Geoffrey de Mandeville, and he illustrates the process very well. He was also the next owner of the palace site.

Geoffrey was an established if modest landholder in Normandy, where he commanded sufficient resources to back William's invasion project with both coin and men. Most likely his fief was concentrated around the village of Manneville, south of Dieppe, and in the years before the Conquest his name appears occasionally as witness to William's charters.[6] The scattered evidence suggests that on the occasions when he actively supported his duke during the endemic fighting there, he did so cannily, as suited his own interests best. Let other men chance their lives and inheritance in the slippery alliances of guerilla war; Geoffrey preferred to consolidate what he possessed, doing just sufficient to establish himself in the duke's eyes as reliable. That William did consider him both efficient and reliable became apparent as soon the English invasion was successful.

This view of Geoffrey de Mandeville as essentially a cautious man must be set beside the likelihood that he decided very early that his duke's invasion plans offered him a chance of profit which was simply too good to miss, and he gambled heavily on a successful outcome. The ability to recognize the single chance in a lifetime on which fate hangs, and then risk everything to grasp it, is a not uncommon characteristic among self-made millionaires.

Statue of William the Conqueror in the main square of Falaise, Normandy, where he was born. (Courtesy, Office de Tourisme de Falaise)

Geoffrey de Mandeville is not recorded as present at the Battle of Hastings but he must have been there, and also during the advance on London, because he was one of the first Normans William rewarded after his coronation. That early gift of land was the first of many, and Geoffrey eventually owned no fewer than 118 manors in England, mostly concentrated in the strategically vital counties of Essex, Suffolk and Middlesex. Just as important, he seems to have been appointed custodian of the new Tower of London,[7] and definitely as Sheriff of Middlesex, an area which included Westminster and land immediately outside the City's walls. Put together, Geoffrey's collection of honours, manors and offices launched him as one of the three or four most powerful men in England after the king, with the additional significance that he controlled its very heartland. Quite when he received the Manor of Eia is uncertain, but probably immediately after the death of Queen Edith in 1075.

The surprise is that William did not retain it for himself. The causeway to Cow Ford remained the only way out of Westminster not circumscribed by the Thames or London's walls, and the extent of the king's confidence in Geoffrey, as uncharacteristic as it is interesting, is heavily underscored by this gift, which greatly increased an already powerful subject's grip on London and its outskirts.

If Geoffrey is an elusive figure to track through the records in Normandy, he remains tantalizingly so as a great magnate in England. Clearly, whatever his fortune before, it had been transformed by the Conquest. He was personally responsible for the practicalities of establishing the Tower as William's own fortress and for rebuilding it in stone, to rule surly Londoners and to exercise jurisdiction as sheriff outside their walls. When most of the City burned down in 1077 he would have been deeply involved with its inhabitants in re-establishing prosperity with all possible speed.

By 1086 ten men, of whom Geoffrey was one, held a quarter of England by direct grant from the king. Yet as an individual he left remarkably few records behind him; it is as if once his one great gamble triumphantly succeeded, Geoffrey de Mandeville reverted to his Normandy habits of oozing almost unperceived into the cracks and interstices of power. Sound judgement, loyalty, and discretion in the exercise of authority were valuable qualities during the years when William's hold on England remained only superficially impressive. At base, however, Geoffrey remained a crafty and avaricious Norman baron.

As Sheriff of Middlesex, the only appeal from his judgements was directly to the king; his revamped office one of several shrievalties held by a tight group of men the English described with horror as ravening wolves.[8] Defence, the law, accountings for tax, forced labour; all came within their remit. If Geoffrey de Mandeville is not recorded as indulging in particular excesses, this probably only demonstrates his skill in the uses of power, although on one occasion he forfeited some land in London, in his absence given by the king to an Englishman.[9] Since the Conqueror was not capricious in such matters, there may have been a warning here, all the more pointed because an Englishman was the beneficiary. If so, Geoffrey seems to have accepted it as such. No doubt he was angry over being humiliated, and losing anything went against the grain, but there is no sign of the suicidal pride which threw others into rebellion over trifles. He simply continued to extend his possessions, and a case from Essex shows him as prepared to trample on the rights of fellow-Normans as on those of the English, when he set up his own mill on an ex-soldier's land. There is also a cryptic entry from Barking, where the local people tried unsuccessfully to testify against him.[10]

There can be no doubt that Geoffrey enjoyed an outstandingly successful career, establishing the house of de Mandeville as one of the great baronies in England. He left sons to succeed him, survived to see the Conquest established on solid administrative foundations and to fortify his lands with castles. He would have been scandalized had he known that his grandson, another Geoffrey, would throw away all these gains in a spectacular life of crime, when his behaviour was likened to that of 'a vicious and riderless horse, kicking and biting in his rages';[11] when he luckily died from a sceptic cut following an attack on Cambridge, his body lay unburied for twenty years because no priest dared to touch it. The first Geoffrey was buried beside his wife, Athelys, in Westminster Abbey. He died just before the Conqueror himself, probably in 1086, and on his deathbed showed the usual but not excessive concern for his sins: 'For his soul and the soul of Athelys his wife buried in the cloister of St Peter ... [he] gave to St Peter of Westminster the manor near the church he had held, namely Eia, in perpetual heritage.'[12] This bequest would bring stability of ownership to the palace site for the next five hundred years.

At the time of Geoffrey's death information was being collected throughout England to be incorporated in 'Domesday Book', and for the first time this describes Eia in some detail, and therefore the Buckingham Palace lands. The eastern, northern, and southern borders of the manor were established before Queen Edith's day, but that to the west was still pushing outwards as more land was cleared, until it reached a natural boundary, descriptively called Outer-Edge-on-the-West Stream, or in modern terms, the Westbourne. This was a flagrant encroachment on royal rights, which in lesser personages than Edith or Geoffrey de Mandeville would have been a capital offence; that it slipped past unrecorded only demonstrates the position of power each occupied. On the whole, Edith is the more likely culprit, since William pounced on crime, whoever committed it.

The pressures of an increased population at Westminster made such reclamation well worthwhile, and it is likely that a drain known as the 'The Old Ditch' dates from this time too, documented in the 1130s as a completed work. Its exact location is uncertain, but probably it ran from the curve in the Tyburn near the palace site into marsh between there and the Thames in an attempt to drain some of this lower-lying land.

In 'Domesday Book' half the Manor of Ebury* is shown as being farmed directly for the benefit of its lord, by twenty-four landholders and one landworker. There were around 1,000 tilled acres but no woods, in contrast to the manor immediately to the north, later to become Marylebone, which remained partly forested. Probably a great many trees had been felled in Queen Edith's day for use as fuel or in the building works at Westminster. The palace area was ragged open fields, almost certainly still obstructed by the huge tree-stumps eleventh-century tools could not tackle, its fertility slowly increased by the pigs which were used to rootle (the word itself is suggestive) ancient clutter out of the soil. Seven plough-teams of oxen, around sixty-four beasts, worked on the manor, cultivating eight ploughlands altogether. People lived in a village around Cow Ford, and possibly also in the stockade of Ebury. The huts at Cow Ford probably stood mostly within the present palace precinct and would have been constructed out of wattle withies gathered from the forest and plastered with clay from the banks of the Tyburn, their roofs thatched with marsh reed. This village would be called Eye Cross, and may have been known by this name as early as Domesday. A stone cross was later erected on the village green, but the name probably derived from the ford across the Tyburn. The village green is generally thought to have straddled the southern corner of the palace forecourt and grounds, and as late as the seventeenth century a tangle of tiny closes indicated the likely ancient presence of those Domesday huts and gardens.[13]

---

* Just as Tyburn derived from T'Eia Burn, so Eaia, Eia or Eiaburgh elided over the centuries into Ebury, the present-day survivor from their past. Changing names are confusing, and for convenience it seems simplest, if not chronologically accurate, to use Ebury from now on.

The settlement was certainly very wet. The Tyburn overflowed in winter and there would have been a great many ponds which stubbornly refused to drain, bringing all the diseases associated with stagnant water. How many people in total lived around the palace site in 1086 is difficult to estimate. A few will have made a living out of the busy ford crossing, selling ale, helping to haul loads up from the water, extorting coins when vehicles became mired. The rest subsisted on the land, and it would not be unreasonable to guess that there were between twenty and thirty huts actually at Eye Cross, containing around 100 men, women and children. Then there would be barns, ox-stalls and corn baskets propped out of the wet on stilts, a not inconsiderable settlement for the period.

Every person living there would have been delighted when their owner-ship was transferred from the de Mandeville heirs to the abbey. A more distant foundation would have been preferable, since distance conferred some immunity from interference, but the church was far less subject to violent change than barons with their unpredictably quarrelsome sons, and provided help to the poor in scarcity or sickness. The Westminster monks would prove throughout the existence of their community to be ambitious and invariably indebted: some forgot their vows for decades at a time, but among them were a few spiritual or outstandingly scholarly men, and as a foundation it rarely overlooked Christian principles entirely.

Only a few months after Geoffrey de Mandeville's death, word came from Normandy that the Conqueror had been killed when his horse reared, frightened by a spark in a burning town. Word spread as fast as messen-gers could travel through Normandy to England: up the causeway from Westminster and across Cow Ford they raced, seeking out the late king's officers and shouting out snippets of news as they passed.

This illuminated initial graphically illustrates the formal feudal relationship of king and lord which controlled nearly all of William the Conqueror's new subjects in England. (Durham Cathedral Library, by courtesy of the Dean and Chapter: MS A.II.3, f. 225v)

*Ocaptabunt in animam iufti: + fan
guinem innocentem condempnabunt.*

*Once the manor of Ebury was owned by the Church, the daily agricultural round would have
continued year after year, regardless of the political roundabout at Westminster. Here, peasants
are shown ploughing.* (Mansell Collection)

People everywhere were stunned. In all his life William had hardly known
a day of illness, his energy phenomenal in an energetic age. Now the leader
of wolves, whose presence dominated England and Normandy for a generation, was dead. William had been merciless and was not greatly loved, but his
majesty inspired respect in the remotest corner of his realm. At Eye Cross, the
villagers lived close to a hall where he often came; they had seen him ride
through their ford and across their ploughlands to hunt, as he liked tirelessly
to do. And as he rode past they must have felt his magnetism, sensed his
ruthlessness, admired the way he forced his detestable barons to carry out
his will. As they watched the messengers gallop past, there would have been
many uneasy whisperings about what might happen next.

It was mid-September when word of William's death reached Westminster
and on Ebury Manor the harvest was nearly gathered in. The forest leaves
were touched with bronze and oxen harnessed ten or twelve to a team had
begun to plough the moist dark earth. The shrill cries of boys carrying goads
pierced the autumn air, without varying staid ox paces by a fraction. The
skill of a drover was to keep his beasts going steadily forward past obstructions and through the shallower pools, putting off the task of turning such a
long team. The strips and baulks of individual holdings made his task more
difficult, but with luck a few furrows might stretch across the whole site of
the modern palace, its courtyard and gardens. Then the oxen would pause
to breathe, before stepping slowly and with a great flurry of cries, sideways
and sideways until with God's good grace their drover was able to set them
off towards the village again, with the same narrow wave of soil breaking at
their heels. Day after day, season after season, this was the reality of life.

At Westminster, and sounding very close across the marsh, the mourning
bells began to toll for William, King and Conqueror, whose achievements
were reality too, and would echo down the centuries.

CHAPTER 4

Fashion and Forgery

From a moralist's point of view, William's son, Rufus, must be considered the worst king ever to have sat on the English throne. His Court was legendary for its wickedness, his followers notorious for lust, brazen opportunism and cruelty. Perhaps characteristically, the English did not at first dislike him; they greeted his accession with enthusiasm and rallied to his banner when a revolt threatened his rule. Only later did heavy taxation arouse discontent.

Rufus had been educated by Archbishop Lanfranc, one of the most notable churchmen of his time, but every honest teacher admits to failure sometimes. Lanfranc died soon after he consecrated his pupil as king, lamenting that after all his toil Rufus was not even a Christian. He was in fact that rare phenomenon among rulers, a boastful atheist. Even nowadays, few political leaders outside the former communist world actually proclaim religious disbelief, and it is out of fashion there; in medieval times it was unimaginable.[1]

After Lanfranc died, no one remained at Court with the courage or, in most cases, the inclination to criticize the king's conduct, which during his reign became more unbridled. His Court so appalled monkish chroniclers that they described its homosexuality and abominations in coy Latin phrases they hoped only scholars understood, a practice for a long time followed in English by later historians.

To make matters worse, Rufus borrowed from the Jews and instead of being repentant about it, he defended them from an outraged, persecuting church. Their cash was useful and he delighted to find yet another way of infuriating his bishops. A new-fangled idea called fashion appeared in his time too, which Rufus's cronies contrived to get labelled as mortal sin from the outset, when they dressed in skirts and wore their hair long, even inventing shoes with pointed toes. The monks who called down damnation on such perversions have not lacked successors to echo their feelings ever since.

So far as the tenants of Ebury were concerned, for some years they were probably not too dissatisfied by Rufus as a monarch. Salacious gossip about vice in high places is always agreeable, and they were close enough to its source to be constantly amazed by what they heard. As the years passed and everywhere people were squeezed for money to pay for his wars in Normandy the grumblings increased, as did the fear that such impiety might call down a curse not only on the king but on his subjects too. When Rufus was killed in the New Forest, the monks of Westminster, who were normally aggressive over their right to crown and bury monarchs, gracefully yielded to Winchester the honour of burying this particular king. They must have congratulated themselves on their foresight when, seven years later, Winchester's tower fell down.

Like other rip-roaring kings, Rufus enjoyed spending money. Especially on new buildings. When London burned down yet again in 1088 he became involved in grandiose plans to rebuild a much finer city, but since he expected the Londoners to pay for it, these were overtaken by its citizens' practical need for shelter while continuing to earn a living; a sequence which repeated itself many times, down to the aftermath of twentieth-century blitz. One lasting change did result from this particular fire: a stone-built bridge across the Thames which took thirty years to build (at private expense) and was finished in 1209. This hastened the process of sucking business travellers away from the Westminster boat-crossing, and therefore from Cow Ford. Even so, administrative traffic continued to be attracted westward, and the Archbishop of Canterbury's residence was built at Lambeth, where it remains today.

Miasmic wetness made life at Westminster wretched when it rained and occasionally left the whole island of Thorney swamped. This did not trouble Rufus, and he replaced the Confessor's old hall with a splendid new building 270 feet long, boasting that this was a mere bedchamber compared to the palace he would soon construct. He died before his ambition could be fulfilled, but, rebuilt and reroofed three centuries later, the hall's foundations still survive. Enthusiastic architect though he was, Rufus never wasted money on churches and since Westminster was ruled by a principled abbot during part of his reign, it lost rather than gained during his lifetime. Rufus's successor was not much interested in it either and also evolved the useful dodge of leaving the abbacy vacant so he could enjoy its revenues, but at least he brought the relative respectability of mistresses back to Court. On the debit side, he married a nun, which tempered the church's satisfaction over Rufus's death.

All this time, the administration of England and Normandy was becoming more complicated. A constantly travelling king began to need hierarchies of officials to help him govern, and permanent stores for his treasure. In addition, his staff already included marshals, whose impossible task it was to prevent bloodshed under the royal roof, constables to repel thieves, and minstrels to soothe the royal temperament. A queen attracted a different establishment, mainly of women to keep her out of mischief, but an energetic consort required grooms, tumblers and almoners, not to mention cot-rockers and wet-nurses for her children. The larger the Court, the loftier the names occupying these offices and the less inclined they were to do the work attached to them, a tradition carried down, untouched, into Queen Victoria's reign.

During this time Ebury's landlord, Westminster Abbey, often found itself in an extraordinarily difficult position, and partly as a consequence the next character in the history of the palace land is a monk, who doubled as an expert forger.

The community lived even closer to the Court buildings than modern maps suggest, with only a wall instead of a road separating the holy from the profane, and the abbey's offices were often used as a secretariat. Westminster's ambition to be the premier Benedictine foundation in England as well as its coronation church also meant that its abbots were unable, or did not wish, to distance themselves from the Court when it camped next door. And if proximity made it difficult for monks to avoid being drawn into politics, kings, too, particularly resented moral censure from a source so close to home.

There was a further, racial, tension. Abbots and priors were usually Norman, like the barons and officers at Court, but for some time after the Conquest the majority of monks remained English, often recruited from the sons of peasants on the abbey estates. Among these, Ebury was exceptional in being close at hand and because of it, royal and priestly needs constantly encroached on life there. Crops were trampled during hunting, beasts driven off for slaughter if stewards miscalculated their quantities, girls were more at risk from lustful squires. The Conqueror had required the abbey to provide knights equipped for combat as part of its feudal service, and Ebury's fields were convenient for hurried, last-minute gatherings of this force. Since most monks were affronted by their forced involvement in arms, chaos was the common factor on such occasions, ecclesiastical knights being widely derided as scrubs rejected by more warlike lords.

After Henry I's death in 1135 the country slid into the civil war in which Geoffrey de Mandeville's grandson mirrored the general disintegration by his career of brigandage. The palace lands do not seem to have suffered greatly during these years, in which London stayed loyal to King Stephen, but attempts by successive abbots to improve the management of their estates floundered in the prevailing anarchy. Once war became endemic a general truculence set in too, and the Westminster monks plunged deeply into debt.

One of the brothers at this time was called Osbert de Clare, one of several ghosts inhabiting the palace site who nowadays would be locked up as a criminal. He was born around 1100, the year Rufus died, and made no secret of his disgust that his abbey should be forced into perilous expedients simply because it had been denied the wealth which Edward the Confessor intended it to have. It did not occur to Osbert that these shortcomings might be a sign of that king's parsimony rather than subsequent fraud or double-crossings. To Osbert, Edward was perfect. Previous communities who had not pursued his canonization were traitors or worse, because once Westminster possessed its own very English saint its problems would be solved. Pilgrims would come, its revenues increase, all other foundations acknowledge its supremacy. To a fanatic like Osbert, it was as simple as that. How to achieve it was the only question.

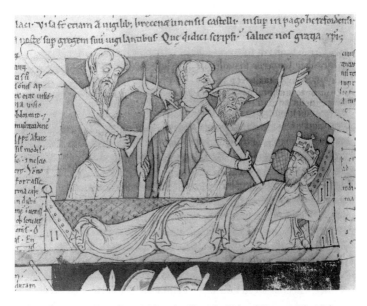

Peasants in arms at a time of anarchy, from the Chronicle of John of Worcester: 'The Nightmares of a King'. *As war and chaos spread, everyone became more truculent in defence of their rights. In the same way that monks were sometimes forced to forge documents in their own defence, peasants resorted to guerilla war.* (By permission of the Master and Fellows of Corpus Christi College, Oxford: MS 157, p. 282)

For several years Osbert astonished his fellow monks by producing a jungle-growth of ideas for solving their crisis. Not content with domestic matters he plunged into larger religious controversies and incurred the censure of his abbot; while still in his twenties he wrote to no less a personage than Anselm, Archbishop of Canterbury, chattily complimenting him on his return from exile.[2] It is not difficult to picture Osbert in the cloister, where the monks took their leisure and much of each day's business was transacted. A pest always pulling at sleeves to suggest some new scheme, his daring furiously mixed with madcap foolishness. Rarely satisfied by objections, but if he was, then plunging off after some different, more outrageous plan. Whispering to his neighbours at Mass if he remembered a fresh argument he might have used.

Around 1127, the abbot had had enough of Osbert and he was banished from the abbey. For several years he wandered disconsolately around other Benedictine houses, firing off complaints about his treatment. Even so, he assured his brothers at Westminster, however poverty-stricken he might be and unjust his exile, he had not and never would sully his hands with trade: disheartening evidence that the English sin of snobbery was already well entrenched.

And all the while, at Westminster the situation was getting worse. King Stephen needed money to fight for his crown, and was so often unsuccessful that his servants used the law as a weapon to extract increased assessments. A barbaric ferocity too, lay closer to the surface of life, riding roughshod over custom or undefended ownership. Previously, you lost if you were caught on the losing side in war; now you lost on the winning one as well.[3]

Westminster's titles to land, like many others, were often difficult to defend or missing altogether: eaten by rats or beetle, made indecipherable by floods, or written in derided Anglo-Saxon. In such turbulent times the abbey was in danger of losing manors to which its right had never previously been questioned: around this time a hospital dedicated to St James was set up by some citizens of London, its grounds hacked out of marsh which Westminster monks knew was theirs. As stagnant bog, this particular loss might not matter much, and a Christian hospital was annoyingly difficult to challenge, but to lose even marshland within sight of the abbey was deeply disturbing.

In their extremity the monks remembered Osbert de Clare, the one man who was convinced he knew how to save them. Now they craved his leadership above everything, to shine as light in their darkness, and forgot that they had considered him a dangerous freak before. In 1136 Osbert was recalled to Westminster and elected prior, only narrowly losing a contest for nomination as abbot. Once back in what he called 'his own country' of Westminster, Osbert settled with relish to the task of securing it from its enemies. While England's rulers were distracted by the war, the monks under his direction engaged consultants and turned themselves into a cooperative of highly skilled forgers.[4] How far this was a plan Osbert had long been advocating or whether it was only the latest strategem his busy imagination produced, is impossible to say. The fact remains that Westminster Abbey soon became known on the monastic grapevine as the place to go for good quality forgeries, and modern analysis traces Osbert's hand in nearly all of them.[5]

Ambition grew with success. Royal seals were feloniously struck and applied with abbey wax and home-made strings, a heinous capital offence. Existing but obscure deeds were usefully augmented, or cunningly scrubbed and reused; Osbert realized that by using original vellums he added veracity to his forgeries. Once launched, the scope of fraud continually widened. Spurious histories were composed and embellished,[6] a visit to Westminster by St Peter himself triumphantly sworn and publicized. Export enquiries from the continent offered the ultimate accolade, since competition there in ecclesiastical forgery was particularly keen.

In extenuation, Osbert was only introducing economies of scale to a practice which was widespread. At times it seemed almost the duty of a cleric to forge, and only natural to look indulgently on a practice to which a large proportion of the educated class was professionally addicted, in the same way as the aristocracy were sympathetic towards their occupational hazard of murder under arms. Forging the king's seal, on the other hand, was definitely treason, and cheating him of his proper dues almost equally dangerous. But monks were protected by benefit of clergy, which in effect offered at least one offence free of penalty, though Osbert had no intention of being found out. His objective was to authenticate the abbey's rights and being found out would only cast more doubt on them than before. History was there to be used.

In this perilous and daring enterprise, he was dazzlingly successful. There were a few mutterings from other monasteries about the notion that St Peter had personally consecrated Westminster, but these were easily shrugged off. From Osbert's time until recently no one seriously questioned charters dating back in some cases to the eighth century, which between them confirmed sweeping privileges for the abbey and gave the community a much stronger grip on their lands.

What had happened at St James's made the monks especially anxious about Ebury, which had already proved uniquely valuable to their community. Since animals and even geese must walk to market, often for long distances, it was the only place they owned sufficiently close at hand to bring them back to prime condition. Barns at Eye Cross stored the abbey's reserve of corn, and hay for horses could be brought in each day sweet from the stack. It is not surprising therefore to find that one of Osbert's most creative efforts relates to Ebury, and (from the abbey's point of view) one of the most useful. Kings, too, saw the advantages of land just across the Tyburn once their Court settled for longer periods at Westminster. Some of them would try to occupy it, only to find the ghost of Osbert de Clare waiting to trip them up.

The forged deed which relates in part to the palace site was dated from the time of King Edgar in 951, a charter which craftily included a definition of what Osbert considered ought originally to have been the western boundary of the abbey lands. Since Geoffrey de Mandeville's grant had been confirmed by the Conqueror, it was as nearly safe as any grant could be, and Osbert's charter was designed to show that the abbey already owned everything up to the place where his bequest began, that is to say, the Tyburn. It was too late to overturn the loss to St James's, but Osbert did not intend to lose any more of this valuable adjoining area, which in summer grew lush grass and here and there was beginning to be drained.

The description he wrote[7] in this spurious charter is interesting not for what might have existed in 951, but for what men living in 1138 knew existed in their own time and believed could reasonably be projected into the past. In Osbert's day a few monks would remember talking to men who had sung the Confessor's requiem, and it is their memories which are being used in the detail confirming the abbey's ownership of land on their own doorstep:

First up from the Thames along Merflete to Pollarstock, so to Bulinga Fen and along Old Ditch to Cow Ford. From Cow Ford along Tyburn to the Broad Military Way, then following the Military Way to the stock of St Andrew's Church, then within London Fen, proceeding south to the Thames and along by stream and strand to Merflete again.

Some of these places are guesswork now, but the outline is clear and in Osbert's day could not be bettered; if he could have thought of more explicit landmarks he would have used them. The abbey claims everything within a line roughly from Vauxhall Bridge (Merflete) through the morass of Bulinga Fen around Victoria Station to Buckingham Palace forecourt at Cow Ford, then northward to Oxford Street (Military Road) and back by way of St Andrew's, Holborn, to the Thames again. In the event, the more they claimed towards the City the more difficult it was to defend, but along the middle course of the Tyburn this forgery bolted on securely to de Mandeville's gift, except where St James already held part of the marsh. The Old Ditch, as mentioned earlier, must have been dug some time previously, to start draining fenland south of the palace gardens.

Osbert next turned his attention from manorial grants to his most cherished project: the canonization of Edward the Confessor. Undoubtedly his main motive was devotional. He believed that Edward was a saint, a man whose chastity had been a supreme sacrifice to God, and he wrote as many documents as he considered necessary to prove it. In 1141 he set out for Rome, to argue the Confessor's cause in front of Pope Innocent II. Unfortunately, although Osbert had seen to it that he did not lack documentation on his cause, he was more than a little short on humility and tact. Rome was awash with forgeries, fanatics and the peddled relics of saints, and even to obtain a papal hearing required a great deal of diplomacy. Innocent discounted unimportant supplicants on sight and was disinterested in England; after months of delay, his verdict brought all Osbert's hopes crashing down in a landslide of disappointment. When there was some evidence of a widespread English wish for Edward the Confessor's canonization, rather than a little local agitation, Innocent said crushingly, he might consider it. Certainly not now. Perhaps never.[8]

There is no record of Osbert's response, which is a pity. Egotistic at the best of times, his arrogance must have been increased by success, and it would be surprising if his argumentative boldness had not burst out in open fury. Significantly, Edward cruised to success as St Edward only a few years later, when the request to Rome was more coolly argued.

Osbert dallied in Rome for a while, making a nuisance of himself as he used to in the cloister, but eventually he tramped resentfully home to Westminster. There, during his absence the monks had come to realize how much pleasanter life was without him. Their forgery business was soundly established and you never knew with Osbert what he might think up next. In this very different atmosphere of smug achievement, he was soon at odds with everyone and again banished. He lived on until he was about seventy, a great age for the period, but only a few vitriolic letters survive, calling on heaven to witness the wickedness of the Westminster brothers, who had sold their Joseph into exile.

There is no reason to suppose that Osbert felt he had behaved criminally. Rather, he appears oblivious to ethical considerations; driven by conviction, by curiosity in debate, and an incurable cantankerousness which alienated even his supporters. He was faithful to truth as he saw it; not unlike a modern policeman who fabricates evidence because he is convinced of a suspect's guilt. He was certainly an exceptionally useful man to have around a twelfth-century abbey, and particularly Westminster, situated as it was at the eye of a disorderly and acquisitive storm in a time of civil war.

A very different contemporary of Osbert's, Eadmer, Archbishop of Canterbury, a saintly scholar who could not have failed to know he was taking part in a charade, showed a similar attitude when he rejoiced over a forgery, supplied by Westminster, which purported to prove the supremacy of Canterbury over York.[9] And that, too, has endured to the present day.

CHAPTER 5

Burglary

Around 1175 a priest called William Fitzstephen, who had been Thomas à Becket's confidential secretary, wrote the earliest description of an everyday London street scene. Fitzstephen began to write his master's biography soon after his murder, but both he and Becket were Londoners born and it almost seems as if, in the middle of this labour, he decided that a dry recital of events was not enough. He wanted to offer a last joyful saunter around their former haunts to a man who had also been his friend, in tone quite different to the rest of his book.

What he wrote[1] gives a vivid if somewhat idealistic view of the daily life along the Thames eight hundred years ago, and a distant glance at the palace site as well:

> Westminster rises on the river bank, [the King's Hall being] of the greatest splendour with outworks and bastions ... outside their houses are the citizens' gardens, side by side yet spacious and splendid, and set about with trees. To the north lie arable fields, pasture land and lush, level meadows with brooks flowing everywhere within them, which do turn the wheels of water mills ... Close by is the opening of a mighty forest, with timbered copses and the lairs of wild beasts, stags and does, wild boars and bulls.

In Fitzstephen's opinion, Westminster attracted a class of resident 'everywhere respected above all others for their civil demeanour, their good apparel, their table and their discourse'.

A more acid judgement from about the same time, by Richard of Devizes,[2] offers the perspective of a visitor rather than a native son:

> All sorts of men crowd together (in London) from every country under the heavens, and each brings his own vices and customs. No one lives there without falling into crime ... the number of braggarts and parasites is infinite. Actors and jesters, smooth-skinned lads, Moors, flatterers, effeminates, pederasts, belly-dancers, sorceresses, extortioners, night-wanderers, magicians, mimes, beggars, buffoons; all this tribe fill the houses. If you do not wish to live with evil-doers, do not live in London.

He says he is complaining about the City, but his list is more suggestive of Westminster and the Court, which perhaps he preferred not to criticize openly.

As Fitzstephen makes clear, drainage work between Westminster and the Tyburn had begun. The small mills he describes were probably driven by such currents as existed in the streamlets criss-crossing the area, or by muscle-power, and were used for a variety of purposes, including helping to shift some of the water. Windmills are not positively recorded in England until after Fitzstephen's death[3] and corn mills around the abbey were tidally driven.

The actual 40 acres or so which comprise the Buckingham Palace property today was at that time owned in three separate ways. The whole of the gardens and most of the area covered by buildings belonged to Westminster Abbey's Ebury estate, and was directly farmed for the daily needs of its monks, one of whom acted as land steward. The extreme eastern portion, nowadays part of the forecourt and frontage of the palace, then lay on the Westminster side of the Tyburn and was owned by the Hospital of St James. Cow Ford and the marshland surrounding it, where the south-eastern corner of the palace faces Buckingham Gate, relied on Osbert's 951 charter for clear title.

During this time the old causeway route from Westminster was slowly becoming wider, and a gravel bank roughly midway along it, which had always been slightly higher than the rest and consequently was rather extravagantly known as Toot Hill (Tothill), dried out sufficiently to grow a squatter settlement surrounded by tiny closes. This was probably further raised and extended as soil became available from building works at Westminster, in the first instance to provide an outwork on which a beacon could be lit to give warning of raiders: an eloquent testimony of the unsettled conditions. The old word 'Toot' meant a place from which warning could be given, as is quaintly demonstrated in Wyclif's translation of the Bible, when he rendered the phrase 'Nevertheless David took the stronghold of Zion,' as 'Forsooth, David took the totehill Syon.'

Early in the thirteenth century, a growing population drove City of London aldermen to seek a way of improving their supply of drinking water; their solution was to trap Tyburn's springs and bring them by conduit to Cheapside.[4] It was a remarkable contemporary feat of engineering, but as a result the lower Tyburn more or less dried up. Brackish marsh water still drained into it and after heavy rain it ran in spate as before, but its cleansing currents vanished; in summer, it became mere scummy pools which bred mosquitoes. Westminster Abbey solved this problem by bringing water all the way from the Westbourne in hollowed timber pipes, but the village of Eye Cross died. A few huts and possibly a tavern lingered on beside the ford, but the manor's peasants moved away from a stream that had become little more than a sewer.

Thorney ceased to be an island and expanded across the Tyburn delta, although the monastery retained its tidal ditches. Coincidentally, the abbey church was being torn down and rebuilt, and the numbers of men employed there added to the pressure on living space. The king's Court, too, when it came to Westminster brought more people with it, though months or years occasionally still passed while the royal halls rotted emptily in the damp. These factors gave added urgency to land reclamation at Ebury and by about 1260 someone had the clever idea of deepening the Old Ditch, reversing its flow, and extending it to reach the Thames near Chelsea. This meant that instead of curving to reach Westminster, the new Tyburn flowed directly south[5] (where modern Tachbrook Street marks its course), adding some badly needed scour to an otherwise stagnant area. Rich alluvial land began to surface, like Dutch polders, as the diggings progressed, the earliest huddled in a tentative patchwork around Eye Cross. As confidence grew these increased in size, pushing south into fenland, and two new farmsteads emerged, probably populated by migrants from the tumbledown old village: Eybury Farm and Neate Farm. Ebury was on the site of the present square – probably coinciding, too, with Saxon Eiaburgh – which still reflects the shape of this old farmstead from which the palace lands were cultivated. Neate Farm developed further south where there had long been an islet above the swamp. The old English word 'neate' meant cattle, which reinforces the idea that Ebury Manor was widely used for fattening beasts before consumption at Westminster. A later inventory reveals large numbers of cattle and sheep there, together with pigeon houses and goose pools.

Henry III ruled England for much of the thirteenth century. He was one of those kings always at odds with his subjects, alternately obstinate and weak, a clash of personality which made his Plantagenet rages not so much terrible as annoyingly capricious. He also made the mistake, from an English point of view, of choosing a grasping French hussy, Eleanor of Provence, as his wife, who cherished extravagant ideas about baths, glass in the palace windows and courtly manners. Since Henry reigned for fifty-six years and both of them were spendthrift, the Exchequer plunged seriously into debt.

They started by throwing an immense nuptial party. This was held along the causeway and at Tothill; in spite of the recent drainings, still a ruinously wet location. Huge quantities of sand and bundled twigs were thrown down to try and dry it out, and it is easy to imagine the bustle at Ebury to dig and haul these loads, and the fervent prayers of officials for fine weather. Galleries were hung with banners, green boughs slung to shade the ladies, jousting barriers precariously strutted where the boggy ground kept sucking posts out of sight, feastings lugged across the marsh. Great tournaments were the spectacle of the age for rich and poor alike, in atmosphere like a bullfight and Cup Final flung together, but afterwards the grumblings about royal extravagance rapidly increased.

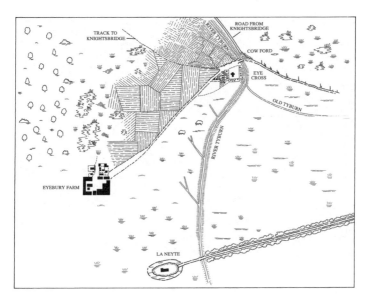

Sketch plan showing the slow extension of reclaimed land around the palace site. Eye Cross began to decay after Tyburn springs were captured to feed the City's water supply and the settlement probably shifted nearer Ebury Farm. To the south, the island of La Neyte had become the Abbot of Westminster's country retreat. Details included for this period can be speculative only.

Henry's particular weakness was architecture rather than tournaments, and he was forced to borrow at ruinous rates to finance his projects, which never prevented him from squandering money where he chose. Such conspicuous consumption soon changed grumbling into fury. Even worse, the king spent valuable tax money on Eleanor's foreign relatives, whom Londoners rudely considered to breed like lice on the body politic. One name which remembers them still is the Savoy, gifted by Henry to Eleanor's uncle from that duchy, and not long afterwards, as she approached Westminster by boat, a mob gathered on London Bridge to pelt her with offal, dung and rotten vegetables.

In this climate, the huge costs incurred on Westminster Abbey were deeply unpopular even in a religious age. Perhaps Edward the Confessor's building did look a little old-fashioned by then, but it was reasonably weathertight and the English have seldom taken kindly to change for change's sake. Not so Henry and Eleanor. Their temperaments came together in genuine artistic excitement as the work progressed, not least because the techniques of design had changed dramatically since Norman times: thin walls, flying buttresses, roofs branching in stone like forest trees, there scarcely seemed an end to the experiments they could try.

Craftsmanship keeps faith with the past: Mason's Yard, Westminster Abbey, August 1995, towards the end of another great rebuilding and repair programme. It is hard to spot many differences in tools or skill from Henry III's thirteenth-century rebuilding of the abbey. (Author)

For the occupants of the Buckingham Palace lands these were strenuous and profitable years, as proximity to Westminster gave them opportunities too. The quantity of materials and workmen required for such an enterprise was enormous. Hundreds of boatloads of stone must be unloaded and carted, wound up on pulleys, heaved from place to place. Tin was brought from Cornwall, marble from Dorset, lead from Derbyshire, stone from Kent and Normandy, timber from Essex, coloured glass from Flanders. Ebury was the nearest source of clay as well as food, of reeds for thatching workmen's huts, skin for parchment and leather, goose-quills for reckonings. In one mid-century week no fewer than 391 craftsmen were at work on new Westminster Abbey, not counting casual labour, which must have been two or three times greater.[6] When the families of these men are added in, together with the Court when resident, the pimps, whores, stallkeepers, taverners, itinerants and mountebanks attracted by boom-town conditions, upwards of ten thousand people needed to be fed in Westminster every day at the height of the building season. Some idea of the local spin-off may be gathered from the case of William the swineherd, probably an Ebury man, who was paid 12s 7d for digging and carrying a thousand cartloads of sand between April and December 1253. He must have acted as entrepreneur, hacking out a new career for himself away from pigs if he succeeded in what sounds a formidable task. And if the sum seems miserly, it represented eighteen weeks' pay for a skilled craftsman.[7]

The central purpose Henry cherished in his rebuilding of the abbey was to create a shrine for St Edward the Confessor, whom he considered a personal, if spiritual, friend. The Westminster monks, while approving his purpose, found its practical inconveniences very great as they were forced for years to live in makeshift sheds while their abbey was pulled down around them. Their devotions were interrupted, their lives made wretched by dust and mud not to mention whole gaggles of painted, tittering women, who kept coming to gawp at new stone, confusing their monkly vows to chastity. Some of the brothers no doubt found this agreeable, but when Henry started keeping his clothes in a side chapel and took over their new chapter house for his Great Council, the litany of complaint increased. The royal jewel box and treasury followed his wardrobe into the abbey, and abbots were more frequently sent away on royal errands. On the whole, these began to enjoy their more secular life, but within their community and on their estates discipline unravelled fast.

Henry III died in 1272 and was buried in the empty tomb from which Edward the Confessor's body had again been translated into something more splendid, but the abbey was still unfinished and its nave boarded up; more worryingly, the new king, Edward I, had different priorities to his father. Immediately, his coronation lined a great many pockets, on Ebury and elsewhere. No fewer than 380 oxen, 450 porkers, 278 bacon pigs, 430 sheep and 22,000 fowl were consumed at the feast which followed it. The meal lasted a fortnight and during that August of 1274 the area around Cow Ford must have been a hell's kitchen of slaughtered animals, terrified bleats, squallings and lowings from beasts scenting blood. Women knelt where the palace gardens now are, scraping skins for curing; others washed wool in inadequate water, boiled hoofs and bones for glue, tallow with ashes for soap. Everyone was exhausted by haste, and the summer heat made offal stink faster than it could be removed, snapped tempers and kindled mighty thirsts for ale. The by-products of such gigantic slaughterings were too valuable to be lost and yet inevitably they were lost under such conditions. Bailiffs covertly took their cut, stray dogs and flocks of gorging gulls settled in a dirty, fighting plague wherever they weren't kicked aside, several modest but triumphant fortunes no doubt made by pilfering Ebury villagers.

To begin with, Edward kept court as usual at Westminster, but wars in Wales and Scotland soon drew him away. His deserted halls and a debt-ridden abbey brought economic ruin to people who until then had been fairly well-off, though the City continued to thrive for a while on war-time profits. Immediately, the Jews paid the most obvious price for high interest rates and prejudice, and were expelled entirely from England, with further dire consequences for the economy.

For these and other reasons rents at Westminster nose-dived, although it is impossible to know whether sentiment or hard times made landowners Alice and Muriel exact a rent of only one rose yearly from Nicholas of

Longditch, a deed witnessed by John of Eia (Ebury).[8] Properties lay empty, the numbers of people working on the abbey dwindled from lack of funds, a disastrous fire devastated part of the king's palace and only just spared the chapter house and abbey. By the late 1290s the royal tax assessors, never a breed notable for discounting value, classified Westminster as a village.[9] Even the City by then was suffering, and when yet another forced contribution to the king's war chest was announced, the Dean of St Paul's fell dead where he stood from shock.

Edward transferred the remaining elements of his government to York in 1298, leaving behind him at Westminster only some stored treasure in safe custody at the abbey, the last reserve of a near-bankrupt crown. His palace was left in the care of a part-time keeper, and a bold and disreputable mob made up of both sexes was soon squatting there, abetted by the remaining staff.

★　★　★

The ghost of Richard Pudlicott haunts Westminster rather than Buckingham Palace, but his story does offer a sideways glance at the frenetic excitements which occasionally enlivened the drudgery of everyday life around Cow Ford; besides, it is simply too good to miss.[10]

Richard began life as a clerk in holy orders, but a devotional life soon bored him and he drifted into trading, first in cheese and butter, eventually in wool. Wool was England's great medieval export and dealing in it took Richard to the Netherlands. He enjoyed seizing chances and probably went in the hope that King Edward's presence on campaign would help open up the market to outsiders. In fact, it continued to be dominated by far larger traders than himself, but Richard apparently succeeded in making a little money around the edges of what, for the time, was a highly sophisticated economy. Then disaster struck. King Edward's campaigning was unsuccessful and he returned to England leaving a great many unpaid bills behind him. When the Flemings cast around for means to make him pay up, they hit on the notion of locking up English merchants as sureties for the debt. They could either pay a ransom for release, or their howls of anguish would compel their king to settle what he owed.

Almost inevitably, Richard was among those arrested, an expendable man without friends in the City of London, which even in extremity remained sufficiently powerful to protect its richer citizens. Unluckily for Richard, he was expendable to his king as well; weeks went by without any indication that Edward was willing to pay his debts and obtain freedom for his subjects held in stinking Ghent goal. Richard tried wheedling his captors, since not only his person was at stake, but all his recently earned profits. Nothing worked, until eventually he escaped from prison without securing the release of his property.

Manuscript drawings depicting Richard Pudlicott's daring robbery of royal treasure from Westminster, and his subsequent arrest by Richard Droxford. (British Library: Cott. Nero Dii ff. 193–4)

He was reduced to beggary, but somehow reached England. All his bright hopes were blasted, and, nursing a bitter grievance, he turned up in Westminster, where he joined the horde of squatters in the palace courtyards. He considered he had a right to be there as a petitioner to the king for restoration of his losses, and it is hard to disagree with him. The snag was that all the king's Courts and his Exchequer were now in York, but Richard seems to have found some satisfaction at least in living at royal expense. He was not satisfied for long.

It was all very well to enjoy good followship with harlots and drifters in shelter from the winter rain, but Richard had hoped to claw away from itinerant life. He wanted better prospects than free drink and a pallet out of the damp, and his attention was soon caught by the silver plate being carried in and out of the monks' refectory next door. A king had founded the abbey, hadn't he? By a very considerable jump of ideas but without difficulty, Richard convinced himself that it would be only justice to repay his losses by 'coming at the goods which he saw'. Thus a king's foundation might, somewhat irregularly, settle the king's debts.

He used a ladder to scramble through a window into the chapter house; from there he tiptoed to the refectory, choosing a time after the plate was in position and before the brothers came to eat. Hastily, he slung as many dishes, cups and ewers as he could carry into a sack and returned the way he had come. It was so easy, God must have helped him; in retrospect, it is difficult to avoid the conviction that at least one of the monks must have helped him too.

If Richard Pudlicott had ever been a shrewd businessman, this success destroyed such capacity as he possessed for rational calculation. He sold his booty, probably at a huge discount, but was so exhilarated by making such easy money that far from discreetly vanishing back into trade, he remained at Westminster, roistering in the king's hall. Within a few weeks he was broke again, and looking out for something else to steal.

A greater intimacy had grown up between him and the monks during this time as drinking companions. From them he learned that the king's reserve of treasure had been left in the abbey's care, well secured in the Chapel of the Pyx, to be sure, where the only entry was guarded by several locks and a stone trap built into the staircase, but temptingly close by. Later, Richard Pudlicott would swear that he had robbed the royal treasury alone, without accomplices; that he hacked single-handed through 13 feet of solid stone within easy earshot of the cloister to reach the underground treasure chamber, and merely sowed some hemp seed to hide the gaping gash he made in the abbey's masonry. This is plainly incredible, if only because hemp would have needed to grow to wilderness proportions during the winter months of December to March 1303. The slackest of abbots, the most uncovetous of monks and uninterested of Westminster inhabitants would have had to hear nothing, notice nothing for weeks on end.

But by whatever means Pudlicott obtained entry to the treasure, and probably he simply borrowed the sacristan's keys, he remained inside the Chapel of the Pyx for two days, leisurely sorting its contents and passing it out to accomplices in the churchyard. They carried it to the Fleet prison, where William the Under Palace-Keeper moonlighted as warden and could offer a safe haven. As they did so they became more and more elated by the size of their booty, drinking, shouting, ostentatiously clinking sacks, hiring horses to carry such a bulk of precious metals, and finally holding a two-day celebratory feast inside the Fleet. Not only the monks, abbey servants and custodians of the palace, but most Westminster residents and a great many of those who lived along the Strand must have been aware of what was going on, long before the haul was finished. Yet only the almost hysterical indiscretion with which the conspirators sold off their loot eventually forced sluggish authority to take notice of what by then was common knowledge.

The robbers carelessly strewed silver cups and silver plate around; they threw valuable jewels at onlookers, drank toasts from goblets and hurled them into the Thames afterwards, paid taverners and peasant hucksters in gold and silver. Some of this found its way to the huts at Eye Cross on the palace site, where boys discovered pieces hidden in the hedgerows. Goblets were hauled up in fishermen's nets or found where they had bounced off gravestones. Rings sparkled on the fingers of whores – one of them swearing later that hers had been given to her by Adam the Sacrist in the abbey, 'so that she would become his friend'.

City of London goldsmiths, respectable traders within the medieval sense of the word, happily acted as receivers for quantities of precious goods, and new gold florins changed hands as far afield as York and King's Lynn. It was as if the haul had been so easy to obtain, and was so far beyond anyone's previous experience, that joy spun everyone who touched it quite literally off their heads.

The robbery became almost a joke in London and Westminster, and laughter spread with the florins along the moneychangers' routes eventually all the way to Linlithgow, where the king was camped in the course of his Scottish war. As soon as Edward heard the rumours, he appointed a commission to investigate, and the keeper of his private monies, John Droxford, was sent hotfoot to London with a posse of armed men and the keys to Pyx Chapel crypt.

When Droxford arrived in a clash of steel to announce his mission, the monks threw up their hands and were suitably dumbstruck when he opened the Pyx door to discover the void within. Instantly, Droxford ordered a search throughout Westminster. Protests about clerical privilege were disregarded, no time given for concealment. Soldiers were placed on guard, floors ripped up, bedstraw speared; all Thorney was like an overturned beehive. Citizens jerked out of their dreamlike state of celebration to realize with horror that only minutes remained in which to decide how best to save their lives.

The only answer was to get rid of damning evidence fast, and cups and plates were hurled higgledy-piggledy into middens, dumped in sacks, thrown out of doors. The goldsmiths of London swore oaths that they had not recognized the king's possessions and handsomely gave back such pieces as were still in their possession, the most fantastical excuses cobbled together to account for goods identified as belonging to the royal treasury. Anyone slow off the mark, or too close to Droxford when the search began, was caught. A haul of plate was discovered beneath William the Under Palace-Keeper's bed, and a great deal more in the lodgings of Richard Pudlicott and his mistress; clearly he was betrayed by someone saving his own skin. Adam the Sacrist, probably a key figure in the burglary itself, and several other monks, were seized in possession of jewels, silver and gold.

A Victorian drawing of the Chapel of the Pyx, the treasure house raided by Richard Pudlicott. (From Wolford (ed.), *London Old and New*)

By the time Droxford finished checking his lists a week or so later, much of the treasure had been recovered or returned, though some disappeared for ever. Pudlicott and William the Under-Keeper were in prison, together with thirty-two other lay persons. The City goldsmiths presented a united front, a great many specious lies and a handsome bribe, which successfully allowed them to walk away from trouble, possibly in overall credit.

On the other hand, Droxford was in absolutely no doubt about the abbey's complicity and he arrested the entire Westminster community, lay and otherwise, including the abbot and forty-eight monks. Modern tabloids could not ask for a greater scandal, and in an age when clergy enjoyed relative immunity from the law, Droxford's action caused uproar. Much against his will, he was forced to release most of his clerical prisoners on bail; only ten monks and half a dozen seculars, including Pudlicott, stood trial a few months later, when Pudlicott took the whole blame for the affair. Whether this was out of pride in his achievement or from chivalry is impossible to guess. Certainly he must have realized that for him there was no escape. Juries were empanelled from Westminster and every hundred in Surrey and Middlesex including Ebury, where a few secret and spectacular winners may have survived, because Droxford's search inevitably reached there late.

Nearly a year was spent in investigations, at the end of which Pudlicott was found guilty. William the Under-Keeper, Adam the Sacrist and several other monks were condemned as accomplices. In March 1304 William and five lay culprits were hanged, but Droxford lacked the authority to hang priests. Accordingly, the monks and Pudlicott, who had been a cleric in his youth, were reserved for sentencing until the king could be consulted. Edward, however, was a dangerous man to rob. He furiously resented being made to look a fool, and was notorious for disregarding caution where his honour was concerned. When he returned to London, Richard Pudlicott was summarily hanged, regardless of his clerical background, and some reports declare that his corpse was flayed and the skin nailed to the door of the Chapel of the Pyx.

But in not untypical medieval style, after this exemplary revenge Edward's wrath simmered down and Richard's staunch avowal of responsibility was used as a way discreetly to forget about the monks. A few remained in prison for several years, the rest were released within months, including the abbot, Walter of Wenlock.

Morale at the monastery was not improved by these happenings. An atmosphere of strife and distrust prevailed for nearly a generation afterwards, during which time the monks were usually hostile to the reigning king. This state of affairs gave the kings concerned an outstandingly bad press and also resulted in their personal treasury being transferred to the Tower of London. In fairness to the monks, there was a great deal about Edward II, in particular, to which they could reasonably take exception.

CHAPTER 6

Triumph out of Disaster

When the inhabitants of Ebury Manor looked back on the thirteenth century, they must often have exclaimed that those were surely good years to be alive. Of course their monastic landowners poked their noses where they weren't wanted and paid niggardly wages, but there had been work for a growing population then. Cultivated land on the manor probably doubled, the ancient tree-stumps had rotted, the remaining pools were convenient for watering the herds of cattle shuttled in from other abbey estates. Until the 1290s an extravagant Court and daring building projects gave humble people the chance to deal on the side in timber, clay and filched foodstuffs, not to mention the occasional stolen cup hidden in a hedgerow. There was a whiff of freewheeling hope in the air and many girls, too, would have set off with a bundle in their hands to try their fortune in Westminster as servants, petty traders, harlots or entertainers.

With the new century, conditions nearly everywhere in Europe changed sharply for the worse. Populations had slowly been rising for a long time and a largely agrarian economy was increasingly stretched to feed them all. Storage of surpluses from good years was difficult too, particularly when shortages quickly led to riots in which such stocks as existed often vanished in a day. Even in good times, too many people depended on seasonal labour for their livelihood, eked out by begging, theft or charity. Every year needed to be a good growing year, and weather was not so much a topic of conversation as a matter for prayer, frantic hope or despair, and semi-pagan rites.

From around 1311 there began a series of poor harvests, and the situation became sufficiently serious for Edward II to proclaim a schedule of maximum prices with severe penalties for exceeding them, but in a time of critical shortage this may only have driven them higher, as people traded clandestinely. Prices continued to climb and in the devastatingly wet year of 1314 alone, they nearly tripled.[1]

In 1315 cold grey skies clamped down over the whole of Europe north of the Alps, while in England torrential rain began falling in mid-May. The Archbishop of Canterbury ordered a barefoot pilgrimage through the streets of London, and so great was the people's terror of calamity that some in the procession were reported to have stripped naked and danced like heathens to propitiate the downpour. Relics were paraded and entreated. Dogs were pursued in the streets and eaten by starving mobs. The rain continued through into autumn, temperatures plunged, and such grain as could be gathered failed to nourish man or beast. Cattle plague, infections and virulent dysentery followed.

By this time the people of Ebury were in desperate straits. The rains were such that Thorney returned to being an island where its inhabitants used boats to get around, even inside the abbey nave. The whole area between Westminster, St James and Chelsea on its shingle bank became a lagoon, topped up at each high tide by the Thames. Work on the abbey ceased altogether, nobles turned off retinues they were unable to feed, and the king's own stewards sometimes could not find enough bread to satisfy an attenuated Court. For many people wholesome food was unobtainable. Eggs vanished from market stalls, stored grain sprouted before the next harvest, milk and meat were no more than a memory. Salt, a crucial preservative, ran away to nothing. The poor ate rats and cats, the dung of doves and their own children. Cannibalism was reliably reported from all over Europe.

By June the following year the price of wheat had reached 150 pence a quarter, from 25 pence three years before, yet wages had dropped. A monk, John Trokelowe,[2] tells how he was forced to pick his way between dirty dead bodies whenever he went out; prisoners were not given any food, and ferociously attacked anyone newly arrested, devouring them alive.

At Ebury, the work of generations was wiped out. Dykes collapsed under the weight of water, reclaimed fields were covered by a swirling, brackish tide whose currents destroyed enclosures, barns and huts. The present palace gardens may have remained above tidal level but were sodden, the pools there enlarging into lakes. Its heavy clay was a nightmare task to cultivate when beasts and men were weak with hunger. The old course of the Tyburn was in spate, its new outlet to the south submerged, fenland again stretched into the distance.

All hope was fixed on the next harvest. Emaciated people fought their own and other people's hunger to save and sow seeds they were ravenous to eat, stood armed with sickles and clubs to guard their remaining breeding stock from robbers. That year too was grey, but in England's southern counties it was better than before. Men and women prayed a dozen times a day as clouds piled up in the west, hiding a fickle sun. Grain swelled with agonizing slowness, and cattle fared badly on the dirty, sappy grass. In frantic haste towards the end of August the harvest was begun, while everyone looked over their shoulder at a threatening sky and shuddered in thin autumn winds: scarecrow figures staggering across the fields, slipping, falling in weakness but somehow swaying back on their feet to work again, until at last a crop of sorts was gathered in. Prices remained high and disease prevalent, with above-average death rates, but slowly life struggled back closer to normality. Elsewhere, disastrous shortages persisted into 1317.

Within this short period of 1311–17 perhaps 15 per cent of Ebury's inhabitants died.[3] Work, too, continued to be lacking, while for the first time the king became almost their neighbour, occupying La Neyte Farm instead of his own mud-laden hall whenever he visited Westminster. With an unerring eye to comfort, abbots of Westminster had turned this into a private hall away from malcontent monks, and linked it directly with the abbey's west door by another causeway, planted with willows instead of posts. Today, unromantic Warwick Way runs exactly where abbots, kings and queens rode to and from La Neyte along what they more elegantly knew as Willow Walk.

Successive abbots angrily objected to the king's high-handed occupation of their property,[4] although there may have been some sniggers in the cloister. A superior who enjoyed snug comfort while, only a mile away, his community endured wet floors and leaking roofs could scarcely expect their whole-hearted support. But as Edward II's power waned, an acknowledgement was finally forced out of him that 'he did not hold the manors of Ebury and Neyte unless at the will of the Abbot at Westminster'. Two years later he was horribly murdered by his barons, and his son, Edward III, prudently gave the abbot back his manor, perhaps with more than half an eye on getting himself crowned in the abbey, by then essential for legitimating a succession. Osbert de Clare's forgeries continued to be useful in many workmanlike ways.

These disputes gave rise to a number of documents[5] which offer glimpses of what the Buckingham Palace area was actually like in the 1320s, by which time Ebury Farm had almost certainly become the major settlement,[6] although sheriff's courts continued to meet by the cross at Cow Ford. In 1354 John Potter (who came from as far away as Durham) was outlawed there, and his family 'made to be waifs' after they broke into the houses of William Lounde and John Pecche at Eye.[7]

Among the place-names mentioned in the documents are Windmill Hill, whose mill most likely creaked around on the nearest dry ground to the old village; Pourte Lane, possibly the track across the palace grounds from Cow Ford; Causeway Haw (enclosure), which speaks for itself; and a garden called Burgoyne, tentatively identified with old 'Bulinga Fen'. The crofts around Eye Cross were jealously guarded as personal property, since anything cultivated there, however minute in quantity, could be privately sold on Westminster's stalls: eggs, beans, honey, capons and herbs would all fetch premium prices. Goosepool Field is impossible to place but again shows the type of use to which the palace area was being put.

Another name of interest which appears around this time is Rosamonds, because Rosamonds Pool was a renowned eighteenth-century lover's trysting place and can be pinpointed almost exactly, since it was only filled in shortly before Victoria's palace was built. It lay just outside the palace railings to the south of the Queen's Memorial.

Abbot Nicholas Litlington's initials were proudly displayed in stained glass on a window head among his additions to the monastery buildings. (From 'Sketches of Norman Westminster' in the *Gentleman's Magazine*, 1861)

Edward III was very different from his father, and like Rufus before him, a devotee of chivalry and fashion: by this time tights were all the rage instead of skirts. Tights, moreover, which were designed to emphasise the genitals, and moralists found them quite as disgusting as skirts. Edward's wars intermittently bankrupted the treasury, but at random intervals triggered citywide revellings when trumpets blew on London Bridge and carts full of campaigning loot rumbled off the king's ships, followed by drunken gatherings of knights and men-at-arms. Suddenly everyone scrambled after furs and velvet gowns, and the rumour of glorious caperings in stolen finery might bring whole families hurrying in from Ebury to try and snatch what they could from the disorderly rejoicings. With luck, even a ploughman's wife might boast a piece of cutlery grabbed from the spoils, or scurry home delightedly to hang up a fragment of embroidered cloth.

The king and his Court were a city in themselves; a roistering nonsensical city, brimful with schemers and strolling players, where people from Ebury earned what they could and gawped at candlelight winking on fingers knobbled with gems. Pine-tar torches blazed along the Thames, extravagant desires clamoured for satisfaction, bishops tacked craftily for advantage and servants acted as disdainfully as their masters. When the hunt rode out across Cow Ford it carelessly trampled down crops while whooping after hares; one day as a chivalric joke, each lady on her palfrey led a knight by a length of silver chain, and heaven only knew what peasants on Ebury thought about that. Then, in 1348, plague struck.

Recovery after the great shortages earlier in the century had always been fragile. Epidemics raged more fiercely, there were more cold, damp summers than before, but the Black Death brought a different dimension of misery altogether. Victims usually died in agony within hours, and no one knew where this unknown terror came from, why or how it struck, or if it would cease before every soul was dead. It truly seemed as if the end of the world had come, in which the Devil triumphed over God. The stench and pus of plague poisoned Christendom itself, and hysteria sent still healthy people mindlessly running. Some abandoned their families if a member became infected: since nothing could be done to save a victim, courage seemed quite purposeless. Vice flourished, morals were abandoned like so much baggage, the trappings of civilization kicked aside.

Alongside the horror stories, many people behaved as well as despair allowed, a few with saintly heroism, and daily life somehow struggled on. Westminster suffered badly; the autumn and winter of 1348 was again relentlessly wet and the king, his followers and clerks, even his courts of justice which had been settled there for years, fled into the country. The abbot and twenty-seven of his monks died, together with unnumbered servants and two visiting archbishops. Estimates vary, and Westminster had always been subject to rapid fluctuations in population, but perhaps up to half its permanent inhabitants perished, a higher figure than for the country as a whole. Many more fled in fear or through lack of work.

Figures for Ebury are uncertain. At first the manor may have increased in population as refugees camped on the palace fields, hoping this unknown visitation would pass. Soon it was apparent that the infection followed wherever people went, and the wet season made conditions especially dreadful where the only materials for temporary accommodation were withies, reeds and mud. Some idea of mortality in such conditions can be gained from the Hospital of St James, which was at least weathertight, where all the inhabitants died except one.

Plague raged throughout 1349 before partially burning itself out, but other epidemics followed in 1361, 1362 and 1369. Continuing foul weather and the natural calamities connected with it further increased the almost universal misery, and by the mid 1360s the island of Thorney would have become a ghost town, leaving Ebury to flounder out of its morass as best it could, had it not been for two men who succeeded each other in office at the abbey.

Nicholas Litlington became prior of Westminster in 1352, and abbot when the previous occupant, Simon Langham, went to Ely as bishop, eventually to become Lord Treasurer and Chancellor of England. Langham and Litlington worked together to pull the abbey back from calamity after the first onslaught of plague, recruiting fresh monks, reorganizing manors stripped of their peasants, reintroducing order into chaotic finances. While Langham possessed piety, scholarly habits and, surprisingly, an accountant's eye for fraud, perhaps because he was personally wealthy, Litlington had a dynamic way with people. In many ways he was an unusual man to find as a monk. Good with his hands, and practical; not contemplative at all, he liked always to be busy. 'A great stirrer-up of men' was how a contemporary described him,[8] and for years the monks said a prayer of thanksgiving on the anniversary of his election.

In the winter of 1361, not long after Litlington became abbot, a great gale blew, booming against stonework in gusts that shattered glass, and when the wind dropped, half Westminster was flat. The Thames had backed up and flooded Thorney as well as the marsh, leaving behind a scum of timber, thatch and bodies floating in its market place and lanes. People were stunned by this fresh catastrophe; they could not take it in. They had no money, no work. They were sick and undernourished, their families dying again of plague. It seemed the final sign that God had forsaken them, and was received with the apathy of defeat.

Out at Ebury, every hut and building was either destroyed or damaged. Some had blown away entirely in a scatter of planks and thatch, leaving mudstained people to grub in ditches after their few possessions. Cattle lay injured, geese had been flung into the Tyburn drains, fields were again lost to the Thames. The month was January, and as the gale spun away eastwards, a bitter cold was sucked in from the north. Christ Jesus, Mary, Mother of God, have mercy: the prayers still came, but few believed in mercy any more. Some fractured words scratched in a Hertfordshire church where building work was abandoned through fear and lack of labour, speak for Ebury's despair as well:

> The first plague was in June 1349 . . . In 1349 there was a plague . . . in 1350 a pitiable fierce violent plague departed . . . a wretched population survives to witness [it and] . . . in the end comes a mighty wind . . . Maurus, the evil one, and thunders in this year of the world 1361.[9]

Apathy was shattered by Litlington's energy and Langham's money. Ebury was not alone in losing most of its shelter, and desperate messages poured in from the abbey's estates all over southern England. The only available building materials were timber, lime-plaster, wattle, mud and thatch; bricks, which had been extensively used by the Romans, were only occasionally employed again before Tudor times. Stone was rare except in churches. Bad drainage weakened foundations, which were often very shallow, and this had been a tempest which pulled up grown oaks by the root.

As prior, Litlington had seen Ebury's value to the abbey, and had already pressed forward with reclamation after shortage of people allowed its drains to clog and bracken to spread out again from the nearby forest. Now he came back, cajoling, making light of discomfort, bracing fainthearts with faith in God and the future. His achievement in rebuilding the abbey's shattered estates inside three years, including Ebury, was acknowledged at the time as extraordinary. His decision simultaneously to resume massive building operations at the abbey can only be explained in terms of faith; financially, it was a lunatic choice. Rents could not be regularly collected, serfs had everywhere died or taken advantage of the general chaos to run off; the whole system of feudal farming was dissolving in this utterly changed world. To spend out recklessly on an extension to the abbey's nave, on new cloisters, outbuildings and transepts, to design and complete new abbot's lodgings there and at La Neyte, invited the administrative collapse of the monastery itself. Nowadays it would be considered fraud.

Yet in less than twenty years, this was what Litlington achieved. His passion to build was unbounded; to him magnificence in stone epitomized faith transcendent, and for starving people it meant work again. Yet even for them, the click of hammers on scaffolding high above the abbey also affirmed that evil had not triumphed and Christendom was still a banner streaming against the wind, though hundreds lay dying in the streets below. Litlington understood this. Repairing the abbey estates fast was good business, but in extremity what people craved most of all was spiritual comfort and confidence renewed. No one could cure the sick. No one understood disease or price inflation or disastrous climatic changes. Why should plague strike one year and vanish the next? Or rain fall in torrents and rot the harvest, when the sun had always shone before?

Only the Church offered an answer, of life again after suffering. Priests might be hypocrites and venality riddle their hierarchy; both were irrelevant. It was the hope Christianity gave that mattered, and people everywhere had come perilously close to losing it; now, in Westminster at least, hope was rekindled. In 1368 plague broke out again, but work on the abbey never stopped entirely. In that year particularly, when the people who lived beyond Cow Ford rose for work at dawn, they must often have strained their eyes to see if black dots were again precariously climbing upwards against the sky. Some earned wages there, although for unskilled workers the pay was poor, but in such an atmosphere the lure of working on a great religious shrine was irrestistable. Only a mile from Eye Cross, pinnacles were rising up to heaven and to the glory of God, offering fulfilment as well as pay.

Tomorrow, fever might kindle in your blood and by evening you would be dead. Meanwhile, just swinging up baskets of mortar made the humblest a part of something greater than himself. And if by luck or skill a man, sometimes a woman, gained the chance to chip a fold in stone, or press designs into wet plaster on a wall, their life gained a dignity it never had before. Because later, if you survived to follow an ox again on Ebury's fields, or sat spinning beside your door, you could look across at the abbey and think: I'm there. I shall always be there; my mark is given to eternity.

Nicholas Litlington was in his forties when he succeeded Langham as Abbot of Westminster, an elderly man by the standards of the time. This made no difference to his drive and right up to his death, impatience for results appears his leading characteristic. He also fell into serious dispute with the king, whom he crowned as Richard II in 1377, when, not long afterwards, a man called Hawley escaped from imprisonment in the Tower. He fled to claim sanctuary at Westminster, hotly pursued by royal officials, who burst into the abbey during High Mass and fatally wounded a sacristan before murdering Hawley on the steps of the high altar. The scandal shook the young king's government to its foundations. Litlington was naturally enraged by such sacrilege, and to make matters worse the abbey was barricaded by royal sheriffs while accusations, threats of excommunication and anathemas exploded like cannonfire between him and the royal council. The Pope was dragged into the row, and the next parliament was summoned to meet in Gloucester rather than Westminster, always a bad sign.

Although by then in his late sixties, Litlington rode there himself, only to find that the king's advisers planned to defend the indefensible by attacking other abbey privileges, which, with some reason, they considered excessive. This attempt he reduced to rubble, using words as he would one of his builder's hammers to stun the assembly into penitence. Westminster Abbey's rights were affirmed and royal officials paid a hefty fine to settle the affair.

In the longer term, this contributed to the growth of a disorderly slum clinging to the abbey's skirts, which eventually straggled along drying ground all the way to the Buckingham Palace site. Considerable immunities from royal justice remained even after the Reformation, when no less a churchman than Sir Thomas More exclaimed in outrage:

> What a rabble of murderers, and malicious heinous traitors . . . unthrifts, and debtors gather there! Yea, and rich women flee thither with their husband's plate . . . Thieves bring in stolen goods, and . . . nightly go to rob and plunder and kill, and come in again as though those places gave them not only safeguard from the harm they had done, but a licence also to do more.[10]

The contrast between later, prestigious developments west of Buckingham Palace and slummy hovels between it and Westminster was stark right into the nineteenth century, when bands of robbers infested St James's Park and the journey to Chelsea remained almost as dangerous as when a remote causeway crossed the marsh.

In Litlington's day other discontents were brewing: king's ministers were impeached for evil conduct, religious radicals preached disaffection, and a shifting, unsettled population was precariously beginning to increase again.

Typical of many people on the edge of destitution was Isabella Puddyngwyf, the next character from the palace site's past. She tried to support herself by selling meat pies in Westminster's lanes and rookeries, but never seemed able to make ends meet. Wages were low and the cost of food high; she struggled to sell pies which were either too expensive for people to afford or kept cheap by using such foul fillings that no one fancied them. She was desperate and her child wailed with hunger, while in the streets around her preaching friars proclaimed that the poor had a right to seize wealth from the rich. So, one harvest night in 1377 Isabella resolved on theft.

It was after midnight when she and her child stole along the causeway towards Ebury, shying in terror at the eerie splash of creatures in the marsh. At Cow Ford, she found that the Tyburn had been reduced to a muddy trickle by summer heat and the bridge was broken down. She could not know that the great Abbot of Westminster himself was in trouble for not maintaining it, but as her legs sank into the stinking quagmire the Tyburn had become, she was terrified afresh by the noise she made. Really, Isabella would have liked to run back to Westminster and safety, but if she did, how could she and her child then live? Holding hands for courage, they clawed out of the Tyburn somewhere near where Buckingham Palace's grand staircase now rises and scampered over to where threshed grain was piled ready for carting to the abbey. These were tithings from Ebury's crop, demanded by the church in addition to rent, and Isabella's temptation had begun when she saw the carts carrying it creak past her through the streets of Westminster. Sweet Jesu, by using stolen grain, she could earn enough to feed herself and her child as if they were fat earls! But she also thought: I shall burn in hell for stealing from the church.

Isabella had not reckoned with this panic and flutter in her mind, nor the difficulties of carrying loose grain bundled in her skirts, the crackle of straw underfoot, the swallowed shriek when her child thought a corn-stook was a hobgoblin leaping out of ambush. Someone on Ebury heard them, and when they tried to escape the steep Tyburn banks became a trap into which they blindly ran.

Instead of eating well that winter Isabella Puddyingwyf was hauled in front of the manor court, and she and her child separately fined. No one recorded what happened to them afterwards, but probably they died. A double fine in their circumstances and with winter coming on, left little chance of survival. Contemporaries probably thought Isabella lucky not to be burned in the hand for theft, but just possibly as repentant sinners they were given alms from the abbey and lived to see another spring.[11]

One of the radical friars Isabella may have heard preach was John Wyclif, a personal enemy of Abbot Litlington after they clashed at the Gloucester parliament, and in 1381 his incendiary words helped to bring peasant armies marching into London. The Archbishop of Canterbury was murdered, order utterly broke down; everywhere, fear and violent anger raged. Ebury as usual seems to have been a gathering point for people on the move, and when sheriffs later charged such malefactors as they could catch, William Peche, a clerk of St Clements, was accused of wickedly stirring up and consorting with rebels at Eye Cross.[12] It is interesting to remember John Potter of Durham, whose family was 'made into waifs' after he broke into the house of John Pecche at Eia, so probably this later William Peche was native to the manor.

Although in 1381 the peasants went home after being courageously outfaced and then tricked by the king, afterwards the dissolution of feudalism continued faster than ever. The survivors of this bitter century were different to their forebears; more turbulent and self-confident, more aware that ordinary men and women possessed power too. People of all degrees took advantage of the near-frantic demand for labour after more than a third of the population vanished between 1315 and 1370. A seemingly endless war with France demanded credit and startling quantities of goods, which fuelled more skilled employment and a different kind of change. The new king too, was one of those intermittent unfortunates on the English throne: a lover of luxury and art.

By the time Nicholas Litlington died at La Neyte, these changes had reached Ebury. Cultivation directly under the control of monks for their community's profit was finished and a few rich tenants had taken their place, above all at Ebury Farm, from where most of the Buckingham Palace site was farmed. These families welcomed a more uncertain world with its wider opportunities, and as Litlington's uncompromising but stirring rule ended, they looked with hope for what would happen next.

CHAPTER 7

The Witch of Eye

What actually happened next was a witch, the most tragic spirit to haunt the palace site. Margarie Gourdemaine was born around 1390 and probably lived all her life at Eye Cross. In her childhood Rufus's old hall was rebuilt, the splendid flying angel roof, which still survives, something to marvel at. In the late fourteenth century its size, the span of its timbers, the extraordinary work of winching whole oaks high into the sky, made it an awesome feat of engineering and Richard II's Court celebrated its completion with characteristic extravagance. The king wore a gown embroidered with pearls and paraded the new habit of using a handkerchief to blow his nose, while the popinjays around him outdid themselves in doublets slashed so deeply that one observer considered they might as well have used rags stitched together.[1]

Whenever Margarie walked from Ebury to Westminster market as a child, she would have seen a bustling community at work again. The permanent population remained small, probably no more than two thousand people lived around Thorney in 1400, but the spirit of the place had recovered from the devastating shocks of plague and scarcity. Fine metal-smiths worked in odd corners and bookbinders, illuminators, poets and scriveners found the atmosphere irresistibly congenial. Administration was lax compared to the City, and the Court attracted scholars as well as scoundrels. Geoffrey Chaucer lived in the abbey's shadow, and when Abbot Litlington commissioned a splendid new missal for his personal use, the scribe who produced it could not bear to leave once his task was finished, and became a monk in order to continue his trade in tranquillity.

Consequently, as Margarie wandered between the market stalls, she saw more varied goods offered for sale than the size of Westminster justified, and one day there was a great furore when Maud Smith, a purse-maker, nearly scratched out a rival's eyes. But what fascinated Margarie most of all were the stalls offering potions and spells, some of them tawdry and hung with dried foetuses or bats, others more secretive for fear of the church. It was commonplace to buy cures from a sorcerer, but beyond such semi-lawful magic lay a diabolic world. Demons hovered like pirates at the edge of everyone's consciousness, ready to cut out any lagging soul, and Margarie

Witches, devils and the tortures of the damned were everyday realities in the fifteenth century; spells and maledictions a source of hope or revenge. (Bibliothèque Nationale, Paris: B 67/295, f. 105v)

would have been forbidden to linger where scented smoke drifted out from behind drawn curtains. As she grew older it became easier to steal away to Westminster alone; only a mile along a drying causeway and there it was, full of brawling life. It had drawn other girls away from rural Ebury and now it drew her; already her interest in spells and curses made her strange to youngsters her own age.

Witches inherited or learned a skill in herbs and the best of them were indispensable as midwives, bone-setters and hypnotists. Many were scarcely witches at all, merely women who believed as everyone did in superstitions essential to their trade. A few were slapdash poisoners who mixed ingredients almost guaranteed to kill, others possessed specialist skills and acquired the showmanship to display them. Only a minority actively practised blasphemies and waited in hope for Lucifer's triumph over the angels, but it was their heresies which contaminated all the rest. The contradictions of this situation are well illustrated by a magician of Westminster who was granted sanctuary in the abbey, presumably because his magic was considered harmless to Christian teaching; once there, he conjured up the devil and drove his boy assistant mad with fear.[2]

It is impossible to know how or why Margarie Gourdemaine became known as a witch. She was later always referred to as the Witch of Eye, which probably means she continued to live at old Eye Cross and the events of her life swirled around the present palace buildings. And if a semi-deserted village at the Tyburn crossing was convenient for clients, its eerie atmosphere would have increased the sense of dread felt by suppliants whose teeth were already chattering after a night-time journey across a marsh flickering with ghostly shapes.

For most of her life Margarie probably practised the kind of magic her landlords, the monks of Westminster, would not have seen as a danger. Around 1420 this situation changed. War, social upset and populist preachers were fuelling a veritable explosion of deviant belief, in which the Devil's fatal swagger captured hearts as well as minds. And if the price of apostasy was burning in hell for evermore, why, it was no more than Christianity promised for less exhilarating sins. The church felt so threatened that it launched a furious onslaught on heresy, which kept taking on new forms. There were flagellants who whipped each other to exhaustion for their sins, Waldensians who denounced the Pope as the Whore of Babylon, Brethren of the Free Spirit who likened themselves to God. Above all, there were the Lollards. John Wyclif taught that righteousness alone gave the right to govern: a simple proposition whose logic challenged the entire existing framework of order.

In this hothouse atmosphere, witches became more extravagant in their claims. Some admissions were extorted under torture or reflect their persecutors' questions, but there is no reason to doubt that many practitioners enjoyed hysterical-mystical experiences: an early example of demand-led marketing response. They kissed the Devil's buttocks, had intercourse with him, adored him in the form of cats and goats and bulls. There was a different, patriotic hysteria at this time too. In 1415 English longbowmen shattered a French army several times larger than their own at Agincourt, and Henry V laid siege to town after town until by 1420 he became in effect King of France as well as England. The legend of Henry's invincibility was rhymed, sung and told until the English became drunk on glory and unreason.

Then in 1422, at the age of twenty-seven, Henry V died of dysentery, leaving a perilous inheritance for his successors. The Crown was heavily indebted by the soaring cost of ultimately untenable ambitions in France, the population as unsettled by success as by past disasters, and the infection of wild heresies made the towns dangerously volatile. Worst of all, the throne was inherited by a child.

For nearly twenty years the Regency Council was remarkably successful in preventing its personal disputes from exacerbating public disorder, but a remorselessly losing war in France did nothing to calm tempers. Then, just as the regency was ending, a single spark threatened to ignite all this tinder. That spark was Margarie Gourdemaine, the Witch of Eye.

The young king, Henry VI, was simplistic-minded, pious and annoying; later, he would be shuttled around his realm like unwanted baggage, but in 1440 he enjoyed general goodwill. The exception was Eleanor, Duchess of Gloucester, wife of the heir presumptive to the throne, Humphrey of Gloucester. She was disgusted that Henry, her husband's nephew, had not succumbed to a childhood illness which would have elevated her to queen consort of England and France. Nevertheless, his survival shows that neither she nor her husband plotted against him during the temptingly long years of his minority.

Gloucester was regarded as an erratic politician, known to have been extremely dissipated during his youth. He was also a man of wide interests: a soldier and patron of the arts, a scholar who enjoyed the company of learned men, a bibliophile whose collection founded Duke Humphrey's Library at Oxford. His first marriage had been a *cause célèbre* which led to war and a specious declaration of nullity, by which time he had fallen in love with a woman in his ex-wife's household – handsome, impetuous and grasping Eleanor Cobham. She was almost certainly his mistress for some time before they married, a ceremony thought to inflict such infamy on a great man's honour that Eleanor was widely considered to have used sorceries to confuse his judgement. Later, the Witch of Eye would be accused of assisting Eleanor[3] to bewitch the duke into marriage, along with other, more serious charges.

As wife to the Duke of Gloucester, Eleanor was first lady in the realm until the king married, and she revelled in her position. 'Whence arose shame and more disgrace and inconvenience to the whole kingdom than can be expressed,' wrote a chronicler disdainfully.[4] Eleanor was frankly ambitious. She could not help wanting to be queen and her husband to be king, an ever-present possibility which further envenomed Humphrey's quarrels with the Regency Council.

From the moment that Margarie Gourdemaine was drawn into this political maelstrom, she was set adrift in a storm she could not see.

There is a possibility that the whole affair was fabricated to discredit Gloucester through his upstart wife, but the best propaganda is founded on truth and there can be no doubt that Eleanor had made her interest in the king's health entirely plain. Nobody was surprised by this; she would scarcely have been human if she had not at least imagined a death which would benefit her so greatly, and Eleanor was riddled with human frailties. Perhaps she became so obviously impatient that the idea of entangling her in black arts was born in someone else's scheming brain, and insinuated into hers. A similar conspiracy had been hatched against Henry IV's queen only thirty years before, with limited success.

The evidence is contradictory, but Margarie was said to have been consulted early in 1441, and to have predicted that Eleanor would become queen in June, a sufficiently specific prophecy to be regarded as treason. There were allegations, too, that she made a wax model of the king to help prediction on its way. Incantations were chanted, herbs burned, spells spoken, and there must be a strong suspicion that if Eleanor did visit the Witch of Eye without covert encouragement by her enemies, then her purpose was discovered and an agent-provocateur planted to encourage her into further, betraying risks. Roger Bolingbroke, a hanger-on in Duke Humphrey's household, joined Margarie in her divinations and, so it was said,[5] boasted afterwards that the king had only months to live. He also said that the Witch of Eye had spoken further spells to make sure that Eleanor carried a living, legitimate child when Duke Humphrey inherited the throne.

Eleanor Cobham, the Duchess of Gloucester and Queen presumptive of England, forced to walk in penitential procession through the streets of London. (Mansell Collection: from *A Chronicle of England*, 1864)

It seems unlikely that Margarie personally ever came inside Westminster Palace. She would have said her spells and made her divinations, moulded her wax model[6] and impaled it with thorns in her hut where Buckingham Palace's courtyard stands today. She received her reward and waited there with professional suspense to hear if the king had indeed been taken ill, while someone better able than she to pass scrutiny around the Court performed additional magic closer to where he lived. That person was most likely Bolingbroke, but could have been another of the accused, Thomas Southwell, astonishingly a Canon of St Stephen's within the royal palace.

If these allegations were true, it is worth asking what made a witch like Margarie agree to use her skills to murder by intent. In Eleanor's case the motive for an initial foolish inquiry is clear, and the ambition which may have led her to try and ensure the king's death, but why should Margarie Gourdemaine, a old woman with little to gain beyond some coins she might never be able to spend, agree to help her? How did witches make the psychological leap from skill in potions to cursing people they often did not know? A few would always have been known for skill in malediction, and perhaps a chance success, in a world where people often died, first made their reputation. Traders thrive on success and conscience could be lost in professional triumph if a victim sickened, and nagging fear about lost powers if they did not.

Leeds Castle in Kent, where Eleanor, Duchess of Gloucester, was imprisoned before her trial in 1441. Often called the most romantic castle in England, this winter setting makes it easier to imagine Leeds in the role of a medieval political prison. (Author)

Margarie may have belonged to this fraternity, but most witches were more prosaic unless, for a few, their careers developed. Then they were led on by pride, by the practical difficulty of refusing help to petitioners who could easily betray them to an angry, vengeful church. Only complicitous guilt made everyone safe, those easy steps from one thing to another. Conjuring up a date was nothing, after all. Christians prayed for miracles every day, and a witch might say she too entreated fate, with equally arbitrary results.

In the case of Margarie Gourdemaine, the Council either set a trap for the Duchess of Gloucester, into which the Witch of Eye also fell, or its members heard rumours about the king's forthcoming death begin to sweep through his palace. Bolingbroke and Southwell were arrested, together with a secretary to the duke, John Home, although nothing was done until June was safely passed, leaving the king still healthy – a delay perhaps calculated to reinsure risk in case the spells worked and Humphrey indeed became king, as well as to avoid public panic. In fact Henry VI troubled his realm for nearly another thirty years, before he finally was murdered.

The accused were interrogated and on 16 July 1441, Roger Bolingbroke was set in pillory at St Paul's Cross with 'his sorcerer's instruments and wizard tooles'[7] hung around his neck. There, in the presence of a huge crowd, he created a sensation by accusing Eleanor, Duchess of Gloucester, as the instigator of witchcraft and conspiracy. When Eleanor heard that the London mob was screeching for her blood, she fled for sanctuary into Westminster

Abbey, only to be seized when she tried to escape down-river in disguise. She was examined on charges of 'necromancy, witchcraft, heresy and treason' and after a brief imprisonment in Leeds Castle, Kent, was arraigned with the other conspirators, including Margarie Gourdemaine, before a special commission where all of them were found guilty.[8]

Bolingbroke was drawn on a hurdle through disorderly crowds to Tyburn for execution; Southwell died in prison the night before he would have endured the same fate; John Home was pardoned and released, successfully to continue his career. If the whole affair reeks of malice and contrivance, he has to be prime suspect as the tool used by Gloucester's enemies. As for the duchess, the premier lady of England, she was condemned to three days' public penance of the kind usually reserved for common whores, and life imprisonment afterwards. The duke was not mentioned, but an edict forbidding interference with the proceedings may have been aimed at him; if the accusations were a conspiracy against him, it had been successful.

On Monday 13 November 1441 Eleanor was taken by barge to Temple Stairs. There her ladies took off her hood and gown, wrapped her in a white sheet, tied a handkerchief over her head, and placed a wax taper in her hand. In this shameful costume and with trumpeters walking in front of her and behind, the sister-in-law to Henry V was forced to walk barefoot through the filthy roads of London, past tumultuous crowds and windows sold to ribald watchers. Old scandals were revived by this prostitutes' ritual, and people shouted out that the great Duke of Gloucester had married a whore because she and the Witch of Eye used black arts on him, too. Next day Eleanor had to endure again, and then again the Friday following; perhaps when she set out she was sustained by scornful rage, but by the end she can only have been numbed by the horror of it all.[9] The one exception to the general execration was the Lord Mayor of London, who with his aldermen, decided that rank mattered more than questionable guilt and met her with the ceremony due to a royal duchess at each of her entries into the City.

When it was over, Eleanor was sent away to a variety of strongholds until she died in 1452. Humphrey died under arrest at Bury St Edmunds in 1447.

Long before any of this, Margarie Gourdemaine was ash, trampled into the dust of Smithfield. No one questioned her guilt. She was a witch, she was old, she had no friends outside Eye Cross, and past clients dared not admit they knew her. In intent she may have been a murderess, also ignorant and steeped in superstition. Just possibly she had not been a party to anything at all, and her only crime was to distil potions for an illustrious patron.

Alone, and surrounded by the hate of people who in their hearts believed as implicitly as she did in the magic arts, Margarie Gourdemaine, the Witch of Eye, 'was brent at Smythfield ye 27 October 1441'.[10]

Today, when the guard changes at Buckingham Palace, they probably march across the place where her hut stood.

CHAPTER 8

Royal Return

By the middle of the fifteenth century Westminster's population still only numbered around two thousand, but there was no longer any doubt that this boggy Thames-side village had become the administrative capital of England and Wales.

For centuries English kings had felt little need for any permanent base. What centralized control there was accompanied them on their travels, and few kings stayed more than two consecutive weeks at Westminster. Their subjects, on the other hand, found it increasingly tiresome to trek around the country searching for justice, tax receipts or commissions of authority. Treasure dribbled mysteriously away when it was hauled around in carts; not to mention the peculations of monks who were entrusted with parts of it. Accountants in all ages prefer precise habits and resent getting their records wet, or blown away in a gale, or stolen by the Scots.

By the late fifteenth century English kings were still by no means regularly based in London, but they had acquired residences close by: Sheen, Nonsuch, Havering, Eltham, Greenwich, Brentford, Richmond, Windsor, all were picked up jackdaw-like and occasionally used. The Treasury was locked up in the Tower but household finance, Chancery, Common Pleas and the Exchequer settled at Westminster, and parliament rarely met anywhere else. Medieval governments were not exacting over the office space they required. Churches, the homes of high officials, disused buildings, all were considered suitable and Westminster Hall housed a bewildering variety of activities: common pleas were heard in one corner, pleas to the king in another, and in a third the Chancery used a large stone table to carry out business that nowadays requires half a million civil servants. All this surrounded by a mob of people consuming fast food sold by pedlars and nagging about their grievances.

The continuous development of Westminster into a national administrative capital had a significant effect on Ebury. Its farm tracks grew into rudimentary highways and the bridge at Eye Cross became a short cut for messengers. The monks, its landlords, were often involved in politics and perhaps as a consequence their community became riddled with fraud and sex-scandals. Abbots were indicted at frequent intervals for civil misdemeanours connected with those parts of Westminster's communications that ran through the

Unsprung, unarticulated heavy vehicles churned up the highway around the palace site for centuries, creating a widening area of waste which proved crucial to the eventual development of a gentleman's residence there. Often, as here, iron or wooden blocks attached to the wheels for grip only made matters worse.

Buckingham Palace site: for not maintaining the rights of way 'within Eye', not scouring its ditches or clearing conduits, for allowing the highway to flood, and failing to repair the bridge at Eye.[1]

Another consequence of a collapsing administration at the abbey was the stranglehold individuals could exert on farming profits, even in a nearby estate like Ebury. The present palace site and the land adjoining it were farmed by two men named John Norreys, almost certainly father and son, for sixty years between 1421 and 1481, during which time they were also bailiffs for the abbey.[2] In theory they accounted for stock and service, received rents and repaired its highways and bridge; in practice they found better uses for their time and the monks' money. There are cryptic references to shortfalls in cash and paddocks sublet to London merchants. It is easy to visualize the Norreys family developing lucrative private sidelines, while their own rent was negligently left by the monks at £21 per annum, plus twelve carts of hay and a boar they probably poached from the forest.

Conditions remained lax until after 1500, when John Islip succeeded Abbot Eastney and drove through reforms. Eastney did, however, rent a shop to William Caxton, who picked Westminster for his new venture into printed books, enjoying great success before he experienced that most enviable of deaths for anyone of full age who loves books: collapsing while at work on a manuscript. In 1491 the accounts for St Margaret's, Westminster, record the expenditure of '6/8d for torches to accompany atte bureying of William Caxton . . . and 6d for belle atte the same'.[3]

Henry VII's Chapel and the Palace of Westminster, taken from the abbey roof, 1995. From this perspective a historic hub of government might almost be the dreaming spires of Oxford. (Author)

John Islip entered Westminster monastery around 1480 and was elected abbot in 1500, by which time he had become personally friendly with Henry VII, the first Tudor king; a relationship which to some extent contradicts the accepted view of Henry as a cold fish. Tuns of wine were regularly rolled from the royal cellar to the abbey as gifts, and Islip made sure the monastery kitchens sent back a supply of the king's favourite marrowbone puddings, at 2*d* the pair.[4] They met often, and not only to discuss affairs of church and state. Both were meticulous men, precise in discharging their duties and calculating towards the result of their endeavours; they enjoyed speculative discussion in the company of another exacting mind, particularly one which did not threaten their own position. They also shared the original sin of kings and Westminster abbots, a love of extravagant building, but with one fundamental difference from their predecessors: neither intended to be made bankrupt by indulging it.

Henry VII's miserliness with money is legendary, and like many legends is at least partly untrue. He spent lavishly on occasion, but without ever losing sight of his cashflow. Islip inherited a badly run, indebted and incomplete abbey, and took the bold decision to spend his way out of trouble: he completed the nave, cleaned up its shrines as a tourist attraction and started work on foundations for twin towers which for the past four hundred years had only been talked about, although foundations were as far as he got. He zealously drummed up revenue from the monastery's estates, lifting rents, tightening obligations, insisting on the abbey's rights. For the Norreys at Ebury, it was all a highly disagreeable shock. But in land management above all, tenacity in cunning belongs to those who actually farm the soil, and a new family called Whasshe was soon assiduously making itself indispensable there.[5] They leased most of the palace site and became bailiffs for the manor; after Islip's death they moved into his snug old house at La Neyte.

Immediately, however, Westminster bounced back into solvency and as a fashionable place of pilgrimage, helped by a new, nationalistic interest in Edward the Confessor. When Henry VII decided to build a great shrine there to house the bones of his murdered Lancastrian forebear, Henry VI, Islip realized at once that the abbey was about to gain a splendid new visitor attraction, gratis, and eagerly cooperated by wholesale demolition of huddled dwellings beyond the chancel.[6]

There is every indication that Henry and Islip enjoyed themselves hugely, planning and building a chapel of innovative new design, and Islip personally laid the first stone. So far as money was concerned, Henry VII ran true to form. In all, his chapel cost around £14,000, an extravagant sum for the time, but he found it by successfully negotiating with the Pope to close several small monasteries, on the excuse that the money was needed fitly to enshrine a saint. When the Pope later demanded too high a price for the canonization ceremony, that part of the project was cheerfully abandoned, poor Henry VI being pushed aside as so often in his lifetime, while his cannier successor used the raided cash to glorify his own dynasty. There he was interred beside his queen, and his friend Islip not far away.

In his lifetime, Henry VII occasionally travelled out to Islip's refurbished country house at La Neyte. At that time, it was as convenient to ride across Tothill Fields to Cow Ford before turning south, as to use Willow Walk. For wagons it was different. Increased traffic had very much widened the highway around Eye Cross, and since the bridge was usually in disrepair, heavy goods had to splash across as best they could. The unmade verges churned up in wider and wider arcs as drovers struggled to find drier ground, until, by the time Henry VII rode that way the highway around Eye Cross was probably 50 yards wide. The old village green had all but vanished into the slop and the few remaining inhabitants fought a losing battle against the juggernauts of the day, a situation with which many modern roadside residents will sympathize. Only the stone cross remained in place until the 1540s, when that too vanished, knocked over by a cart or with its foundation disintegrated in the mire. As a Westminster court declared in 1533:

> The hyee way goyng into Tothill . . . lyeth so fowle of downg & caryen . . . and other fylthiry to the great infeccyon & noyaunce of the King's liege people comyng or goyng . . . it stoppeth also the common sewer there [old Tyburn] so that water maye not have its course.[7]

The spelling may be rocky but the picture is clear, and at Eye Cross the widening area of 'fowle waste' was later to be of crucial importance to the history of Buckingham Palace.

When Henry VIII succeeded his father in 1509, he recognized Islip's usefulness, but the two men were never friends.[8] Instead, Islip became close to

Cardinal Wolsey and was lucky to survive his fall. Lucky, that is, to possess the means to buy himself out of trouble, since he only retained Henry's favour by transferring to him all the abbey's land along a growing thoroughfare later called Whitehall. Henry VIII possessed a vulture's eye for property and a blackmailer's ruthlessness over securing it, and this was one coup which proved of lasting profit to the state.

Islip died in 1532, and it was as if the medieval age died with him. Like Litlington, he received the last rites at La Neyte, and afterwards his funeral procession stretched down Willow Walk all the way to the abbey's west door. Banners floated in the wind; scarlet, gold and azure hangings splashed against grey stone. Monks chanted in a nave he had at last completed, high clear notes that had hardly changed since the Edward the Confessor founded this holy place. Afterwards there was unashamed feasting on 'spiced bread, suckett, marmylade . . . and diversse sortes of wines in plentie'.[9]

On the day John Islip was put in his tomb his monastery must have seemed eternal, but it had only eight more years to live. The processes of Henry VIII's acquisitive reformation were already set in motion, and within months of Islip's death Anne Boleyn's child, the Princess Elizabeth, would be christened only yards from where he lay.

The abbey's former properties along Whitehall were added to a royal development scheme for a new palace centred on York Place, Cardinal Wolsey's magnificent town house, also seized by Henry. As a compulsively active king, Henry also wanted space for bear-pits, tournament yards and tennis courts, mews for his falcons, stables for his horses and deer in a park, and a love-nest to share with Anne Boleyn. His acquisitive stare moved westward, to the marshy fields around the Hospital of St James, with Ebury beyond, and in December 1531 Eton College was forced to transfer St James and its land to Henry, in exchange for derisory compensation. This bargain brought part of the Buckingham Palace site back into royal hands for the first time since the Confessor gave it away; but it was a small part only, on the near side of Tyburn, on which part of the forecourt and visible facade is now built. Luckily, this brings the spectacularly scandalous monks of St James, whose community was originally dedicated to abstemious Christian care of the sick, into the pattern of ghosts around the Buckingham Palace site.

The difficulty was that the sick they cared for were exclusively female, described as 'leprous girls or virgins and no others'.[10] This limitation proved too great a temptation, and the girls soon became notably unleprous and very far from virginal. The monks were also able to exploit Westminster's sensitivity towards an intruded foundation on their land, after the crown claimed rights there too. As a result, St James went unsupervised for decades at a time.

There is evidence of trouble before the end of the thirteenth century, when the brothers were formally prohibited from fraternizing with the virgins in their care, which to the cynic immediately suggests the opposite. One of the rare visitations discovered too much dissipation and 'clamer' at

St James's, and another killjoy reported them for brewing extra-strength beer. Not long afterwards, senior monks of the hospital conspired to steal the offertory money and some resident sisters were suitably astonished to learn that it was illegal to sell the church's property for their own profit. The prior of the time appears particularly blameworthy, an aggressive drunk who referred to any brothers objecting to his habits as mangehounds.[11]

From a religious point of view, matters continued to go from bad to worse, although it is hard not to feel that St James may have been the best place in London in which to attempt to sit out the calamitous fourteenth century. Chic little Alice of Paris was imported for the Master's especial comfort and records show Prior John of Sydenham busy purchasing trashy books for light reading;[12] at the same time, dormitories were partitioned to replace communal living with separate bedrooms, a highly suspicious circumstance where monks and resident virgins are concerned. When the inhabitants of St James looked out across their slab of marsh and saw the rain still falling, they can have had little difficulty in deciding that comfort came before labour: there always seems to have been another silver cup they could sell instead of trying fruitlessly to farm a bog. The next visitation remained defeatist, the only difference of substance being that the new Master's harlot was reported to be English rather than French. By 1340 her lover was in prison on suspicion of murder, only to regain his position as Master after being helped by his monks to escape.[13]

But even St James's was not immune to plague and all the inhabitants except one died in the first outbreak. Outside predators then moved in, in this case a rival clerical gang who looted comforts they had previously envied from a distance. As it happened, the buildings exacted their own revenge, because the raiders caught the plague there and by 1353 the hospital was entirely deserted, and rotting in the rain.[14]

Recovery came under a series of royal clerks who were granted leases there by the king.[15] The buildings continued to house a small community of monks and were also used as secular apartments, until Henry VI gave them to his favourite new foundation, Eton College, in 1449. This shifted the remaining monks elsewhere but made few other differences, except that the college Master also used it as an occasional town house, assuaging his conscience by dedicating some rent to maintain four poor women there. In true St James's style, these paupers soon mysteriously changed into wealthy widows enjoying a peaceful retirement on cheap terms, and there is no reason to suppose that Henry VIII was particularly unjust when he finally turned them out in 1536, each with a pension of £6 13s 4d a year.[16]

Eton had not yet become its later self, when a forced exchange amounting to theft of its property was likely to cause more trouble than it was worth. To Henry, St James's was a plum ready for the picking. And as events were to show, even a fully fledged and highly successful contemporary old-boy network like the church was no match for King Harry in his prime.

CHAPTER 9

Entry of the Speculators

The king's acquisition of St James's was followed by other gains, even more significant to the evolution of the palace site. In 1536 Henry received the manor of Ebury, including its subdivisions of Hyde and La Neyte from Westminster Abbey in exchange for monastic lands in Berkshire which cost him nothing.[1] On 16 January 1540 the abbey community itself came to an end. For nearly a year after closure its buildings stood derelict and unused, stripped of moveables by the royal commissioners. Gold from the Confessor's tomb was melted down while onlookers stood by, waiting for a thunderbolt to strike down the destroyers. When nothing happened, they too began to look around for moveable loot to steal.

After Henry VIII's death, the Duke of Somerset, regent for the boy-king Edward VI, seriously considered converting the abbey into his personal residence, but fell from power before the deeds could be drawn up.[2] For the inhabitants of Ebury, these events fundamentally altered their lives, though few peasants probably changed their beliefs for another generation. The changes may not immediately have seemed particularly significant compared, for instance, to the opportunistic way in which the Whasshe family used the upheaval to extend their grip on the profits of the manor. Quite soon the very landscape changed, as the king began draining the marshes of St James's, preparatory to enclosing it as his private park behind

> a sumptuous wall of brick . . . Wherein his majesty devised and ordained many
> and singular commodious things, pleasures and other necessities, most apt and
> convenient to appertain only to so noble a prince, for his singular comfort,
> pastime and solace.[3]

Henry often visited these works and his principal minister, Thomas Cromwell, personally supervised both drainage and the rebuilding of St James's as a royal hunting lodge. The new buildings were scarcely finished and 300 ounces of gold used to entwine the initials H&A into every corner of it, before

Queen Anne Boleyn was whisked away to be beheaded in the Tower; after this, neither Henry nor his later wives cared much for the place, and spiteful courtiers mocked that all those gold initials spelt Ha-Ha as an epitaph on royal romance.

Thomas Cromwell was an efficient man, and at least partially succeeded in draining the malarial swamp between St James's and the Tyburn for his king's pleasure, where generations of monks – with varying enthusiasm – had failed. Trees were planted, deer brought in, a bowling alley and tilt-yard constructed, a park-keeper and staff appointed. A new catchment pond near Cow Ford immediately attracted the name of Rosamund's Pond: Rosamonds has already been noticed as a description of land close to the palace site. Possibly under Henry but more likely in his daughter Elizabeth's time, an artificial mound and belvedere were constructed there, where the queen liked to snack alfresco and view the steeples, mansions and palaces of her capital.

She often rode out as Henry had done through Ebury to hunt, and unlike him, enjoyed strolling through the pleasant meadows she owned there. The Whasshes were by then securely settled with a long lease on 'Eyeberrie Farm', whose fields extended for some 400 acres around and across the palace site, and while no doubt humbly welcoming the queen on their knees as was only fitting, they had no intention of allowing her to interfere with a highly profitable tenancy. The Whasshes were businessmen and already distanced from their peasant ancestors; if they farmed at all it was by supervising others, and they intensified the previous practice of subletting to

> divers persons, who, for their private commodity did close up the same and made pastures out of arable land, thereby not only annoying her majesty in her walks and passages, but hindering her game and offering great injury to the common which at Lammas was wont to be laid open.[4]

In fact, the queen was so seriously annoyed that she granted a thirty-one year lease of Ebury Farm, including the palace site, to William Gibbs, one of her gentlemen-pensioners, to take effect when the Whasshes' lease ran out in 1584. Reversionary interests were a cheap way of rewarding service, but Elizabeth probably also intended to reduce the Whasshes' ability to exploit their lease by signalling that it would not be renewed. If so, her hopes were disappointed. Within a week William Whasshe demonstrated his purchasing power by buying up Gibbs's lease for £450, thereby securing his tenancy until 1615. The grant to Gibbs nevertheless created a new legal interest in the palace lands, and in 1585 Elizabeth, who continued to be exasperated by the impunity with which her will was flouted by the Whasshes, granted a further lease to a favourite, Sir Thomas Knyvett. This took effect from 1615, for a further sixty years, a valuable future term which could and did change hands as an investment.[5]

The Swan Inn at Enford, Wiltshire, would still look familiar to the generations of Rolfes who lived around Enford at least from the sixteenth to the eighteenth centuries. (Author)

If ancient leases are tedious to read about, they were bewildering to people trying to earn a living off the land at Ebury, and threatening too. Their common grazing lands had been enclosed by the Whasshes, and St James's marsh, where they had been accustomed to trap eels and fish, was lost behind a wall. Meadows which had always been thrown open at Lammas tide were shut up for profit behind hurdles. Ordinary villagers no longer knew when some unknown might not ride over Cow Ford holding a paper in his hand, which he said gave him rights over their lives. Even the queen could not prevent William Whasshe from rack-renting them. In 1592 they rioted, spilling out in a tumult over the palace site and 'With pickaxes and suchlike pulled down the fences and brake the gates', whereupon the Whasshes laid a fierce complaint before the queen's treasurer, Lord Burleigh.[6]

But riots made little difference once new-style transactions created a market in legal rights. Land that its inhabitants regarded as part of themselves became a commodity, ancient certainties were replaced by faceless traders in investment, and it was the fraudulent inter-relationships among six such speculators which finally transformed old Eye Cross into a site that kings would covet for their palace.

The eldest of these, William Blake, was born around 1570, probably in Hampshire but possibly in London. Either way, he can first be positively identified in London, making money in any way he could.[7] Lionel Cranfield was five years younger and definitely a Londoner, the second son of Thomas Cranfield, a struggling mercer who renounced his trade for religion. When Lionel started work at fifteen he had already decided that he wanted to be rich, really rich, primly declaring that he must peruse how the debts his father owed had grown, in order to avoid such foolishness in the future. In spite of being apprenticed to a grocer, since money was lacking to place him in his father's more prestigious mercer's trade, Cranfield was dealing on his own account before he was twenty, with capital exceeding £2,000.[8]

Not far away from the Cranfields and two years after Lionel's birth, another second son was born, this time to John and Margaret Audley. Like Thomas Cranfield, Audley was a mercer but in an altogether better way of business, and he married into a similarly wealthy family. The young couple were able to buy a pleasant house in Wood Street, off Cheapside, as well as invest in property at Sutton, Kent, and they succeeded in rearing three daughters and two sons to adulthood, a good average for the time. Hugh, the younger of these two sons, was admitted to Inner Temple in 1604 and called to the Bar in 1611,[9] but his real talent lay in money-lending.

In Wiltshire, about the same time as William Blake, Hugh Audley and Lionel Cranfield were setting out on their careers, a certain William Rolfe married Sara Blake, probably a cousin and certainly related to William Blake. Their son, another William, was born at Enford in Wiltshire around 1595; apparently no other children survived. Rolfes had lived around Enford for a long time, and in decreasing numbers continued to live there into the eighteenth century. They were humdrum people; husbandmen, craftsmen and weavers who only appear in the records if one of them was killed by the kick of a horse, or picked up dead in a field, or bound over to keep the peace after brawling with the relatives of a girl he fancied. One drunken Rolfe turned over a cart 'and was killed on the spot'; another, Anne Rolfe, became a tithingwoman in 1581.[10]

The two youngest players in the drama which, within the first thirty years of the seventeenth century, would change peasant plots around Cow Ford into a potential palace site, were William Blake's son, yet another William, and Anne Hawker, ultimately the most crucial of them all. She was probably born in 1606,[11] at Heytesbury, a small cloth town on the Salisbury–Warminster road. The Hawkers had only recently come into Wiltshire from Somerset and almost certainly had risen in the world by making and merchanting cloth, the one great industry of the area. When Thomas Hawker bought the manor of Heytesbury in order to expand his enterprise, it was a natural migration up the social scale and along the cloth routes.

The early years of Anne's childhood were peaceful, although her sisters' scattered birthdates suggest the usual tragedies of stillbirths and deaths in infancy. If Anne's later life reflects anything of her earlier character, then she was a stubborn, single-minded and courageous child, probably ambitious too, as her father had been before. She could read, write a good hand and express herself fluently,[12] but like all girls of her time was trained to defer decisions to her father, the head of the household and its only male.

In 1614, when she was about eight years old, a door slammed shut on tranquillity when the London merchants suddenly stopped buying cloth. No one in Wiltshire entirely understood why and the details are irrelevant, but the basic cause was an impudent and incompetent fraud. Some months earlier a new scheme for raising tax had been put to the king, cunningly packaged to appeal both to his need for money and his canny sense of economic advantage for his realm. In fact the proposers were interested only in their own profit, but no such crude design appeared among the arguments put forward by their leader, Alderman Cockayne, whose scheme would forbid the export of unfinished cloth. When some privy councillors expressed doubt, because so much English cloth was unfinished, Cockayne breezily guaranteed that his syndicate would fulfil all outstanding contracts. After the ban, finishing cloth in England would boost jobs and increase royal revenues. The council remained unconvinced, but once Cockayne transferred his attention to King James, he was instantly successful.

By instinct James loved quick fixes. In the London taverns too, the idea of dislocating the trade of established merchants for the gain of lesser men was widely welcomed, and the promised work in new finishing trades made Cockayne and his allies popular with the poor.[13]

None of these hopes were realized. In cloth-producing regions like Wiltshire, the consequences of conspiracy struck like a thunderbolt out of a sunny sky, ruining manufacturers, merchants and farmers alike. Very little skill in finishing existed in such an area and when the Dutch reacted by banning English cloth altogether, the market plummeted. Clothiers were ruined overnight and whole families put out of work who relied on weaving for a living. Carters, pack-horse drovers, gear-cutters, shepherds, dealers, fullers' earth diggers; everyone was affected.

Some time before this, Lionel Cranfield had grown bored with making money on the City markets, and embarked on a new career in royal service. The chaotic Jacobean crown finances offended his sense of order, but basically his change of career was a profit-making venture. By the time Cockayne's schemings had brought about a sensational collapse of general trading confidence, Cranfield occupied the modestly lucrative position of Surveyor General, where his business experience had quickly told him that Cockayne was a crook.

The two men fought the matter out before a by now thoroughly frightened Privy Council.[14] Cranfield won decisively, but in front of the king it was a different matter. James hated to admit he was wrong, and Cranfield was shown the door. Another disastrous year followed before the government was forced to revoke Cockayne's changes, a vindication which boosted Cranfield's career while at the same time planting a distaste for him in James's mind.

For Thomas Hawker in Wiltshire, a future which had recently been filled with hope and the bustle of affairs, by 1620 looked very bleak. He had three daughters to settle and no son to carry on his trade; interest rates were high, the price of cloth continued very low. Eventually he decided there was little point in risking more loss by trying to keep on trading as a clothier, and life must often have been gloomy at Heytesbury Manor during these later years of Anne's childhood. Her older sister, Elizabeth, married – probably cheaply – back into their Somerset connections and her other sister, Lady, was still a child; plans for her own marriage were in limbo now every family she knew was scraping to pay debts.

These discontents were scattered when William Rolfe rode into Heytesbury as the Earl of Pembroke's candidate[15] for the parliamentary election of 1623 and Thomas Hawker apparently offered hospitality to a man who came with a great earl's patronage to represent his town. Rolfe had left home early to be apprenticed as a scrivener in Fleet Street, probably to his mother's relative, William Blake. He was a quick-witted boy and cunning by instinct, traits he may have inherited through his mother's Blake blood; unfortunately, he also inherited a streak of naive Rolfe simplicity together with over-confidence in his own ability, which lured him into believing that he could swim with impunity among the killer sharks of Jacobean London.

To Anne Hawker, then seventeen years old, William Rolfe must have seemed like the answer to her dreams when he came to eat a meal at their house. Wiltshire-born like herself and therefore less intimidating than a true Londoner would have been, he possessed the charm of a man who had risen by his wits. He wore city-tailored clothes, and fashion in the 1620s had become almost incredibly lavish; men curled and scented their long ringleted hair and even boots were cut to sag artistically in folds. In Heytesbury, Rolfe was an exotic, and chatted about the king, his great ministers and the Earl of Pembroke with easy familiarity. Had the Hawkers heard that when King James visited the Earl at Wilton, they hid a piglet in the royal chamber pot? In revenge, 'twas said, for him putting a toad down Pembroke's neck at Whitehall Palace. Everyone knew his majesty possessed as great a horror of pigs as Pembroke did of frogs.

In a more sober vein, he probably talked to Thomas Hawker about the forthcoming parliament, where the many discontents of the kingdom must surely be addressed. Lord Treasurer Cranfield might even be impeached for corruption there and, modestly, Rolfe looked forward to playing a part in these stirring events. The Hawkers were fascinated. Never before had they heard such gossip, and Rolfe rode back to London in high feather, assured that arrangements for his election were well placed in the hands of Thomas Hawker. He need not worry about it any more; instead he was mulling over a fresh idea for profit.

Rolfe had come a long way from being a scrivener's apprentice, partly through a lucky marriage to an alderman's daughter.[16] He applied himself, he had few scruples, he was eager to climb the slippery pole of success, but his rise in fortune basically still depended on his relative, William Blake, who, during the recent years of tight money had over-extended himself while Rolfe's more modest ferreting in the market-place continued to flourish. In reality both were indebted and their debts were intertwined, a situation made more precarious when as a gesture, Rolfe bought his birthplace manor of Enford in 1621.[17]

Above left: *The peaceful River Avon runs through Enford Manor, a title briefly acquired by William Rolfe during his meteoric rise as a London property speculator, when his dealings included a fraudulent interest in the Buckingham Palace site.* (Author)

Above right: *Wiltshire sheep country between Enford and Heytesbury. Thomas Hawker's dowry of his nearby manor to his daughter, Anne, was criminally converted by Blake and Rolfe to provide the capital they needed to build the first house of any size on the Buckingham Palace site.* (Author)

Blake was twenty years older than his ex-apprentice, an apparently solid citizen living at Hale House in Kensington, 'a religious, charitable good friend to this church & parish' as the register later described him.[18] He acted as Hugh Audley's man of business, a position filled with possibilities as Audley rose to become the richest property lawyer in London and bought himself the position of Clerk to the Court of Wards. There, land and heir-esses were dealt in wholesale, ostensibly for the benefit of the Crown but in practice to the significant gain of its officials. Some of this largesse had already come Blake's way when he was appointed Master of the Fines Office: a sinecure he estimated to be worth £700 a year. The information Audley nowadays knew could make Blake rich again, but he needed to be careful. Hugh Audley was a dangerous man to cheat.

When he was not handling Audley's business, and probably quite often when he should have been, Blake dealt in land on his own account, a cun-ning operator who used stacked-up debt to support a comfortable lifestyle. Now, as economic depression persisted, the slightest whisper against him could bring the whole ramshackle edifice crashing down.[19] When Rolfe came to Blake offering Anne Hawker as an heiress for negotiation, by luck or judgement his timing was exact. Blake believed he could solve his financial difficulties if only he could find some ready cash, and a pliant heiress with a conveniently distant father was exactly what he needed. Not for himself; Blake was a married man, but for his son.

William Blake the younger was a disappointment to his father. All the toughness seemed to have leaked out of him with the easier life his father's successes brought and he was growing into a park-saunterer, a fashionable fribble, but at least that ought to mean he could more easily turn a country girl's head. Then the word would get around that old Blake had landed a fine fish, and he would have won the time he needed to confound his creditors – if Anne Hawker was really and immediately rich.

On this point Rolfe was shown later to have elaborated with his customary confidence. He sensed Blake's eagerness and settled delicately to reel in his catch. Not long afterwards Rolfe returned to Heytesbury, and the moves began which led to the first house of any size being built on the Buckingham Palace site.

It is impossible to know when William Blake was first struck by the potential of Eye Cross, but living as he did in Kensington and with business he must conduct with Audley in Westminster Hall, he would often have travelled the direct route between the two, across Cow Ford. He could not fail to notice the trampled width of the highway there, on both sides of the Tyburn. To the east lay St James's Park wall and remnants of the old causeway, noted as still visible in 1638;[20] to the west around the palace site there were only fields, small enclosures and perhaps a windmill. Then the perils of passage began, as his horse slithered on eroded banks to reach what was called the King's Private Road (the far end is still King's Road, Chelsea), little more than a disagreeably wide wallow trapped with remnants of old Eye Cross. Builders had burrowed here too, illegally digging free gravel in the boom years of construction and leaving their pits to fill with water. Altogether, Eye Cross had become an unsavoury place where squatters clung on in a wilderness.

But a property developer's imagination never rests, and what William Blake saw was a site. A site he need not pay for. Wasteland, where ownership could be endlessly confused. Legally too, this noisome slop possessed advantages no one else had the wit to grasp. During the past hundred years London had grown so explosively that kings and ministers had come to fear its size, the potential for trouble seething through its streets, and issued proclamations forbidding new building there, except on old foundations.[21] The penalty for transgressors was demolition. In Stuart terms, at worst this meant developers must pay a significant bribe, at best grease a few subordinate palms, but corruption kept growing more expensive.

At Eye Cross there had incontrovertibly been a village. People still living could swear that a cross had marked its green, even if precise locations of its hovels were a matter of opinion. Blake knew how the law could be used; he realized that old Eye Cross offered him a licence to build, squatter though he might be. Another factor was the King's Mulberry Garden which blocked off the area to the north, leaving just half an acre of pitted wasteland between it and the highway at Cow Ford which Blake might conceivably exploit.

Then, probably during the course of that same year of 1623, Blake picked up the first hint that the whole of Ebury manor might come on the market.[22] Feckless King James needed to realize more capital out of Crown lands and Ebury was one estate which would be sold. This in itself made little difference to Blake. He could not hope to raise sufficient cash to purchase a manor now. What frightened him was the probable purchaser, since Ebury had not been picked for sale by accident. From the king's point of view it was an absurd choice when anyone of reasonable intelligence could see that land there was bound to appreciate in value if London continued to grow. It had been chosen because Lord Treasurer Cranfield, now principal royal minister, planned to buy it for himself at a knockdown price, which, even in the freewheeling England ruled by James I, would be considered sufficiently corrupt to ruin a minister already disliked by his king. This may initially have made Blake hope that Cranfield would abandon his plan as too risky, but by the late autumn of 1623 he knew any such hope was misplaced.

Almost certainly, Hugh Audley was Blake's source of information. Knowing secrets was Audley's business, and Cranfield was his direct master at the Court of Wards; from his perch there Audley's instincts already told him that the Lord Treasurer's days in office were numbered. As a consequence he became more than ordinarily interested in Cranfield's covert dealings, because when any great minister fell there were always good pickings to be had. Audley may even have encouraged Cranfield to purchase Ebury for the scandalously low price only a chief minister could arrange, in the belief that afterwards, through pressure of events or blackmail, he could squeeze it out of Cranfield for himself, also at a suitably concessionary price.

If he knew about these subtleties, and probably he did, Blake would have been more alarmed than ever. He might not be as important or self-confident as Cranfield, nor anywhere near as rich as Audley, but he understood the London underworld of property-related crime to a nicety. Either Cranfield or Audley would own Ebury within a year, and Blake's experience told him that Audley was the likely long-term winner. If he, Blake, was to establish possession as those precious nine points of the law over a small but tempting sliver of the manor, he had only the next few months in which to do it, while ownership of the whole remained in doubt.

When he rode home after his discussion with Rolfe about the possibilities of Anne Hawker as a bride for his son, Blake would not have been human if he had not drawn rein at Cow Ford Bridge and gazed at the swampy patch between where he sat his horse and Mulberry Garden wall. Christ's Blood, what a chance, but what a risk as well! To level and drain such a site would cost at least £200, and before a brick was laid. The burden of debt was beginning to wear Blake down, but he knew he needed one last deal to clear himself for retirement. Probably he was enough of a property man to feel the old excitement stir once the development game began. Life was a mill-race and not easy to fish in, but only faint-hearts gave up trying.

CHAPTER 10

Anne Hawker of Heytesbury

There could scarcely have been a greater contrast than that between Queen Elizabeth I and her successor, James of Scotland and now England too. The only similarities were that neither saw absurdity in the most extravagant flattery, and both enjoyed surrounding themselves with handsome male favourites. At first the sense of change came as a relief, and James brought south with him a fresh vision of two united kingdoms. He could be canny, generous, judicious, and was not hampered by set ideas; there was no reason at the outset to believe that his reign would tar and feather the monarchy with contempt.

The scheme to establish a Mulberry Garden on part of the present Buckingham Palace site illustrates in miniature much that ultimately went wrong in his reign. On the surface, setting up new manufactories in silk looked like a good idea, although borrowed from Henri IV of France, who publicized his new industry by keeping silkworms in the orangery at the Tuileries. James, too, wished to set an example and, while regretting the absence of an orangery in Whitehall, decided to make a garden for mulberries as close to his palace as he could. James was familiar with Ebury, since he enjoyed hunting with a fanaticism rare even in a king. He believed that the blood of freshly killed beasts held magically restorative powers, and several ambassadors, after searching for his majesty through the woodlands of England, were startled to be greeted by a bloody royal head poked out of the slit belly of a stag, where James was wallowing in warm guts. Whenever he stayed in Westminster he rode out in the forest beyond Ebury, which had the additional advantage of adjoining St James's Park, turned by him into a cross between a zoo and a nursery for game.[1] As a recreational area this had become significantly more private since crocodiles were introduced into its swamps, from where they malignantly eyed passers-by and shared the deer nursed up for the chase. A new gate and bridge across the Tyburn there would enable him to keep a royal eye on his new silk enterprise, which would, he announced, 'by discourse of his own reason and by information gathered . . . wean the English from idleness and the enormities thereof'.[2]

During 1608 a wall was built to enclose 4 acres of open fields[3] where the north wing of Buckingham Palace now stands, the ground inside it was levelled and mulberry trees were planted. This was only part of a more ambitious whole, as shiploads of mulberries were imported and distributed to officials who were instructed to insist that landowners bought and planted them. A few responded, and Robert Cecil loyally planted a whole new orchard of mulberries at his great house of Theobalds, but arrangements were rudimentary and willingness to purchase sickly saplings for an indeterminate purpose understandably remained minimal.

In James's own Mulberry Garden matters looked more hopeful, where a man called William Stallenge[4] was selected as lessee, a previous sinecure-holder at the Customs House who had experience of breeding silkworms as a hobby. Small quantities of silk were already woven in England, but the industry relied on imported yarn and only a few amateurs, like Stallenge, knew anything about producing it. Even in France, experience suggested that cultivation could only be reliably achieved in the warmer south.

None of these considerations worried James. He wanted results and he wanted them fast. Stallenge was paid the handsome sum of £935 to establish a silk garden at Ebury, together with a fee of £120 a year to look after it, and there has to be a suspicion that he was the real promoter of the scheme. He was there, waiting, when the idea was born; he possessed knowledge which cost the king a great deal of money; and he and his family continued to benefit while the king's losses grew. It is a scenario repeated with variations throughout James's reign.

Stallenge received a licence to import mulberry seeds and set them in any part of the realm, but his real gains came from a cosy manager's house in Mulberry Garden. If he needed money to keep the enterprise afloat, then regardless of his fee and annual payment, he expected the Exchequer to pay. In 1611 for all charges 'without account' given; as the years went on for more buildings, labourers' wages and 'other particulars,' even mulberry leaves.[5] For the minor inconvenience of living beside sheds inhabited by worms, Stallenge achieved at royal expense what William Blake schemed to accomplish on borrowed money: a convenient lodging on someone else's site.

Stallenge's son inherited the post of Keeper to the Worms and continued to enthuse about prospects for silk, also to submit expenses to the Exchequer. There was controversy too over the mulberry trees, with the deceiving French suspected of supplying the unsuitable Black Mulberry instead of White, but as long as the king remained personally interested all would be well, and an outwardly impressive show of activity prevailed on the site. Only dividends continued to be lacking, and by 1623, when William Blake was covetously considering the wasteland lying beyond Mulberry Garden's southern wall, the Stallenges were growing nervous of the future. King James was old and ill, and no one could tell what his successor might think about silk.

Heytesbury High Street with its seventeenth-century coaching inn, where Rolfe and Thomas Hawker would have needed to arrange for Rolfe's election to parliament. (Author)

It was during that winter that Blake's plans suddenly hurried closer to success. Although Rolfe encountered a tougher negotiator than he expected in Thomas Hawker of Heytesbury, when matters finally reached the point where William Blake junior could travel to meet his proposed bride, a contract was clinched.[6] With parliamentary elections imminent Rolfe's talent for obliging others at profit to himself had rarely encountered better circumstances in which to prosper. When he promised Thomas Hawker that he would 'do great matters'[7] for his young kinsman, William Blake, no one doubted his ability to make his promise good. It was as if the Earl of Pembroke himself had spoken. Probably Hawker was capable of estimating young Blake's abilities as mediocre at best, but the boy was agreeable, good tempered, and richly dressed. If he was easy-circumstanced as well, he should make an obliging husband and give Anne a step up in the world.

On this point Rolfe was definite, as he had been to Blake about Anne's prospects. As proof, he suggested that William Blake senior should put at the couple's disposal, in addition to an entail on his estate, either land worth £700 a year or his own position as Master of the Fines Office, at their free choice.[8] This clever device appears to have settled Thomas's doubts. He belonged to the provincial gentry, a clothier who in the nick of time had bought into landed prestige. A Mastership of the Fines Office was quite outside his experience, except he knew that place-holders fattened like ticks on their sinecures; to him it offered just the kind of opportunities a pleasant idler like young Blake should be able to exploit.

On this basis a bargain of marriage between Anne Hawker and William Blake was struck, and only the details of settlement remained to be haggled over. Here Thomas proved generous, but without forgetting to insure his generosity. He proposed to convey his manor of Heytesbury, probably his

Heytesbury Church, where Anne Hawker and William Rolfe were probably married during the spring of 1624. (Author)

only remaining asset of any significance and valued at £12,000, to Blake senior for a sum of £5,000 only. The balance of £7,000 represented a £3,000 marriage portion for Anne, on which Blake was to pay her £300 a year, together with annuities to Hawker and his wife for their life, and to a Lady Gayes,★ jointly worth £390. Since Anne's allowance was clearly calculated at 10 per cent, Hawker thus craftily ensured that Blake benefited, on paper at least, to the tune of only £10 a year for his trouble. He also meant to tie up the whole in trust. Thomas Hawker understood business, even if his judgement of people such as Blake and Rolfe might be suspect.[9]

Blake senior must have suffered an unpleasant shock when he read these settlements, after euphoria when he learned that Hawker, having no son to inherit, was willing to assign his entire manor as a settlement on Anne. A manor worth £12,000 represented a pledge he might use to lever out three or four times its value in credit, but a different matter altogether once set in trust. Clearly, Rolfe and Blake thought long and hard about proceeding further, before deciding on straightforward fraud. Trust deeds were complex and their wording notoriously obscure; there were ways in which Hawker's country lawyer ought to be deceived. Rolfe was definitely back in London for Christmas with everything concluded, because during the festivities some inebriated young gentlemen of Inner Temple perpetrated

★ Since Lady was a Christian name in Anne's family, it is likely this was Anne's grandmother, not a title.

sundry wrongs upon him, perhaps a sign that where he was known, he was not particularly liked.[10]

So far as Anne Hawker is concerned, the following few months can only be pieced together from documents later submitted in evidence during embittered wrangling between herself and her husband. She and young William most likely married early in spring 1624, for which year Heytesbury records are missing. The marriage settlements were signed and the Fines Office sinecure assigned to William junior, which gave the young couple a pleasing sense of independence. In addition, Blake willingly entailed his son's inheritance. He knew young William and did not trust him with sale-able assets.

There is no indication in their later depositions how long the young Blakes were happy together, but Anne later wrote that during this time she was easily persuaded to do whatever the Blakes wished; a hint that she was indeed content and had no reason to feel suspicious.[11]

There was also the excitement of a new house her father-in-law was building beside the Chelsea road at old Eye Cross. The trick about building on wasteland – and squatters tried it all the time – was to have your dwelling built and someone living in it before legal wheels could turn. A poor man could cobble together a hovel in a night, and Blake's house would not take a day longer than he could help. Anne may not have understood the need for haste but it would have been difficult to overlook the whiff of daring attached to the project; the elder Blake's feverish impatience to overcome every hitch, followed by anxious expeditions if bricks or glass failed to arrive on time. There were angry scenes too, whenever they visited the site. Carters yelled about the dangers of an illegally narrowed highway, and ragged families shook fists which said there was too little room now left for them between churning wheels and Blake's new wall. When later that same year the Blakes moved in, Anne may have dreaded leaving Kensington for such a hostile place.

No authentic view of Blake House survives, but the evidence suggests that it was very simple: a glorified farmhouse with a single downstairs room either side of the entry and bedrooms huddled in the roof-space. The servants would have slept haphazard in the stables, outhouses and kitchen, and even after occupation there remained a great deal still to be finished. It is not clear if Anne and William alone moved in, or the whole family lived together to save expense. Blake senior retained ownership of Hale House[12] in Kensington until his death, so with or without her mother-in-law, Anne became mistress of the first household of any size on the Buckingham Palace site.

What she did not know was that it had been built with her money, and the credit Heytesbury represented among the London money-lenders.

CHAPTER 11

Corruption

So far as can be established, Cranfield's interest in land around the Buckingham Palace site began in 1618, when he was still rising in the royal service and privileged information had begun to yield a dividend. He had long been a judicious purchaser of property, the classic example of a man who squeezes his debtors while spreading payments to his creditors as thinly as possible, and Ebury's title could have been tailored to suit a man of his instincts. The freehold belonged to the Crown, and James had enclosed 4 acres to make his Mulberry Garden without caring in the least that it was subject to other interests, but in reality the reversionary lease on the manor as a whole, granted by Queen Elizabeth to Sir Thomas Knyvett, was not due to expire until 1675. This had been divided, and one half assigned to Cuthbert Lynde, a grocer in the City, the other to Edmund Doubleday, a vintner who 'distilled sweet waters at the palace of Whitehall, and kept the library there'.[1]

Knyvett and Doubleday seem to have had a fairly regular business relationship and, intriguingly, they jointly and officially discovered the Gunpowder Plot in 1605. On the plot itself there are nowadays a great many doubting opinions, and one senses an additional falseness when a pair like Knyvett and Doubleday, small cogs in the palace machine who snapped up half-leases and similar crumbs of government bounty, stumble on Guy Fawkes, almost with lighted match in hand, 'Which he had prepared to give fire to a train of gunpowder'.[2]

When Lynde's half-lease came on the market in 1618, Cranfield realized the unique value this represented. The inexorable westward spread of London defied all proclamations and there, a mile from Westminster and across its path, lay the wide meadows and smallholdings of Ebury manor. If he could also buy up Doubleday's interest and then use his position get hold of the royal freehold, Cranfield knew he had a bargain. As a king's minister, he should undoubtedly have bought in these leases as a royal investment of potentially great political and monetary worth, and although altruism was rare in a seventeenth-century statesman, he knew he was failing in his duty. When Cranfield bought Lynde's lease he did so through intermediaries; in 1622 he successfully snapped up Doubleday's as well, and his final step was sufficiently dubious even by contemporary standards for him to wrap it up behind not one, but two sets of nominees.[3] In May 1623, while Rolfe still hovered to keep the Earl of Pembroke's favour as his client for election, Cranfield clinched his triple bargain when the freehold of Ebury manor was sold by Letters Patent under the Great Seal of England. The conveyance specifically excluded Mulberry Garden, and was to John Traylman and Thomas Pearson, two unknowns who resold the same day to Nicholas Herman and Thomas Catchmay, both of whom frequently appear in Cranfield's papers as his confidential servants. They conveyed it a few days later to their master.[4]

Quite how Cranfield pulled off this deal for the derisory sum of £1,501 (of which the Crown received only £1151 15s 1d, the balance sticking to the fingers of Cranfield's employees) is impossible to say. Even James ought not to have been blind to Ebury's potential value and certainly he did not know that his principal minister was the ultimate purchaser. The sloppiness in administration cannot simply be written off to the habits of the age. Henry VIII, for instance, kept an unblinking gaze on what pertained to his Crown and its exact valuation, including such trifling matters as his share of profit on the Bishop of Chichester's mule. But with James on the throne, Lord Treasurer Cranfield triumphantly emerged as owner of all outstanding titles to land which stretched from Oxford Street by way of Hyde Park and Mayfair, through the palace site to Chelsea.

The parliament of 1624 began in unusual amity, but quickly degenerated into rancour. The irresponsibility of James's heir, Charles, and his favourite, the Duke of Buckingham, made matters worse, and by then James lacked the stamina and authority to prevent disaster. Rolfe would have arrived at the Commons' chamber full of expectation, if with less than admirable aspirations. Votes were routinely bought and influence used for personal profit there, deals of all kinds whispered among shifting groups of men sharing covert interests. Members like Rolfe, who had done well for themselves and burned to do better, were scavengers among them and only intermittently interested in the great constitutional issues of the day. In the event, Rolfe made no public impact at all on a parliament which saw the impeachment and downfall of Lionel Cranfield, with infinite consequences for the power of the Crown, financial and otherwise. He never spoke in debate, and cannot be traced as a member of any committee. In such company he was no more than a jumped-up rustic elected solely as a client of the Earl of Pembroke, and attempting to trade his vote elsewhere was more perilous than he had realized. Perhaps he tried to do so and was found out, because Pembroke never backed him as a candidate again, and the overwhelming impression has to be that in the Commons, Rolfe was out of his depth.

As a result of his impeachment Cranfield lost all his offices, was imprisoned during the king's pleasure and fined the enormous sum of £50,000. In fact, James showed to better advantage than his son would do when his minister, Strafford, was later impeached; he reduced the fine to £30,000 and on his own authority released his ex-servant after only a few days in the Tower. Even so, such a sudden loss of position and fortune was crippling. Cranfield loved power and mourned for it continually during the remaining twenty years of his life, which were mostly spent defending his possessions. Never had he evaded his creditors with such infuriating skill or prevaricated so convincingly, spinning out miserly instalments of his fine year after year. He hated to sell land and struggled to keep Ebury, selling jewels, his wines, even his richly upholstered bed to try and avoid the necessity, but luck continued to run against him. The depression which had helped him to buy land cheaply, still persisted now he longed for values to rise, and 1625 was a plague year when traders fled from London. Moreover, following his impeachment, parliament had made his estates a surety for his fine, and prospective purchasers beat him down by arguing that they were buying defective titles.

The consequence of all this for the palace site was to leave Blake undisturbed for more time than he can have dared to hope in his new house on manor wasteland, while Anne and young William enjoyed themselves around town until plague drove them away too, probably to spend the summer back in Heytesbury.

Blake senior did not leave London. His reputation, and therefore his credit, depended on his remaining Hugh Audley's business manager and he spent that dangerous summer peevishly travelling through stricken city streets to haggle on Audley's behalf over the purchase of Ebury.[5] It is extraordinarily ironic to find Blake acting for Audley over land where he himself was a squatter and it would be easiest to assume that Audley sanctioned Blake's presence there: men of his kind were kept reasonably honest by kickbacks on the deals they negotiated. But contemporary opinion on Hugh Audley is unanimous in describing him as an exceptionally astute and calculating man, a diligent lawyer with a practical knowledge of real property and conveyancing unequalled in his day. When one considers the confusion that would engulf the palace site as a result of Blake's encroachment, it seems almost inconceivable that Audley could have allowed a man whose fortunes he controlled to inconvenience him in such a way.

And yet doubts persist. Two years went past between the time when Blake began to build his house and Audley's ultimate purchase of the manor in 1626. He must have known what Blake was doing, where his son and possibly Blake himself were living. And if he knew, then Blake cannot have built on manorial waste Audley expected to own without his consent. Why, therefore, did Audley, that clever man, agree to something which later caused him so much trouble? The answer must be, to increase pressure on Cranfield. These were precisely the months when Cranfield was fighting for his political existence and then was forced to start realizing his assets; when he heard about Blake's encroachment he would naturally assume he acted as Audley's business manager, under orders to rub Cranfield's nose in his powerlessness to prevent an impudent seizure of part of his manor.

Lionel Cranfield, Earl of Middlesex, exploited his position of Lord Treasurer to buy the freehold of Ebury Manor for a derisory sum from James I. Cranfield's marble tomb lies in the south ambulatory of Westminster Abbey. (Courtesy of the Dean and Chapter of Westminster; print: author)

Cranfield dared not admit his ownership of Ebury, an undiscovered corruption which would bring the Commons back in full cry after his blood. It was blackmail by Audley. If Cranfield did not sell to him, he could and would betray him, which were useful business tactics when he entertained no fear that Blake would double-cross him. Blake was his manager and financially embarrassed; when the time came, he would be paid off and his house revert to Audley.

Against all reason, Blake defied these predictions. Perhaps he fell in love with his new house and did not want to give it up. Perhaps he held out for a better deal than Audley was willing to give him. Whatever the reason, he refused to quit the site and its entire future history was shaped by that decision.

The negotiations over the eventual disposal of Ebury were tortuous in the extreme. Both protagonists were close-fisted to the point of avarice, and unscrupulous; the difference between them that Audley had unashamedly purchased his office as an investment, and no damned nonsense about service to the Crown. When an acquaintance asked him what his Chief Clerkship of Wards might be worth, his answer reveals both realism and caustic humour:

> It might be worth some thousands of pounds to him who after death would go instantly to heaven; twice as much to him who is willing to go to purgatory for a while, and nobody knows what to him who would adventure into hell.[6]

If the theology is surprising in a protestant, there is every reason to suppose that Audley risked adventuring into hell, since by the time he died his fortune was estimated at around £400,000, or roughly a year's revenue to the Crown. Cranfield complained that he had never before dealt with so barbarous a man and, more interestingly, since no portrait of Audley exists, 'that his looks show his disposition'.[7] It was not meant as a compliment and a comment from his agent adds that Audley bore himself 'so lofty, respectless and peremptory' that he was unable to make progress towards effecting a sale.[8]

Hugh Audley was forty-eight years old at this time, and had reached the point in his career where mere accumulation of money could with delicate calculation be shifted towards its multiplication. These complaints, prejudiced though they were, portray a man who was filled with confidence in himself, harsh-featured, sharply sardonic in humour, made aggressive by a success he no longer troubled to conceal. He led Cranfield into a war of nerves which, temperamentally as well as materially, he was far better equipped to win.

On 1 March 1626 Audley paid £9,400 for Ebury freehold, using as his trustees for the sale those same two accomplices, William Blake and William Rolfe.[9] Half this money was paid when the deal was sealed, the balance six months later. This was substantially below a price Cranfield had refused to consider the year before, when he said that Audley must consider him a very young man to put such an absurd bid forward.* Now he was forced to accept unfavourable terms as well, his own trick of delayed payments played against him, as Audley dawdled over paying the balance long after it was due.

For several months after Audley's triumph, Blake's fortunes rocketed in the wake of his master's success. He avoided confrontation over his house, and both he and his son received additional sinecures as chirographers to the Court of Common Pleas, which can only have come through Audley's influence.[10] In celebration Blake bought himself a knighthood and became Sir William, an ostentation Audley probably despised since he never bought one for himself. For Anne and young William this was a carefree time, when just beyond the new Blake House wall, St James's Park had become the fashionable place to stroll and be seen. The crocodiles had gone and in dry weather the trees planted in Henry VIII's reign shaded elegant walks surfaced with crushed sea-shells. Officially, people like the Blakes were not allowed inside the park, but in practice anyone could pass the lodge gates who was fashionably dressed and possessed friends among the other young hopefuls who cruised piranha-like in the shallows of Court life.

This loafing life in an age of extravagant fashion was ruinously expensive, but Anne received £300 a year under the terms of her marriage settlement and William possessed two sinecures – £1,200 of spending money when tradesmen were lucky to earn £30! There was no need to worry about extravagance, and borrowing was easy if funds should run short.

Very likely there was a party at Blake House that summer to celebrate Sir William's knighthood, the first social gathering of consequence on the palace site. In imagining the scene it is hard not to warm a little to an old rascal, smugly greeting guests to his new brick house. Rolfe would have come, and he too was enjoying the fruits of success. If he did not yet aspire to knighthood, he had moved to more prestigious Inner Temple quarters, where he was involved in minor business for the Pembroke family. Best of all, he had been included in the Commission of the Peace for Wiltshire,[11] and as a Justice could expect to rub shoulders with the gentry whenever he rode down to his manor of Enford there. Maybe Hugh Audley came, looking at Blake House with calculating eyes, expecting it soon to be his.

---

* He had of course only paid the Crown £1,151 for it, plus payments for the outstanding leases.

Sir William must have known by then that his instinct had been right: he had indeed picked up for nothing potentially the best residential site in official and fashionable London. What he needed to do now was somehow to hold on to it. Blake may initially have been uncertain whether he could defy his patron, Audley, and keep his house; around 1627 he seems to have taken a firm decision to stay and fight, with ruinous consequences for himself and his family.

By the late 1620s the long economic depression at last was easing, which may have been a factor in his calculation, but conditions remained very difficult. Relations between king and parliament were deteriorating and in 1629 Charles resolved to rule alone; the consequent need to raise regular royal loans sucked credit out of a primitive money-market and interest rates for unsecured debtors rose. From the moment Audley realized that only successful legal action would evict his former manager from his encroachment, Blake's credit was under pressure. Realistically, there could only be one end to such an unequal contest, but as Blake aged and became ill with worry, obstinacy took over from calculation. He loved his house, its views, its country air. He refused to give it up, regardless of the calamities each day brought.

To Anne and young William, the first sign of danger came when her allowance was not paid on quarter day. At first her father-in-law may temporarily have terrified them out of pressing for it, since she described him as formidable in his rage.[12] But disaster quickly multiplied for them, too, as the profits from young William's sinecures also ceased, and he discovered that they were mortgaged as collateral for his father's debts. By then neither bluster nor rage could disguise the situation, although the truth took years to unravel. In essence, when Blake was allowed by Thomas Hawker to purchase Heytesbury Manor for less than half its value, he and Rolfe were supposed to be trustees for the capital balance, from which various annuities and allowances would be paid. Instead they had used it as security for their joint debts and to raise money to build Blake House.[13] The papers Anne had signed when receiving past allowances were now revealed as conveyances of her rights to Rolfe, and her income had been paid out of Blake's borrowings, which had dried up. The Fines Office and chirographer's salary were loaded with prior debt – and, Anne would later allege, the documents fraudulently backdated. No money existed there either.

In these circumstances, Anne grew up fast. She seized the reins of the household and burrowed, begged and quarrelled her way into understanding what, exactly, had happened to her and William's money, before urging him into rescuing it if he could. In this she failed. In his own later depositions William junior appears as decent but helpless,[14] and his helplessness stung Anne into becoming a businesswoman on her own account.

Sir William Blake died in 1630, and around the same time so did Thomas Hawker. Blake's widow renounced the administration of her husband's estate in favour of her son, who at once and very foolishly agreed to be liable for all his father's debts although he had no means to discharge them.[15] Sir William had owned other lands besides his houses in Kensington and at Eye Cross, which perhaps his son believed would cover obligations whose scale he failed to grasp. But these were mortgaged too and selling them to any advantage required more time and skill than young William possessed.

Anne fastened early on the Fines Office as the most likely means of support for herself and her children. Although her evidence differs from her husband's on a number of topics, both agree that she persuaded him to make the sinecure over to her. So far as William was concerned, this was a ruse to keep it out his creditors' hands, and then use any profits to discharge debt. For Anne, the motive was to get her hands on cash, and keep it. She reckoned she had a right to whatever she could find, and putting even a sinecure back in profit was no simple task. She succeeded all the same, and once in possession of William's deed to the office, she defended it with a growing lack of scruple, angrily rejecting her husband's pleas to pay off debt. Until their dispute froze its assets, she accumulated, so William said, £3,000 while he was forced to manage on a £30 annuity: 'leaving him to work or beg and otherwise insufferably abusing him'.[16] Poor William; even in extremity, he continued to equate work with begging.

The fiercest opponent Anne had to defeat was Rolfe, whose affairs were so meshed in with those of Blake that he faced ruin too. The battle to establish who had defrauded whom raged throughout the 1630s, during which time Anne became understandably more shrewish. For a woman who was literate but utterly inexperienced, and who lacked cash resources, to take on a crooked lawyer like Rolfe was difficult enough; to take him on and win while encumbered with children, a useless husband, a sick mother-in-law and a house rich Audley wanted, must often have seemed dauntingly impossible. The details wound in and out of Chancery and are not directly involved in the history of the palace site, but doggedly through constitutional crises, civil war and the triumph of parliament over the king, Anne Blake's cause crisscrosses the records of the time. In February 1642 it reached the House of Lords, sandwiched between messages about riots in Enfield Chase and 'the sin and misery of this afflicted nation'. Orders to examine witnesses were issued during business to raise £60,000 for the defence of the realm, and a despairing petition from William 'that his wife Anne Blake may deliver his goods and an Accompt of the monies which came into her hands and which she hath imbezilled, sold, and sent abroad to places unknowne' was presented alongside information concerning Scottish intervention in England's civil war.

In June 1645, as the war drew to an end, young William died and was buried in the Long Walk of Temple Church. Rolfe was also sick, both men debilitated by a debtors' existence which put them occasionally in prison, where Rolfe still languished. In December all suits were finally withdrawn,[17] leaving Anne triumphantly in possession of the accumulated profits of the Fines Office and entailed remnants of her husband's estate. Rolfe was released from prison, but for him there was no way back from ruin. He returned to his native Wiltshire,

A list of debts owed to Hugh Audley in 1658, when he was nearly eighty. (From C.T. Gatty, Mary Davies and the Manor of Ebury, 1921)

a classic illustration of a man who meteorically outgrew his origins only to fall back to earth as his luck burned out. He had long since been struck off the Commission of the Peace[18] and in 1635 was forced to sell his manor of Enford. He died the year after he returned home, leaving what little remained of his estate to be administered by his principal creditor. On a happier note, another William Rolfe, almost certainly his son, steered a less notorious course through the law and was buried in Temple Churchyard in 1693.

These deaths left Anne Blake and Hugh Audley as survivors from the six protagonists who during this time dramatically reshaped the history of the palace site. Anne with her children vanishes from sight;[19] but Audley, although he had ruined the Blakes to make sure he clawed back their house and encroachment into his new ownership of Ebury manor, still had a considerable part to play, because Audley, for once, had miscalculated.

Events had led the Blakes to cherish a rancorous grudge against him and before he died, old Sir William provided himself with deeds to supplement his squatter's title, which, if his heirs were forced to sell, should enable them to do so at a better price than any Audley was likely to offer. Artistically dated for the short time when Cranfield had secretly owned the manor, these documents were ferociously contested by Audley (and, one feels, with reason) throughout the next twenty years until, in 1653, he was finally forced to pay a substantial sum in order to obtain a judgement. Since the judge concerned was Sir Edmund Prideaux,[20] the son of one of Sir William's close collaborators during his early, swashbuckling days as a property developer, this probably represents Blake's vicarious triumph from the grave.

A more immediate result of old Blake's cunning was that his house had long before been sold, not to Audley but, with the benefit of the deeds he had obtained, to a speculating courtier, Sir George Goring.

CHAPTER 12

A Court of Rogues

George Goring made his name as a fool. In the Court of James I extravagant slapstick became a sure way to fortune, and Goring's fame was established when he marshalled into a banquet 'four large brawny pigs, piping hot, bitted and harnessed with ropes of sausages, all tied to a monstrous bag-pudding'.[1] Thereafter, if a master of festivities was required, King James sent for Goring. He could make people drunk on their own animal spirits, and if his humour was of the crudest kind, so was the king's, who particularly enjoyed the kind of debauches where everyone ended up by vomiting over each other's boots and the ladies sang nude in a fishpond filled with wine.

Within weeks of the incident with the pigs and bag-pudding, Goring had received £2,000 as a gift from the king and a variety of sinecures followed.[2] As James's death approached Goring attached himself to Charles, the king in waiting, and in 1623 followed him, uninvited, on an expedition to search for a royal bride in Spain. When this failed, he insinuated himself into negotiations to bring the French Princess Henrietta Maria to England as Charles's queen instead, a shrewd move which slid Goring rapidly up the greasy steps of favour, at a time when he might easily have fallen to the bottom.

The new king's character was chaste and serious, in most ways a direct contrast with that of his father, and even the most censorious of puritans found it difficult to criticize behaviour at his Court. Vulgar horseplay was out, artists and architecture in. Goring's response to these changed circumstances was to capitalize on his stay in Paris and attach himself to Henrietta Maria's household, moderating his bawdiness into wit, his more grotesque tricks into felicitous jokes. Avarice is generally characterized as a mean-minded, humourless vice, but George Goring was expansively avaricious, unscrupulously amusing, all things to as many people as possible and everything to himself. The Earl of Clarendon, a relentless critic of courtly iniquity, describes him as 'a frolic of pleasant humour'[3] but unfitted for serious enterprise, a judgement the Exchequer records show to be inaccurate, if the enterprise was his own enrichment. He was created a baron in 1628 and Earl of Norwich in 1644, but it was the gains accumulated during the king's personal rule which enabled him to purchase Blake House at Eye Cross and enlarge it into a gentleman's residence, with the changed name of Goring House.

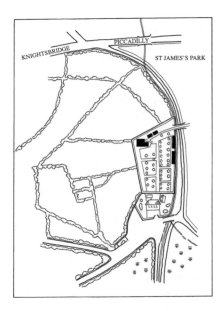

Sketch plan showing the area around Buckingham Palace about 1630, with Blake House inserted into highway waste and gravel workings near old Eye Cross. Mulberry Garden is shown immediately to the north of the house. A slaughterhouse probably existed on the site of the present Royal Mews, indicated near the fork in the road south-west of Blake House.

Where Cranfield had at least worked hard in royal service for the favours he received, wealth simply fell into Goring's hands: duties worth £4,000 on sugar, the right to tax gold and silver thread manufacture, butter exports, taverns. In 1637 he pulled off the coup of his courtly life by landing the sole right to license the import and sale of tobacco, and the following year he fronted a syndicate which displaced City financiers from the Great Farm of Customs. For all the goodfellow image of this next character in the palace site's history, there can be no doubt that Goring was one of the most rapacious exploiters of his time, mostly at Crown expense but also taking bribes from outsiders to use his influence at Court.[4]

When such a third-rate parasite as Goring could pick up gifts which gave him an income not far short of total national expenditure on the Navy,[5] it is reasonable to wonder why King Charles ever needed to embark on dubious constitutional expedients in an attempt to increase his revenues. Jobbery on such a scale and for no return in service was considered scandalous even by contemporaries, but Goring remained always short of cash. Constant novelty of a kind to entertain kings and queens was expensive, as was the extravagance to advertise his position, and the search for more favours never ended. Sharp teeth, a tenacious digestion and unwearying application to pleasure were the vital attributes of predatory courtiers, like so many tiger worms processing garbage.

Goring bought Blake House for an undisclosed sum, using intermediaries to help safeguard what clearly remained a highly dubious title, completing the deal in 1633. Meanwhile he negotiated directly with Audley to purchase more land around Blake's half acre, consisting of two large enclosures known as Upper and Lower Crow Fields, now part of the modern palace gardens.⁶

Why Audley agreed to this sale when he was still violently contesting the title to Blake House is uncertain, but in the early 1630s Goring was an exceptionally useful man to know, always willing at a price to carry out favours within the inner reaches of the Court. Once someone so close to the king was in possession of Blake House he would be impossible to dislodge, and Audley extracted a high price for the 20 acres he sold: at £7,000 perhaps nearly a quarter the agricultural price for wetlands even today. But he knew Goring's spendthrift reputation and offered easy terms, probably calculating that the payments would not be kept up. In fact, Goring paid £520 on taking possession and then no more. In law he was at Audley's mercy, which did not prevent him from spending money as if indebtedness had no meaning.⁷ After 1634, the only land Goring still lacked to complete his ownership of nearly all the modern Buckingham Palace site was Mulberry Garden and the eastern forecourt section, what was then still the course of the Tyburn, the road alongside it, and a segment of St James's Park.

Goring's obnoxious talent for milking public finances was relieved by two virtues: his ultimate loyalty to the king and the vision with which he set his new home in extensive grounds. The house itself was described as 'another pile of building joining south to Sir William Blake's', and like Blake's, it faced south towards the river rather than east over St James's as the present palace does. Clearly, it was an enlargement and elaboration rather than a completely new structure. 'Convenient buildings and outhouses',⁸ a laundry yard and stables adjoined, and since Goring House was by no means large, these additions provide some standard of comparison for Blake's earlier house, which in retrospect appears extremely modest.

Goring also grabbed more highway waste, extending his courtyard entry and landscaping a 'tarris walk and ffountain garden' out of verges and gravel diggings along modern Buckingham Palace Road. He evicted smallholders from the fields he bought from Audley, planted a pippin orchard and enclosed the whole behind a long brick wall, known for many years afterwards as Goring Great Garden. In the 1630s it became a landmark, and one anecdote describes how the Earl of Elgin and Sir William Crofts fought a duel there, without seconds: 'they two only walked into the fields over against Hyde Park by my lord of Goring's garden wall, where they chose a place and fought like courageous men'.⁹

Several small paddocks lost to Goring's garden were marked on an early map as 'poules',¹⁰ which may suggest intensive poultry rearing for the London market. Eviction was a catastrophe for local people, who also raised market crops, fattened beasts for the table and sublet horse-grazing there, but these were not considerations which troubled either Goring or Audley when they bought and sold land.

*Sketch engraving and signature of George
Goring, Earl of Norwich. (From J.E. Doyle,
Official Baronage of England, 1886)*

All these works took place in a relatively short space of time between 1633 and 1639, and they plunged Goring into debt. Not only did he fail to keep up his instalments to Audley, he also mortgaged Goring House to his wife's relatives, the Dennys, and borrowed £15,000 from moneylenders on security of Goring Great Garden. By 1639 the Dennys' original £2,450 loan had rolled up interest to reach £5,000, and the moneylenders' debt had passed £20,000.[11] It would be surprising to discover that builders, landscapers or cabinet-makers working on Goring's new property fared any better, and such behaviour by a man who remained high in the king's favour can only have contributed to the venom revealed among the London mobs during the political and religious crises soon to follow.

None of these debts prevented Goring from casting acquisitive eyes on other land nearby and in particular Mulberry Garden, next door to his house and still leisurely producing minute quantities of silk. Those missing 4 acres were a particular irritant when all his other boundaries reached open country or flanking roads and, most annoying of all, the Tyburn's foul waters trickling past his salon windows were further polluted by this manufacturing settlement close by. Unless something was done about both these nuisances soon, all his expenditure would be wasted and the house become uninhabitable.

When Charles I inherited the throne from his father, he soon lost faith in the Stallenges' ability to deliver a silk industry and terminated their concession, granting to Lord Aston, 'the keeping of his Majesty's Mulberry Garden and the silkworms and houses therewith appertaining, with the yearly fee of £60 during his life and that of his son'.[12] Aston was a rich Staffordshire landowner, and quite why he should have received Mulberry Garden is difficult to determine, since a man whose rents yielded £10,000 annually was unlikely to covet a mere £60.

Possibly Mulberry House held the same attractions as Blake's had done, for use as a residence when Aston returned from being ambassador in Spain; possibly he had become interested in silk manufacture while living there. He was also one of Charles's few personal friends and not a rapacious courtier. In 1635 he went back to Spain as ambassador, which must have marked the end of any pretence at supervision over silk production, and over the following years Goring repeatedly tried to buy out his interest. He failed, but when Aston died in 1639 a contract was clinched with his son, and on the principle that it is never too late to nag for a gift, Goring instantly transferred his attention to the king, who held the Crown freehold. Success there came in July 1640, on the very brink of civil war, but the document failed to pass the great seal before King Charles fled London, which it needed to do for legal execution.[13]

Whatever the discrepancies, legal shortcomings and underpayments litter-ing Goring's transactions, by 1640 he had, at least in theory, assembled nearly all the future Buckingham Palace site into his own hands, the first person to separate it out from the manor of Ebury. There were exceptions, the most significant of which remained the Tyburn frontage. The grant of Mulberry Garden went some way towards rectifying this by stating that Goring also acquired 'all that watercourse in or near the highway . . . and the soil of the same, with liberty to build upon the said watercourse and highway',[14] which probably means that he already envisaged enclosing the land above and around the Tyburn within his site by culverting the old watercourse underground. Whether he actually did so remains doubtful.

The Short Parliament met in April 1640 and its collapse left the king with the impossible task of financing a war against the Scots from his own resources. Goring was among those sent to try and negotiate a loan from the City, which virtually guaranteed failure since he was particularly disliked by its great merchants, who had been fleeced for years by his activities as a monopolist. He also rashly promised to raise a troop of horse for the king's service, an undertaking which plunged his finances into a chaos transcend-ing mere humdrum indebtedness. At once, Hugh Audley pounced and his timing was exquisite. Goring owed him £6,480 plus interest on his purchase of land for Goring Great Garden, and Audley now laid down precise dates for payment, failing which he would resume the title.

In November 1640, a bare three months after Goring believed he had gained the freehold of Mulberry Garden, the Long Parliament settled in at Westminster and a general doomsday began for beggars at the Court of Charles I. Goring lost everything. Sinecures were abolished, monopolies and concessions swept away, the king's ability to pay pensions to his favourites neutered. The extent of cataclysm, which struck inside a few weeks, was fearful.

The crisis deepened throughout 1641 and in the streets of Westminster anyone wearing fine clothes was liable to be booed; ministers were set on and bishops tumbled in the mud. When the first of Hugh Audley's dates for payment arrived, Goring had no hope of meeting it, and Audley's response was instant. He put tenants into Goring Great Garden as if it was still fields, including a Mr French who had planted Goring's orchard and now leased it from Audley for his own profit. Apparently Audley was fond of apples, because he stipulated that part of his rent should be paid in pippins.[15]

Not surprisingly, a violent dispute exploded as a result of these moves, since Goring apparently still occupied his house when the garden was invaded. Audley remained undisturbed. Events had moved decisively in his favour and Goring was still raging ineffectively against him when war finally broke out and he was forced to leave London, as escort for the queen on her flight abroad. He never lived in Goring House again.

For a few weeks after Goring's departure his house remained empty, its ownership contested between Audley and Edward Denny, to whose father Goring had mortgaged it, but parliament soon stepped in. An abandoned building so close to Westminster looked useful, and both it and Mulberry Garden were seized for use as barracks.

A decisive factor in the civil war was the attitude of London, and from his headquarters in Oxford, Charles concentrated his early campaigns on its recapture. As a result a ring of trenches, forts and batteries was constructed around the capital, from Wapping by way of Islington and Hyde Park to Tothill and the Thames, later extended along the south bank as well. Among the sites chosen for fortification was Goring House, that outrider of London's expansion to the west. As a City resolution of 1643 puts it:

> At Hide Park Corner a large forte with flankers on all sides. At the corner of Lord Goring's brick wall next the fields, a redoubt and battery where the court of guard [guard-post] now is; at the lower end of the Lord Goring's wall, the bresteworke to be made forwarder.[16]

From this it is clear that there were already defensive works around the barracks that Goring House had become, and confirmation comes from Audley's tenants, who complained that construction work was ruining their livelihood. Soon, they refused to pay him any rent at all. Anyone who remembers the state of property taken over by an army in time of war will find it easy to imagine the destruction which tore apart Goring's fountain gardens and terraced walks, the damage to panelling, smashed glass, and the clutter in his forecourt. The garden wall was punched with holes for use as firing points and the parkland stripped of topsoil for use in revetments. The new forts would be even more destructive, being built of whatever materials could be scrounged from the house and locality. They comprised a protected mounting for cannon and walls barricaded by turfed clay. The disturbance was enormous, and there can have been little garden left after oxen and people swarmed everywhere in wet spring weather, building them. As if this was not enough, in January 1644 the

Common Council of the City ordered that all trees and hedges remaining near London's forts should be uprooted, all objects in the field-of-fire pulled down, all ditches filled in.[17] If these instructions were even perfunctorily obeyed around the palace site, the result would have been not just more destruction but severe flooding as well.

While all this was going on, Audley and Denny temporarily ceased to fight each other and launched bitter joint complaints against parliament for waste, but without receiving any satisfaction. In the spring of 1643 the Venetian ambassador described the works as being pushed forward at great speed:

> They do not even cease work on a Sunday which is so strictly observed here, but . . . march out with spades, shovels, pickaxes and suchlike tools on their shoulders to assist in the work. On Tuesday last there were 5000 Feltmakers and Cappers, near upon 3000 porters besides other great companies of men, women and children. This day the whole company of gentlemen vintners went out with their wives, servants and wine porters.[18]

It provides some relief from the general sense of tension and vindictiveness to picture the gentlemen vintners of Westminster pausing in their unaccustomed labour on Goring House fort to enjoy covert swigs unseen by puritan demagogues. A Scottish visitor dramatized the scene:

> a novelty beyond novelties and what was more rarer, I found the grasse growing deep in the royall Courts of the King's House at Whitehall . . . and out beyond it people marching to the fields and outworks carrying on their shoulders yron mattocks and wooden shovels, with roaring drummes, flying collours and girded swords; most companies [including] ladies, women and girls; two and two carrying baskets to advance the labour where divers wrought till they fell sick of their pains.[19]

As the likelihood of an attack on London receded, work on its defences ceased. Then the bills came flooding in, and it became apparent that many of those whose labour had been considered voluntary now expected to be paid. Long after the war was over parliament was still struggling to settle claims and demands for damages connected with London's fortifications. Ruin at Goring House was among these, and adjudication became urgent when it was decided to lodge an incoming French ambassador, M. Bellieure, there.[20] Troops were hastily evicted, patchwork repairs carried out, furniture hastily trundled in. Bellieure, as a captious Frenchman used to good living, disliked such makeshift quarters on sight, and after voluble complaints decamped to visit the king in Oxford. On his return he refused to be housed at Goring House again and the Commons thriftily resolved to put in their Speaker, William Lenthall, instead.[21] Since Lord

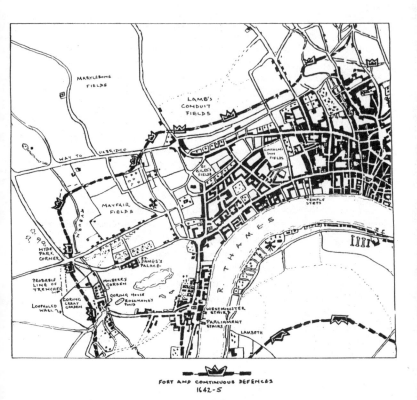

FORT AND CONTINUOUS DEFENCES
1642–5

London's Civil War defences encircled the capital, and included a fort and garrison at Goring House. The garden wall was loopholed and turf dug from the lawns to form revetments and trench parapets. (Author, extensively redrawn from 1927 map)

Goring* returned from exile around the same time, following a cessation in the fighting, the House of Lords objected to this on behalf of their fellow peer, a remarkable sidelight on the tribal loyalties of the time, but Lenthall, not Goring, was the next occupant of the palace site. In August 1647, while Goring was still unsuccessfully pursuing his claim, the Kentish Rising began and he was despatched by Royalist conspirators in London to become its figurehead, not at all a good choice. He was sixty-four years old, and unlike his son of the same name had no experience of leadership in the field, even less of disorderly rustic rebels. But he liked to be agreeable, which at first made him popular, but later exacerbated the quarrels which broke out. As the rebellion collapsed, Goring and

---

* It seems simpler to keep the same name, although he was created Earl of Norwich in 1644.

his immediate followers fled across the Thames to Colchester, imagining they might hold out until support could reach them. Conditions in the besieged town became appalling through the summer of 1647 as these hopes were disappointed, Goring's own conduct varying between courageous determination not to desert his men and callousness towards civilians with whom he had no sympathy. When the women of Colchester came to his headquarters to beg for food for their children, he shouted back in anger that they might eat their children if they liked. During the siege Goring's wife died in London and his daughter was allowed past the lines to bring the news, providing she did not enter the town. The odd sight followed of Goring and his daughter lunching together outside the wall on horseflesh stewed in claret.[22]

On 28 August the Royalist leaders surrendered to mercy, their soldiers to quarter, a critical difference which led to two of the former being shot out of hand as rebels. Goring was sent for trial with three other Royalist conspirators of the time, and the special commission created for this occasion was presided over by Speaker Lenthall, another strange irony from the past, since he was almost certainly living in Goring's house. The prisoners were kept just across the park in St James's Palace, and Lenthall cannot have escaped some squeamish feeling when he returned home each night, to relax in a lodging still called Goring House. When the time came for judgement, all the accused were condemned outright, except the Earl of Holland and Goring, where there was an equality of votes, leaving their lives at Lenthall's mercy. Holland's character was the more pleasing of the two, but in his case Lenthall gave his casting vote for death, in Goring's case for life, and it is almost impossible to avoid the conviction that the ghosts of Goring House had a great deal to do with his decision. Matthew Carter, who had been present at the siege of Colchester, reflected the general surprise and cynicism about a verdict no one had expected to be merciful when he wrote that Goring only escaped with his life because Lenthall was said to have received some past favour from him.[23] After all, the king himself had been executed only the month before for making war on his people. The snag is, that so far as is known, Lenthall and Goring neither knew each other nor was Goring likely to have granted favours to a man whose only fame was to preside over a parliament which destroyed his world.

But a link between them did exist, and it was his house on the Buckingham Palace site that probably saved George Goring's life; one more strand in a pattern which reaches into many unexpected places.

After Colchester fell, dissension between the army and parliament took over from war between parliament and king. In London the Lord Mayor even ordered the citizens to hold the capital's defences against Lord General Fairfax's advancing troops, but they lacked stomach for a fight, particularly against men so recently regarded as their champions against evil.

When the troops came in from the west, they streamed past the empty revetments in Goring Great Garden, camping there and in the open spaces near it, but

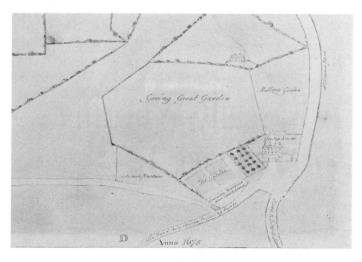

Map dated 1675 showing the property accumulated – but not paid for – by George Goring. The fanciful sketch of his house is the earliest representation of a building on the site, but contemporaries such as John Evelyn indicated that it remained quite a modest gentleman's house, and by 1675 it had in any case burned down. Note entry to the south rather than the east, and absence of the Tyburn, which Arlington probably later enclosed within a conduit. Since there is no trace of it further north either, this may reinforce suspicions of some artist's licence drawn into the house as well. The treed area near the house may indicate some survivals from the slighted fort of thirty years earlier. (British Library Crace Collection: Port. X, no. 32)

in spite of this surrender, the generals very soon decided it was too dangerous to leave forts around a capital whose loyalty to a newly-victorious parliament clearly remained questionable. In September 1647 an ordinance ordered all 'Ramparts, Bastions and other works which incircled the Cities of London and Westminster ... to be forthwith slighted and demolished',[24] but a few remnants remained visible into the mid-eighteenth century.[25] At Goring House, Speaker Lenthall was in a position to urge forward demolition of jerrybuilt constructions which spoiled his view, yet part of the garden could apparently still be described some thirty years later as 'having therein a ... mount set with trees'.[26] Mount Street, Mayfair, commemorates a similar strong point and there seems little doubt that the word does describe the remains of Great Goring Fort; this roughly treed area is placed just beyond the modern palace terrace by a plan dated 1675. There the eager drums had roared, and vintners picnicked in the tatters of Goring's garden; there parliamentary soldiers burned his furniture to stay warm, and kept guard in a spindly timber tower. And one day perhaps, between presenting her petitions against Rolfe and her husband in the Parliament House, Anne Blake came in with the crowd and looked with astonishment at what had happened to the place where she spent the first happy years of her marriage.

CHAPTER 13

'A Rascally Whoring Sort of Place'

By the 1640s Westminster Abbey was a shadow of its previous self. Plundered by Henry VIII, it had been briefly restored as a monastery under Mary, when the monks prudently laid in a store of gunpowder in case they should need to defend themselves from attack by protestant malcontents. This stockpile was rediscovered after the abbey was returned to royal control under Elizabeth, and employed by the dean to blast pigeons out of the nave, after which the building was even less weatherproof than before.

During the upheavals of 1641 the abbey was defended from sacrilegious mobs by the dean's staff with drawn swords and tiles hurled off the roof, backed up by the Archbishop of York's retinue. Puritanism triumphed all the same and in 1643 soldiers were quartered there; an orgy of destruction followed when even the organ pipes were sold 'for potts of ale' and whores.[1]

With peace, the soldiers departed but only to be replaced by religious freaks and fanatics. Fist-fights broke out over obscure points of doctrine, abuse was yelled at opponents during rival acts of worship. Visionaries prophesied desperate tortures for the damned, which sent everyone in earshot into hysterics, and when Cromwell attended a service some rabid dissenters tried to shoot him. Afterwards 'a bold thief' stole lead off the roof while onlookers, who considered the abbey a house of Mammon, cheered him on. Eventually Cromwell sent musketeers to clear the place, but when Samuel Pepys attended the last puritan service held there immediately after the king's restoration, debris kept falling on the congregation from holes in the roof which, as he observed, 'made me wish myself safely out'.[2]

Through all this chaos Hugh Audley pursued his claim to Goring House and garden. A boy of eleven when the Spanish Armada was defeated, he had lived through the follies of James I, through civil war and execution of a king by parliament, which to an Elizabethan like Audley must have seemed unimaginable, though he shared the general anger against royal incompetence. The return of Lord Goring in 1647 must have caused him some anxiety, his departure into exile a satisfactory outcome which helped clear away an obstacle to his title.

As traffic continued to increase, heavy coaches and newly introduced hackneys churned up the roads around Goring House still further. (From Larwood, *History of the London Parks*, 1881)

The sequestrators of the new Commonwealth of England had some time before pronounced that Mulberry Garden remained royal property since the sale had never passed the seal, but the old Blake encroachment of Goring House was different, though niceties of ownership were overlooked while the war still raged. Both Denny and Audley claimed it, Audley arguing that Denny's claim was fraudulent, since it was based on trespass by Blake. If people were stupid enough to lend money on an illegal title, they had only themselves to blame for loss. Surprisingly, considering that Audley lent money to parliament and served as their sheriff in three counties, the administrators of royal and sequestrated lands eventually decided that Denny was the rightful owner of Goring House, and paid their rent to him. Audley promptly went to King's Bench with his documents and won a judgement there, which transferred these payments to him, whereupon John Denny was so beside himself with rage that he broke into the property in 1651, and again in 1652, kicking down doors and 'defacing [the fabric] and ... taking away one fountain of lead and stone, valued at £100'.[3]

The case turned up next in Chancery with the further complication that John's father, Edward Denny, had sold documents detailing his claim to Speaker Lenthall's son, John, described as 'the greatest liar and bragadoccio of the age'.[4] The matter is obscure, but when Denny broke in to Goring House probably the Lenthalls were in residence, and John Lenthall may have offered cash to take over deeds he might later be able to use. Bankrupt and desperate, Denny must have agreed, and perhaps part of his payment was the fountain out of the garden, which cannot have been easy to remove without connivance. The scene is an intriguing one: half-sacked, half-restored Goring House sprawled over by the Lenthalls, those rewarded victors of a war, when their complacence was abruptly shattered by the crash of a door which sent the lamps flickering in a blast of outside air, followed by the appearance of Denny, probably drunk and hurling anything that came to hand against the walls, on the floor, through recently repaired window glass. Screams from the women, shouts for servants to restrain a madman, incoherent explanations and then, secretly afterwards, two young men, Lenthall and Denny, meet to see what they might hatch together. The second break-in when the fountain was stolen, followed.

Soon afterwards the Lenthalls left Goring House and the troops came back to use it as a convenient base from which to launch a campaign against parliament for their back pay.

This was the point at which the whole ravelled affair lumbered off to Edmund Prideaux, Attorney General to the Commonwealth of England, for decision. In 1653 his judgement finally emerged, and in spite of the fact that Blake had certainly altered and very likely forged the deeds on which the Denny claim relied, Prideaux found that Goring and through him, Denny, did have rights in the property, but ducked the issue of precisely what these were. Audley was forced to compensate them all the same, but at last obtained possession of Goring House, as well as the Great Garden land he had sold to Goring.[5]

It is hard to think of Buckingham Palace as sacked and desolate, looted and occupied by soldiers, but that was its ancestor's state when it came into Audley's ownership. A few years later his heir described it as 'in so great decaye that £1500 would not putt itt in repayre', adding that it had been so 'meanely and improvidently Built and was runn into soe great decayes and ruines that scarecely to susteyne the same from fellinge down'.[6]

When the troops finally left in 1657, Audley was becoming very frail. He had never married and nor did either of his brothers, descendants of his three sisters eventually benefiting from his will, although in common with other rich men, one of the last pleasures of Audley's life was to keep changing the disposition of his wealth. As his abilities began to slip he was preyed on, too, by those who wished to take advantage of him. Sums of money were stolen from his rooms, plausible rogues begged to take care of him and plundered what they could while his mind wandered, only to discover that sometimes it remained as sharp as ever.

In 1661, when Audley was eighty-four, he petitioned the Lord Chancellor, stating that he had settled 'a certain farm called Ebury Farm and Goring House' on John Rea, with whom he lodged. He swore that he had been greatly deceived by Rea and begged the Chancellor to ensure that Rea gave back the deeds to these properties, which he was wickedly concealing. This outcome he achieved only months before he died, after paying 20s costs, a notably cheap deal for recovering most of the palace site and Belgravia.[7]

Almost up to his death, Audley worked hard to recover some value into Goring House and garden. He was not so old that his instinct for circumstance had deserted him; he understood that people were weary of opinion-ated and quarrelsome new rulers who attempted simultaneously to enforce killjoy bigotry and raise large sums in taxation. Restoration of a king might be the only way to reach normality again. A king meant a Court, and a Court meant courtiers – men who would appreciate a residence such as Goring House, adjoining royal St James.

But whatever building works Audley ordered, they did not solve structural weaknesses in Goring House, which may have been as much due to continuing wetness on the site as to war-time damage or slapdash building. Refurbishment of a sort was completed by the restoration year of 1660, when Audley began to let out Goring House for social functions, and Samuel Pepys describes how in that July he 'went to a great wedding of Nan Hartlibb's sister which was kept at Goring House with very great state, cost and noble company'. Pepys also recorded the death of Hugh Audley on 23 November 1662: 'I hear today how old rich Audley is lately dead and left a very great estate, making many poor families rich, and did not leave all [his wealth] to one'. A more succinct writer simply stated that Audley had died 'immeasurably rich'.[8] Indeed, he had lived so long and litigated so persistently that he had become a London institu-tion, synonymous with thrift. An anonymous sniping tract was published just after his death called *The Way to be Rich*, which ostensibly praised his virtuous frugality, but its many caustic asides suggest that the writer was familiar with his methods of collecting on a debt. What it does grudgingly make clear is that Audley made money as much by calculation as by rapacity. At a time when anybody who was anybody lived on credit, he underwrote loans secured on these spendthrifts' estates, with the result that over time a great deal of good land fell into his hands.[9] He traded overseas, was vigilant over his own and other men's affairs, outstandingly patient in an impatient generation, parsimonious in a showy age, undisturbed in his pursuit of business by the fanaticisms of his time. The writer of the tract states that he always lived in rooms within Inner Temple or close by; that he ate simply and wore 'unadorned trunk hose with drawyers upon all occasions, a leather doublet and plate buttons . . . all of good cloth, linnen and woolen, the best being cheap'.[10]

If Hugh Audley provides an example of how some men can profitably ride out a great upheaval in history, Mulberry Garden, which also occupied an important area of the present palace site, offers an equally striking insight into the durability of the human wish to seek out pleasure, no matter how adverse the circumstances. Under puritan rule, secular public enjoyment officially vanished. Strong beer, frivolity and dancing were devices of the Devil, yet no sooner had the parliamentary garrison been ejected, than Mulberry Garden was opened by a certain Mr Chipp as a place of entertainment. Since the grant to Goring was regarded as invalid, the garden had been sold as former Crown property to benefit the Republic, to Sir Anthony Deane of Essex, who in turn sold to Mr Chipp.[11]

At a time when Commonwealth soldiers still remained in Goring House and probably Mulberry House as well, Mulberry Garden opened for business. In May 1654 John Evelyn recorded an evening he spent there, sourly adding that it had become the most favourite place in town 'for persons of the best quality to be exceedingly cheated at'.[12] He was particularly shocked to find women with rouged cheeks strolling in its walks. Since puritan nosy-parkering was then at its zenith, spies from the England of the Saints would have been more than just shocked by loose women and rouge, as well as by the strong drink dispensed by Mr Chipp, and it is probable that these diversions were enjoyed only by those who passed scrutiny at the gate. High walls designed to keep silkworms cosily away from draughts had found a valuable use at last.

The discretion required to operate an establishment like Mulberry Garden at a time of hellfire moralism shrouded it in a mystery which almost certainly added to its fame. There were sound business reasons for trying to retain this after the Restoration, and though descriptions of other pleasure resorts then become plentiful, Mulberry Garden continues to appear only in jokes and asides, risqué dramas and sly allusion. Inevitably Pepys went off with his customary curiosity to sample its delights, but was much dissatisfied, having apparently expected a better class of women. It was, he thought, 'a very silly place, worse than Spring Garden and but little company, and that a rascally, whoring, rogueing sort of people, only a wilderness that is somewhat pretty, but rude. Did not stay to drink'.[13] On another visit, in April 1669, in company with his wife and a Mr and Mrs Sheres, he was better pleased:

> We to the Mulberry Garden, where Sheres is to treat us with a Spanish Olio [spiced stew] by a cook of his acquaintance that is there . . . and without any other company he did do it, and mighty nobly . . . Only Mrs Sheres being taken suddenly ill for a while did spoil our mirth, and by-and-by was well again and was mighty merry; and so broke up.

From Pepys' description it appears that Mr Chipp had built bowers among the mulberries where parties of friends could picnic around a provided brazier, even hiring their own cook, although mulberry tarts remained a ready-made speciality. As the establishment boomed, Chipp leased additional land in Goring's old garden, including his bowling green, where various sports could be enjoyed.

Such descriptions as exist of happenings there are full of smut and belly laughs. Charles Sedley, in a drama he called *The Mulberry Garden*, makes one of his characters poke malicious fun at the country girls who do not know that it is only decent to walk there in daylight; another is disgusted to find children playing where he expected 'to find this place so full of beauties that like a pack of hounds in a hare-warren, we could hunt one after another; What think you of an arbour and a bottle of Rhenish?' And they agree that this is an ideal way of waiting until dark, and while doing so ungallantly exchange the names of women they have enjoyed.

A more explicit scene occurs in Sir George Etheredge's comedy, *She Would if She Could*, which features an old alderman called Freeman and a courtier, who hide at dusk in Mulberry Garden to watch the prostitutes gather.

Freeman. Ha-ha, how wantonly they trip it.
  There is temptation in their very gait to stir
  up the courage of an old alderman. Pray thee
  let us follow them.

                    (Exit, and Enter two women)

Ariona Now, there are two men of war that are
  cruising here to watch for prizes.

Gatty Would they had courage to set upon us, I
  swear I long to be engag'd.

Ariona Ah, look! Look yonder, I protest they
  chase us!

Gatty Let us bear away then, if they be truly
  Valiant, they'll more quickly make more Sail
  and overtake us.

                    (The women go out at a run)

Freeman S'death how fleet they are! I'll
  follow directly, do thou turn down that cross-
  walk and we shall meet them

                    (Re-enter the women, chased)

SCENE 2
Lady Cockwood's House
Enter the two women, Ariana and Gatty

Lady Cockwood Your servant, cousins. How have
  you spent the cool of the evening?

Gatty As the custom is, Madam, breathing fresh
  air in the Park and Mulberry Garden.

Lady Cockwood Without the company of some
  relation! or some discreet body to justify
  your reputations! You are young and may be
  insensible of it, but this is a censorious
  world.[14]

Words and atmosphere are full of innuendo; Lady Cockwood is given a name which raises an ironic cheer each time she mouths a moral sentiment; the Alderman's sail is excited by the chase; the ladies are no common whores but revealed as young cousins of quality, yet their nautical metaphors duplicate the slang terms by which their professional sisters were known.

For just over twenty years, from around 1653 to 1675, Mulberry Garden flourished as an agreeable if raffish place of entertainment to which trades-people came in the morning and a fashionable crowd in the afternoon and early evening; at night its reputation was such that respectable women did not visit there at all. As late as 1735, a writer in the *Gentleman's Magazine* recalls as a boy seeing the poet John Dryden there,

> always clad in one uniform clothing of Norwich drugget before he paid court
> with success to the great. I have eat tarts with him and Madam Reeve [an
> actress who was his mistress] at the Mulberry Garden, when our author was
> just advanced to a sword and chadreuse wig.[15]

All these strolling revellers in high wigs and embroidered clothes, who talked poetry and scandal, affairs of state and states of the heart in sheltered booths while sampling dishes from a brazier, relaxed where the private north wing of the palace is today; and whores sailed by moonlight under the windows of the present royal apartments.

Lord Goring, almost as old and durable as Hugh Audley, again returned from exile at King Charles II's restoration and set about trying to reclaim his house and garden at Ebury. He had lost everything as a result of his own improvidence and loyal service to the Crown, and now pleaded for the king at least to recognize the hurried grant of Mulberry Garden, to which his claim was more straightforward than for his house, where in equity and law Audley was now secure. Charles recognized Goring's penury but was reluctant to part with a royal freehold which his own plans for improv-ing St James's Park made him wish to retain. He was about to compro-mise and lease it to Goring for a term of years when Mr Chipp surfaced with his title, bought in good faith through Sir Anthony Deane from the Commonwealth.

Charles was probably glad of an excuse not to alienate land he fancied for himself, and when Goring died, aged eighty,[16] his son's claim to the garden made no progress. Since Lord Aston's son also claimed an interest, Charles announced that he intended to keep the freehold and would compensate anyone who proved a right to it. No one succeeded in doing so. Chipp was forced to pay rent to the king, an appropriate landlord for such an enterprise, and Charles personally leased part of Goring's old 'Great Garden' property for development as a physick garden.[17]

In the end, it would be Charles II's shrewd decision to retain ownership of Mulberry Garden which would become the lever his royal descendants used to take over the entire Buckingham Palace site, together with the much more splendid house which by then was built there.

CHAPTER 14

Marriage Market

Within a few months of her birth, Mary Davies was transformed from being a mere scrivener's brat into an investment. Confidence in her value varied. For years it remained uncertain if she was a high risk for gamblers only, or a blue chip on the marriage market, provided the buyer was not pernickety about birth and breeding.

Mary was the only child of Alexander Davies and Mary Dukeson, born in Westminster on 17 January 1665.[1] Her father was one of Hugh Audley's great-nephews and as such benefited from his will, receiving Ebury Manor as his share in the old man's estate. Alexander had worked as his great-uncle's confidential clerk but had never been able to count on precisely what he would inherit. Ebury, for instance, was willed in turn to each of three great-nephews, and Alexander simply happened to be the latest beneficiary when Audley died. He was not particularly pleased about it either, since he had just been cut out as executor and from what he considered richer land elsewhere. In particular, Alexander's elder brother, Thomas, inherited 18 acres along Millbank beyond the Palace of Westminster, which Alexander had expected would be his. But from being an employee he was now a landowner in his own right, and it was up to him to use what he had learned from Audley about making money multiply. Within months of his great-uncle's death he opened negotiations with his brother to purchase the Millbank land, mortgaging his inheritance to do so and squabbling with his fellow beneficiaries over residuary rights.

As part of his efforts to raise the cash he needed to purchase Millbank and then develop it, Alexander decided to sell Goring House. It was an immediately marketable asset, and he had learned enough about the place while working for Audley to have doubts about its future. The house might look well enough in its smart new paint, but recently had been a sink for money and was still only patched together. Mulberry Garden next door detracted from its potential too, not to mention the stench from the Tyburn along the eastern boundary.

Sometime after 30 May 1663, when a temporary lease to Daniel O'Neill, Charles II's postmaster-general, was agreed,[2] Alexander began discussions with Sir Henry Bennet, a leading minister in the new government, who was interested in buying the property. A price of £3,500 was negotiated for the house and immediate surroundings, and life for Alexander Davies was suddenly all excitement. Secure in the knowledge that as soon as the deal with Bennet was sealed he would have money in his pocket, he did not wait to start on his plans to build along Millbank. He and his wife moved into a new house off King Street, Westminster, where their daughter, Mary, was born; and there, soon afterwards, Alexander died of plague. He was only thirty, but the great epidemic of 1665 was killing thousands everywhere.

Alexander's widow was immediately faced by serious debts, since the Millbank scheme had reached the stage of maximum cost for no return, at a time when prospective purchasers of new houses were frightened away by calamity. She was the daughter of the Rector of St Clement Danes, with whom Hugh Audley had lodged during his last years, and both then and since her husband inherited, she had become familiar with an atmosphere of trade. She appears anyway to have been a hard-headed and rather unsympathetic woman who shared society's view that her baby daughter was a marketable commodity. She married again within months of Alexander's death, to John Tregonwell, who was said to be extravagant; if so, his third wife soon corrected the habit. Means were ruthlessly gathered in, estates managed, creditors avoided, as she steered her late husband's encumbered estate deftly away from the rocks of bankruptcy.

Looked at from a modern perspective, it is difficult to imagine that anyone who could offer Mayfair, Belgravia and Pimlico, not to mention those acres along Millbank, as security could be in financial difficulties over a few thousand pounds. But when he plunged into speculation Alexander had ignored his great-uncle's maxims against borrowing on inadequate cashflow. Ebury yielded very little in rent, the manor being mostly let on agricultural leases whose value was reduced by flooding. The proposed sale of Goring House to Bennet failed because Alexander died before it was completed, and as he had not yet paid either his brother for Millbank or his builders and drainers for work already commissioned there, probate was effectively suspended while public trustees stepped in to line their own pockets and protect his daughter's inheritance by fighting the various claims.[3]

The result was that Mary Davies spent an unhappy childhood. Her mother was preoccupied with business, a new husband and four more daughters, none of whom would inherit a fraction of Mary's potential wealth. Probably they were jealous, and as well as being singular within the family, Mary was strictly guarded. From infancy, she represented credit to the frequently hard-pressed Tregonwells.

A further attempt to sell Goring House began in 1666, but again foundered against the twin obstructions of Mary's protected status in trust, and the continuing confusion in her estate. For the time being, the core of Buckingham Palace lands remained in her ownership, although occupied on lease by Sir Henry Bennet.

Gradually the Tregonwells' fortunes eased. The family moved into one of the new houses started by Alexander along Millbank, although such were

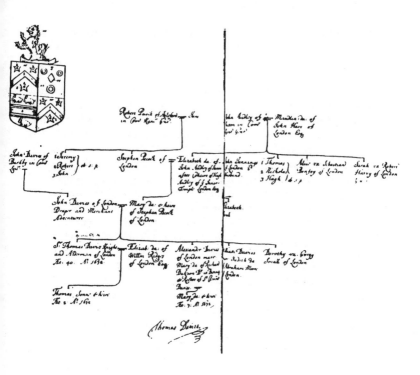

Pedigree showing Davies and Audley relationships, drawn up for the 1664 visitation and signed by Thomas, Alexander Davies's elder brother. The arms are those of Davies quartered with Audley, although there is no record of the Davies being awarded arms. Mary's name appears just above Thomas's signature. (College of Arms)

the skills that Mary's mother had developed in keeping back money, while at the same time creaming off profits which should have gone into trust for her daughter, that the contractor who had built it would not be paid until 1695, some thirty years away.

Long before then, Mary was paraded to advertise her worth. A coach drawn by six horses was dedicated to her use, which can only have stirred up more envy among her half-sisters, and as her mother smugly wrote, 'All things were carried on with the air of greatness answerable to the fortune she was supposed to have'. Mary almost certainly drove in state to the City to watch while her uncle, Thomas Davies, was installed as Lord Mayor in 1676, to the sound of 'trumpets, guns and thundring drums'.[4] Pepys was there as well, having previously confessed himself very much surprised to find an old schoolfellow of such indifferent merit risen so high.[5] Mary was then ten years old and already betrothed, sold for £5,000 cash to Lord Berkeley as bride for his son, Charles. But the Berkeleys failed to find a further £3,000 worth in land as a marriage settlement and Mrs Tregonwell withdrew, triumphantly refusing to repay their £5,000 deposit. Mary's value leapt on the gossip roused by this coup, and again in November 1675 when a private Act of Parliament allowed specified portions of Alexander Davies' estate to be sold for the benefit of his creditors. Among these was Goring House, together with its kitchen gardens, a great yard and pond, and 'all that great garden adjoining the premises containing twenty acres enclosed around with a brick wall'.[6]

Sir Henry Bennet had remained anxious to purchase, but for once Mrs Tregonwell was at a disadvantage when she tried to haggle up the price. Goring House was destroyed by fire only months before the private Act was passed, and Bennet argued that he was only buying site value; as a consequence, negotiations stalled. These difficulties forced one of those swift recomputations of Mary's worth to ripple through London's salons, and she was banished to the continent until more optimistic sentiment re-emerged.

The man Mrs Tregonwell eventually chose for her daughter was Sir Thomas Grosvenor, of Eaton Hall in Cheshire, and her reasons became clear once the betrothal documents were drawn up. The Grosvenors were a long-established landowning family, and for their heir to marry a scrivener's daughter was something of a scandal, especially when Mrs Tregonwell saw to it that Sir Thomas paid a high price for his bride. But Thomas Grosvenor had already displayed a keen interest in architecture and building at Eaton Hall, and the possibilities around Millbank attracted him. Then there was Goring House. This might be burned down and effectively sold off, but its new owner was a principal minister of the king, who had already brought the old house into the centre of London fashion and now intended to replace it with something better. And all around it lay fields owned by Mary Davies. No one in the seventeenth century could have envisaged London's future growth, and part of her Ebury lands remained dauntingly wet, but to any man interested in investing his money in building, the potential of the Mayfair end of her manor was already obvious.

For Mrs Tregonwell, Sir Thomas Grosvenor was exactly right. He could afford to pay in advance for his bride, and even more to the point, he was sufficiently young and proud not to want to examine the shuffling details of her stewardship of Mary's inheritance. In the contract Thomas signed, he undertook not only to repay with interest Lord Berkeley's £5,000 that Mrs Tregonwell had kept, but to settle £500 a year on Mrs Tregonwell herself, for life. To add crookedness to extortion, the document further specified that all Mrs Tregonwell's prior dealings in Mary's estate should be discharged unaccounted for,[7] which must have made the Grosvenor lawyers wring their hands in despair. They did, however, take a keen interest in all other transactions in her manor, and recovered from Lord Berkeley the document which had secured his money on Mary Davies's estate.

Sir Thomas Grosvenor and Mary Davies were married at St Clement Danes in October 1677, the bride being twelve years old and the groom twenty-one. The service was probably conducted by the bride's grandfather, the Rector of St Clement's, whose friendship and protection of Hugh Audley during the last years of his life had led to the marriage of Mary's parents, and therefore indirectly to this later union.

Because the bride was so young, consummation of the marriage was delayed for two years, but Mary was only just fifteen when she drove north to Eaton Hall as Thomas Grosvenor's wife. Unseen, but with her in the unsprung carriage, came all that unimaginably valuable London land which today forms the bulk of the Grosvenor Estate. Only the two Audley Streets and Davies Street, Mayfair, serve as reminders that it was a scrivener's daughter and a canny Temple moneylender who made the Dukes of Westminster, as the Grosvenors later became, possessors of the greatest private fortune in the United Kingdom. Three hundred years later, they have it still.

Poor Mary was overwhelmed by the circumstances of her life. She was still a child when she was sent into a marriage where everything around her would be unfamiliar. Thomas proved more considerate and loving than her mother had ever been, but Mary had never lived in the country and knew nothing about it, nor about the people of whom her husband's circle talked. Her behaviour was occasionally hysterical and became more so; she had children but they were alienated from her, mostly because her disturbed fits distressed and embarrassed them and only partly because a traditional upbringing decreed it. All her life, Mary seems to have found it difficult to give and receive the affection she craved, even when it was freely offered.

The tomb of Alexander Davies, who briefly inherited that part of Hugh Audley's London property which included the Buckingham Palace site before dying of plague in 1665. The fact that he is described as 'of Ebury' on his memorial (although he lived near Whitehall), suggests that by the time this stone was inscribed (probably on his wife's death in 1717) the extraordinary value of his inheritance was fully recognized. His formidable widow remarried and became Mrs Tregonwell but shares his grave, which stands oddly and completely solitary in the grass between St Margaret's and Westminster Abbey. A reference to Mrs Tregonwell's father, the Revd Dr Dukeson, is also inscribed there. Hugh Audley escaped from predators during his last years by lodging in Dukeson's vicarage, with the result that Dukeson's daughter and Audley's heir met and married. When their daughter married Thomas Grosvenor of Cheshire, Audley's fortune founded the immense wealth of what was to become the Grosvenor Estate. (Author)

Mary Davies, painted by Michael Dahl. An unhappy heiress, she owned Goring House and most of Buckingham Palace gardens until her trustees sold the house to pay her father's debts, and her husband parted with most of the remaining garden land to Lord Arlington. (Courtesy of the Grosvenor Estate)

When Thomas died in 1700, aged forty-five, Mary was even more lonely than before. In her search for security she had converted to Catholicism, which appalled the Grosvenors, staunch protestants to a man, and further strained relations with her husband. After his death she set off on an erratic pilgrimage to Rome. A year later, proceedings began in Chancery when the brother of her household priest, Edward Fenwick, alleged that she had married him secretly in Paris and sued for a share in her property. Nor was he the only claimant, since Mary proved an incoherent witness and once the sharks cruising to snap up rich widows realized how defenceless she was, others closed in for the kill. It cost the Grosvenor lawyers, relatives and friends five years' of fat fees before they saw off Fenwick and the rest, and extracted her from Chancery, after which she lived more or less under supervision for the rest of her life. She died in 1730, and was buried at Eccleston, Cheshire.

So far as can be discovered, there was no history of mental instability such as Mary exhibited after coming to Eaton Hall in either the Davies or Audley families, and her children were untainted. The responses Mary exhibited, both extravagantly searching for affection and hysterically rejecting the forms in which it came, would nowadays be recognized as typical of adolescents emotionally disturbed by their experiences in unloving, exploitative homes. The sad life of this owner of the Buckingham Palace site is perhaps a reminder that damage inflicted in childhood could be as pernicious to later happiness then as now, even in a society that was ignorant of the cause.

CHAPTER 15

The First Grandee

Henry Bennet was destined to enter the Church; instead, he became the first unencumbered owner of the palace site since James I was tricked by Cranfield into selling it. Only when Bennet went up to Oxford, initially to study theology, does it seem to have occurred to him that someone intending to take holy orders should have religious convictions, and since he was indifferent to the enthusiasms of the day and disliked the idea of existing on a stipend of £40 a year, he should exercise his talents elsewhere. Uncertain as to where this might be he lingered on at Oxford, writing bad verse and gaining in reputation as a classical scholar, only taking his degree in 1642 when he was twenty-eight years old.[1]

By that time civil war was about to divide the country, and Bennet, a staunch Royalist, was luckily able to go on living in Oxford while offering his loyalty to the king, whose headquarters the city became. Without the war he might eventually have drifted off to try his luck at Court, but lacking influence or a sponsor he would have found it difficult to make much headway there. As it was, the exigencies of war brought an almost surreal world to his doorstep, where crises intermittently tore in shreds those more durable courtly diversions of faction, wit and profligacy. There were plenty of Cavaliers who avoided drawing a sword in anger and Bennet was one of them; instead, he made useful friends. Events swept him into battle only once, when ineptness in a charge left him with a disfiguring scar across the bridge of his nose, and the chance nature of this injury made it the subject of cruel jokes in later years, when other men were respected for wounds taken in battle.

Soon after this skirmish the king's cause went visibly into decline, and Bennet was one of several envoys sent to try and rally support abroad before it was too late, attempts soon revealed as hopeless. He did not return to England until after the Restoration, but far from being wasted, the years of exile founded his career.

The camaraderie of this time when the young king and his brother were as poor as their followers, when hope was ever deferred yet returned to flourish on a rumour, was to prove a solidly bankable asset when Charles II was restored to his throne. Bennet was sent to Germany and Spain on errands and grew to be on first-name terms with the king, who wrote to him as Harry. He developed perhaps the most useful of all qualities in a courtier: adaptability to circumstance, which might more unkindly be labelled as hypocrisy. Since he was not personally libertine in a rakehelly society, he was also able to maintain an intellectual detachment which survived the most gross of occasions, undiminished. Charles's rougher companions considered Bennet cold and arrogant, but his sobriety appealed to elder statesmen and Charles, too, was shrewd enough to value a man who did not babble in his cups, or upset his hosts by seducing their daughters. Much later, Bishop Burnet would give it as his opinion that Bennet had the art of observing the king's temper, and then managing it, beyond all men of that time.[2] There could be no better passport to success.

In 1657 Charles knighted Bennet and sent him as his personal emissary to Spain, where he remained until 1661, kicking his heels in futility and trying to keep himself in the king's mind with frequent despatches. The delay in his recall after the Restoration was particularly galling, and he pulled strings feverishly in an attempt to hurry his return.

When Bennet did return to England he was so poor he had difficulty paying for a lodging, but as a parting gift his Spanish friends had given him a coach and equipage so ostentatious that in Whitehall he at once became the latest joke. His manner too had changed, and the Comte de Gramont commented with sharp French malice that 'he had perfectly acquired the serious air and profound gravity of the Spaniards, and imitated pretty well their tardiness in business'.[3] His artifical stateliness in a notably unbuttoned Court was widely mimicked, his pseudo-Castilian love of magnificence enviously pilloried. As a minister he would later be accused of importing Spanish habits of secrecy, indifference to debt and personal popery into a government that already thrived on all these habits. Only the latter accusation was easily dispelled, when even courtly rancours failed to detect any religious belief in him at all.

In 1662 he became a Secretary of State and reached an even more useful eminence as manager of the king's mistresses: perhaps Charles considered he was less likely than most men at his Court to take favours from them on the way. Created baron and then earl, the title he chose – Arlington – echoed a childhood spent at Harlington, Middlesex, and the dropped 'h' is testimony to the cockney accent shared by gentry of his generation.

Until his retirement from politics in 1680, Bennet, or Arlington as it is now easier to call him, remained a principal minister and intimate with the king in ways which constantly surprised and enraged his rivals. Mistresses and policies came and went. Arlington was widely disliked as insufferably proud, absurdly pretentious, his wit derided as too precious. Yet Charles trusted him. He shone in royal company and it was to him that Charles turned for help in his most intimate family dealings. He also proved that rarest of creatures in Restoration society, a faithful husband and loving father.

The enigma of Arlington: loving husband and father, corrupt minister; 'proud as a Spaniard', witty host. This painting by an unknown artist clearly shows the black plaster Arlington wore over his Civil War wound. (National Portrait Gallery: reg. no. 1853)

Quite when Arlington first occupied Goring House is uncertain, but the previous tenant, Daniel O'Neill, died in 1664, and probably Arlington bought up the remainder of his lease. The first definite date is an entry in John Evelyn's Diary for 29 March, 1665: 'Went to Goring House, now Mr Secretary Bennet's, ill built, but . . . capable of being made a pretty villa.' It is interesting to find Evelyn so quickly picking up the shortcomings of the house, and his description of it even then as a villa further downgrades the size of Blake's original construction.

To Arlington, it was the site that mattered. London's explosive post-Restoration growth had not yet begun and Mayfair was still fields, but Charles was already improving St James's Park and the restless, reviving world of fashion had begun to shift westward in a quest for elegance and space. As early as 1660 Pepys notes that a canal was being dug to better drain the park; The Mall was constructed soon afterwards and walks opened up where undergrowth had become impenetrable during the Commonwealth.

Arlington married in April 1666. His bride was Isabella, daughter of Louis of Nassau, a bastard but respected associate of the Dutch royal family. The match created a flurry of interest around Europe, as evidence that Arlington was a figure of more than passing significance, and as a bonus the bride brought with her a hundred thousand guilders and an equable nature. 'She is a fine, discreet lady, personable and well-shap'd, and will certainly prove an excellent wife. She is not given to coqueterie,' reported an English spy[4] whom Arlington prudently sent to view the lady in advance of a proposal. Evelyn was more temperate, considering her to be obliging, but with inclinations towards ambition and extravagance. Pepys, as ever, could not forbear to drive

> by coach to Goring House, there to wait on Lord Arlington . . . but he was not up, being not long since married, so after walking up and down the house below, being the same I once was in for Nan Hartlibb's sister's wedding, and it is a very fine house and finely furnished . . . and then thinking it too much for me to lose my time to await my lord's arising, I away to Sir William Coventry.

Splendid Pepys; he could never resist an excuse to poke about in someone else's house.[5]

To Arlington, ambition and extravagance in his wife were not sins. He was ambitious himself and wished to be extravagant, even if, for a man who, five years earlier, had returned to England owning only a coach and six, he had already done well on the profits of corruption. The marriage proved remarkably harmonious, and in a Court which became a byword for moral laxity Arlington's name was never coupled with that of any woman besides his wife. Their greatest public enjoyment was entertaining in splendour, and for the first time the palace site became the social centre of political London. Immense sums were lavished on the house, but without curing the defects of its past history.[6] What Arlington and Isabella liked was tasteful ostentation, not mundane things like drainage works or pinning shaken walls, and they spent on paintings, elegant hangings, new furniture and decorations. Evelyn, who became a personal friend, commented that he had never seen such rich furniture anywhere in his life before.[7]

But if the setting was superb, good conversation was what made invitations to Goring House a privilege. In company where he was at ease, and especially while dispensing his own hospitality, Arlington became a different man – amusing, affable, tactful, enjoying thrust and counter-thrust with other clever minds. Lady Arlington excelled as a hostess too, and to the irritation of gossip-mongers could never be drawn to discuss her husband's business or matters of confidence. Undoubtedly the Arlingtons' hospitality oiled many diplomatic wheels but it also aroused suspicion, and as one pamphleteer put it, 'Ambassadors using so Noble a House with so much Freedom, gives cause to conclude that they paid dear for it.'.[8]

In the summer of 1667 Arlington's only surviving child was born at Goring House, called Isabella after her mother. In tune with the bourgeois atmosphere around his marriage, Arlington loved her deeply and openly; she was nicknamed Tata and he forgot his dignity to romp with her on his return after a long day, to the astonished scorn of any companions brought home with him:

> For though with us he's stately like a king,
> He'll joke and droll with her like anything.[9]

In 1670 Arlington became involved in the duplicities surrounding the Treaty of Dover, of which he disapproved, but not to the point of sacrificing office for a scruple. Perhaps partly as a bribe, but also because the king felt genuinely friendly towards him, around this time the idea was first floated of marrying little Isabella to one of the king's natural sons. Arlington was immensely flattered and it never seems to have crossed his mind that a dearly loved daughter was being used as a tool of his ambition. A form of marriage took place when Tata was five and Henry Fitzroy, nine; already ennobled as the Duke of Grafton, he was the king's favourite child by Barbara Castlemaine. John Evelyn witnessed the ceremony at Goring House and did not mince his words over what he considered Arlington's infatuation with royalty and position:

> I was at the marriage of Lord Arlington's only daughter (a sweet child if ever there was any) to the Duke of Grafton; the Archbishop of Canterbury officiating, the King and many grandees being present, but I had no joy of the thing for many reasons.[10]

In the same year his daughter was married and as the small change of goodwill, Arlington received his earldom and, more to the point for the history of the Buckingham Palace site, after long pleadings the king agreed to grant him a ninety-nine year lease of Mulberry Garden. This had become an extreme annoyance to Arlington. No matter how much money he spent at Goring House on mazes and fountain walks, bowling lawns and a dwarf tree garden, his family and guests remained affronted by the smells of outdoor cooking, the racket of coarse enjoyment and squeals of whores drifting across his garden wall. He had wanted the freehold rather than a lease, but ninety-nine years stretched comfortably into the distance. To have obtained so much after the brush-off Goring received, must have been one of the ignoble aspects of Tata's early marriage which so affronted Evelyn.

For twenty years, Arlington patiently re-accumulated the land which today makes up the palace site, most but not all of which had briefly been in Goring's ownership. He suffered setbacks and some difficulties seemed insuperable; snack restaurants along the highway and in Mulberry Garden, prostitutes on the strut, market gardens, the king himself as a lessee interested in physick herbs, the slaughterhouse which occupied the site of the present royal mews, the remains of old fortifications. These were only some of the complications.

Each fragment of title had to be separately stalked, then paid for, extorted or begged as circumstance allowed. The surprise is that anyone could then visualize the extent of site which would one day be needed to safeguard from intrusion what was still only a gentleman's modest and somewhat ramshackle residence. In the 1670s Goring House was still surrounded on two sides by more or less open country, on the others by royal parkland, and far from increasing, the population of London had been savagely cut back by the ravages of plague and fire. Trade was not buoyant either, as war and mismanaged finances upset confidence, and the king suspended payment to his creditors.

Through it all, Arlington never let up on his efforts to secure ambitious boundaries for Goring House. He was helped by his wife's money, but only high office could have so successfully crowned those years of ambitious acquisition. After many vicissitudes under a moral republic, the position of king's minister had smoothly resurfaced as the most reliable road to wealth.

In 1674 the Arlingtons suffered a very personal blow when in their absence Goring House was entirely destroyed by fire, finally breaking the link with William Blake's effrontery so far as buildings were concerned, although his half acre remained the site's heart. When John Evelyn heard about the fire, like any good diarist he raced

> to see the great loss Lord Arlington sustained at Goring House, this night consumed to the ground with exceeding loss of hangings, plate, rare pictures and cabinets. Hardly anything was saved of the best and most princely furniture that any subject had in England.[11]

The Arlingtons hurried back to view the damage and although downcast over a loss reckoned at £10,000, with the enthusiasm of true grandees they at once resolved to rebuild, and in much finer style. The fact that a new house would be known by his name was an added joy for Arlington, and dead Goring was safely buried at last.

Arlington House was built with speed and flair, to be flung open to guests in October 1675, barely a year after the old house was reduced to ash. Silk for upholstery was brought over from Paris, the finest Venice brocatelle hung on the walls, and Lady Arlington enjoyed showing to friends her private chamber where the bed curtains were green damask and every pot on her dressing table made from silver or gold.[12] It would take time to replace the magnificent furniture collected in Goring House, but society agreed that little else was lacking in splendour or for comfort. During the following winter hospitality was offered on a truly princely scale, but the effort had begun to show. Whereas Goring House often leaked or its walls showed cracks, entertainment there had been exclusive, exquisite, stimulating. Now the owner of Arlington House was losing influence, and invited whoever might save him from political oblivion. 'He would ask the Devil if he could serve him!' Ruvigny, the French envoy, exclaimed.[13]

But Courts are forever carousels, and the eclipse of those who had taken his place, together with the king's personal goodwill, soon brought Arlington back to favour, if not to power. In 1679 another marriage took place between Tata and the Duke of Grafton, which suggests that because the children were so young, the previous ceremony was considered a betrothal. Whatever the reason, Evelyn was again invited, and again violently disapproved:

I confess I plainly told my lady Arlington that . . . the sweetest,★ hopefullest, most beautiful child [Isabella was then twelve] and most virtuous too, was sacrificed to a boy that had been most rudely bred, without anything to encourage him but his Majesty's pleasure . . . My love to my Lord Arlington's family made me behold all this with regret, though as the Duke of Grafton affects the sea, to which I find his father intends to use him, he may emerge as a plain, useful and robust officer, and, were he polished, a tolerable person; for he is exceeding handsome, surpassing the King's other natural issue.[14]

Evelyn's tepid hopes were partly realized in that Henry Fitzroy, if he never became polished would at least become renowned for his insatiable love of fighting, in which he conducted himself with reckless bravery. When no war offered, he fought duels. Briefly the owner, through his wife, of a great part of the Buckingham Palace site, Henry Fitzroy died from wounds received at the siege of Cork in 1690, when his wife was twenty-three and mother of their only son.

Arlington was elated by his daughter's elevation to quasi-royalty and seized the opportunity to retire while his blaze of glory lasted. He continued to spend freely on Arlington House, and since his daughter's new husband was immediately packed away to sea, he was also able to enjoy Tata's company there. By this time Arlington House was acknowledged as elegantly well suited to its place at the head of the king's new landscaping in St James's Park: topped with a cupola and graceful rather than magnificent, neither over-large nor too much hung about with decoration. Descriptions suggest that there were eight rooms on the ground floor plus extensive kitchen quarters, since the house was designed as a place for entertaining company. The salons were floored in black and white marble and there was a small private chapel, which caused some laughter, since Arlington apparently continued to regard religion as a kind of psychological affliction. Upstairs there were six rooms, all facing west across the gardens, the missing space being taken up by a gallery which ran the full length of the house, where young people could play and adults take exercise in bad weather. This was lit by large windows looking across the park and fixed to one wall was a frame of olive wood with pins to help compute walking a mile there. The agreeable nature of this gallery and the voyeur's interests it offered, made it the feature of the house, where men like Robert Boyle came to discuss the latest scientific speculation, or to admire Lord Arlington's purchase of a woman's head by Leonardo; others to whisper in 1681 that the

---

★ When she died in 1723, Isabella's cousin, Lord Bristol, wrote: 'Thursday, and the beautiful Duchess of Grafton died in London, in justice to whose memory I can strictly averr, that in above forty years' time that I had the honour and happiness of her acquaintance, I never heard her say anything of any absent person which, had they been present, they would have been in the least offended at.'[15]

A Victorian drawing of Arlington House probably elaborated from a sketch in Larwood's London Parks, which he stated was based on 'a very rare old print'. (From Wolford (ed.), London Old and New, 1873)

king had used an old friendship to bid farewell to his favourite bastard son, the Duke of Monmouth, in the gardens of Arlington House.[16]

The year 1681 was one of many crises, although Arlington took little part in manoeuvrings designed to exclude the king's brother, the Duke of York, from succeeding to the throne. When Charles wished to call a meeting to try and settle the matter, the leader of the excluders, Lord Shaftesbury, suggested they should meet at Lord Arlington's

> . . . as the most indifferent place in the world . . . my lord being neither good Protestant nor good Catholic and his being the best wine, which is the only good thing that could be had from such a meeting.[17]

When the Duke of York returned from a temporary exile the following year, it was at Arlington House that he and Charles met to talk privately about the continuing deadlock in the succession. If these secret meetings testify to Arlington's continuing friendship with the king, they also indicated the convenience of his house. Under Charles II, St James's Park had become the outdoor playground for his Court, an upmarket version of Mulberry Garden once social life, amorous and otherwise, no longer hid behind high walls. The king swam in the new canal he had designed to improve drainage. Boats and musicians could be hired there too, and the Duke of York skated on it in frost. Wrestling matches took place to the accompaniment of frenetic betting, and other diversions ranged from fashionable pell-mell to Mrs Pepys running for a wager against a lady friend, or the Duke of Ormonde killing a browsing stag after 'he had run it to a stand on foot'.[18] Inevitably, the best sport of all was lovemaking after dark, and when Lady Castlemaine was accosted there while sneaking across to the king's bed, the masked gallants who recognized her rudely shouted that the mistress of Edward IV had died on a dunghill.

Arlington House commanded all this from its position almost in the park itself, and when its owner walked in his gallery he could imagine himself in every way superior to the great vista of society spread out before his windows, to damn or command it as he chose. Not at all by accident, Arlington had secured centre-stage from which to act out his last role as eminent spectator of London's political circus, because when he rebuilt on the palace site he aligned his house east-west to face directly over the park, whereas both Blake and Goring House faced south to the Thames. The same courtyard as before served as entry to Arlington House, to one side where Blake's gate had been, and the site remained off-centre to the axis of the park because Arlington prudently did not build on Mulberry Garden land, where he only possessed a leasehold. Only the old garden walls were pulled down to make it integral to his property and admit more light to the house built close beside it. Visitors could then stroll in from the park through a wicket gate and enjoy an exclusivity which was fading from St James's.

In 1681 Arlington bought two further fields from Sir Thomas Grosvenor to round out his grounds along modern Constitution Hill, and Mary Davies ceased to own more than scraps of Buckingham Palace land.[19] By then the site was almost as it is today, and only two discomforts remained: traffic and bad drainage.

While it was true that no courtier or favourite could take his promenade without being affronted at every turn by the sight of Lord Arlington's smug cupola and spyglass gallery, a less happy consequence of this proximity to the park was dust in summer and mud in winter, kicked up from the highways close to its walls. The Tyburn, too, continued to leak water strongly laced with sewage into his lordship's premises, and in the means he took to solve these twin dilemmas, Arlington demonstrated that he had lost none of his adroitness in using government systems to serve his private interests.

In 1682 he successfully diverted the Westminster–Knightsbridge road away from his front windows by cramming it against the St James's Park wall and enclosing verge and waste all along his frontage. As a friend of the king, this

A reconstructed view of St James's from the perspective of Arlington's long gallery, showing the rather bleak effect of Charles II's improvements before the trees had time to grow. The banqueting hall, centre, is a landmark, and Westminster Abbey lacks any towers, which were added by Hawksmoor in the eighteenth century. A pell-mell hoop – through which balls were struck with a mallet – can be seen in the distance. (From Wolford (ed.), London Old and New, 1873)

undoubtedly illegal action was never challenged, but its success depended on a solution to his other problem: the Tyburn.

When Goring first treated to obtain Mulberry Garden, the wording of his abortive grant suggests that he had already considered enclosing the Tyburn in a conduit. It is possible he began this work but if so, it is unlikely he progressed very far, and there is no reason either, to believe that Hugh Audley included any such scheme among what were essentially running repairs to the house. Inconclusive though it is, the evidence points to Arlington as the man who actually confined the Tyburn[20] and enclosed within his garden the considerable space gained by such a project, both above and around the vanished river. Otherwise it is hard to see why he took the risk of building his new house so close to a noxious drain, when he owned more than sufficient land to set it back. The motive for his choice was pride. Arlington was not the man to want his fine new residence hidden by trees or distance. He enjoyed thrusting it under the noses of his political rivals, and saw no merit in holding court unseen.

But whatever he did to lessen the nuisance of the Tyburn, it was not enough. The stream still flooded after a storm, and seeped stinking water into the foundations of his house. So it is no surprise to discover that in the same year he succeeded in confining the highway at public cost, a separate coup enabled him finally to contain the Tyburn, also at someone else's expense. In that year, Mr Frith of Soho was endeavouring to develop some land near a lane which people had begun to call Pickadilly. To succeed, he needed to carry out the inevitable drainage works, for which the cheapest outfall lay through St James's Park and into a creek near old La Neyte. Under normal circumstances it is hard to imagine that Frith would have had much luck in persuading the king that he should be inconvenienced by diggings in his pleasure park for such a purpose, or not without paying an extortionate fee. In fact the king seems to have received nothing in return for considerable annoyance, because Arlington realized that Frith's scheme could solve his own difficulty with the Tyburn; when the licence was issued, Mr Frith's only obligation was to divert the course of his proposed sewer nearer to Arlington House. The reason is left vague, but the Tyburn at last received an outfall of sufficient size to take floodwater.[21]

The year after all this was accomplished, Arlington's beloved Isabella was safely delivered of a son, and his friends were torn between exasperation and indulgent mockery when they observed his delight. As Lady Chaworth wrote ungrammatically to her brother, the Earl of Rutland: 'Arlington is so joy'd with that, some says he will smother itt with kisses.'[22]

Arlington's last years were divided between London and his country estate in Suffolk. He remained a part of politics but no longer laboured in the hothouse of intrigue, enjoying his gardens and continuing to improve them, entertaining his friends for the pleasure of their company alone. In 1685 his friend and master, Charles II, died and Arlington did not long survive him.

A modern view of St James's Park, which was agreeably softened and 'romanticized' under George IV. The contrast with Charles II's more formal French-influenced layout is obvious. (Author)

He lived to carry the white staff as Lord Chamberlain under James II and continued through the early summer to attend the House of Lords, on the way driving past a royal aviary for exotic birds, called Birdcage Walk, where the old causeway had once straggled between mudbanks. In July he fell ill at Arlington House and when he realized he was dying, he sent for a priest to whom he might confess his sins and afterwards be received into the Catholic Church, even if, with typical caution, he extracted a promise that this should be kept secret until he was dead.

The sensation of the Lord Chamberlain's deathbed conversion sent a wave of hilarity through the great houses of England. The old rumour that he had been seduced to Romanism during his time as King Charles's envoy in Spain revived, but the more favoured opinion was that he had paid his fee to ensure entry to the Stuart Court in heaven. In life or death, position was all.

But dying is no Court trick, as Roger North, a Suffolk neighbour of Arlington's, observed,[23] and he believed that as his end approached, Arlington became terrified of God in his judgement seat, and, old courtier that he was, he longed for symbols and ceremonies to reassure him. Each of these interpretations could be true, since Arlington had always lived his life in compartments, which left his conscience stranded somewhere in between. But as he died in the house which bore his name, not looking out on the sauntering crowds of St James's but across gardens and parkland he had gathered into a single whole, perhaps he sensed that out of all his anxious scurryings after power, this would be his monument. Fortunately, he could not know that within a few years the house would be rubble, his gardens laid out in quite a different taste, his daughter and grandson no longer living there.

But the site remained, protected in one ownership only just in time to resist the approaching waves of development which would otherwise have engulfed it piecemeal. The richer sort of building already reached out in streets and squares to cover Mayfair and the pastures above St James's, while slums grew like fungus outwards from Tothill as the inland bog between Westminster and Chelsea was haphazardly drained into noisome pools and sewers.

Perhaps by coincidence, but perhaps not, the man who would take over Arlington's home and demolish it, who ripped apart his lawns and fountain walk, also wrote an epitaph for his predecessor on the Buckingham Palace site:

> The Earl of Arlington met with one thing very peculiar in his fortune which I have scarce known happen to any man else. With all his advancement (which is wont to create malice but seldom contempt) he was believed by most people a man of much less abilities than he really had. One reason I fancy to have come from . . . his susceptibility to ridicule, which at last led to his being left out of his Master's business if not his favour, yet after all he was rather a subtle Courtier than able statesman . . . But to end handsomely with him, he was of generous temper, living splendidly and obliging his friends willingly and warmly . . . because this was the greatest satisfaction of his life.[24]

CHAPTER 16

Buckingham

When James II succeeded his brother on the throne, débâcle soon followed. The waspish comment that Charles could see things if he would and James if he could, had enough truth in it to make everyone who heard it laugh, but in those days even profligate courtiers still possessed religious scruples, however hidden, and they were soon forced to decide whether or not they could support a king who openly took mass. Ministers accustomed to almost any zigzag in policy were examined on their theology, their enthusiasm gauged towards plans they believed to be aimed at oversetting a settlement in Church and State which over the years had served their families exceptionally well.

James also attempted to clean up the court, although the fact that he acknowledged at least six bastard children made this a particularly tricky undertaking. In the past he had been quite as licentious as his brother but without ever enjoying himself with the same shameless panache; now he was surrounded by priests who threatened to refuse him the sacrament if he did not banish the most encroaching of his mistresses, Catherine Sedley, from his presence, a surprisingly puritan attitude in Catholic priests, who around the courts of Europe often moderated damnation to suit the influential. It can most easily be explained by their dislike of the lady's sharp-tongued protestantism, which, they said, blasted their designs.[1]

Catherine was the only child of Sir Charles Sedley, that same rakish dramatist who wrote the romp set in Mulberry Garden, whose pleasures he certainly knew. As Sir Charles's daughter, Catherine was brought up among company who guarded neither their tongues nor their inclinations in her presence, and by the age of sixteen she was already described as not virtuous, but a wit. As Sedley's heiress she was also rich, and an early suggestion was that she should marry the son of distant relatives, Sir Winston and Lady Churchill. The proposal did not prosper. The Churchills valued Catherine's expectations but were appalled by her behaviour, ungallantly describing her as an ugly girl with a squint;[2] even so, John Churchill, who was later famous as the Duke of Marlborough, might have enjoyed a happier private life in her company than with the termagent he eventually married.

After this fiasco Catherine gravitated to court, where she became maid of honour to the Duchess of York, in which position she soon supplanted John

Churchill's sister, Arabella, as the Duke's mistress. Catherine was not particularly attracted to James, commenting with staggering candour that she could not understand the Duke's interest in her, since she lacked beauty and he was too stupid to understand her wit. She did take mischievous pleasure in putting Churchill noses out of joint by taking Arabella's place, and remained disconcertingly outspoken for the rest of her career, often emphasizing her opinions with words learned from her father's drinking cronies. Such a flaunting attitude to wickedness only increased the spell she exercised over James and his infatuation was unshaken by Catherine's scurrilous jokes against a religion to which he was devoted. It is unsurprising, however, to find his priests striking back with an ultimatum concerning her removal as soon as he came to the throne.

But Catherine's outrageous charm was not easily dislodged. She did briefly vanish to Ireland, on whose revenues her courtesan's pension was secured; Flanders had been the priests' first suggestion as a place of exile but this she refused to consider, on the grounds that it must be so full of convents that the very air would oppress her. In any case, she returned to England after only a few weeks and was soon established in Arabella Churchill's old house in St James's Square. Ennobled as the Countess of Dorchester, she coolly turned up again at court as if she had never been sent away.

The importance of Catherine Sedley to the story of the Bickingham Palace site lies in her daughter, another Catherine, given the courtesy title of Lady Catherine Darnley. James always considered her to be his, although her mother occasionally disagreed; these doubts made no difference to the younger Catherine, who from childhood was puffed up by intolerable pride in her royal lineage. In contrast, the Countess of Dorchester retained a frank impatience with hypocrisy to the last. When, as an old woman, she visited the court of George I and happened to meet the Duchess of Portsmouth, Charles II's mistress, and the Duchess of Orkney, the mistress of William III, she exclaimed for everyone to hear, 'My God, who would have thought that we three whores should have met here!'[3]

Catherine Darnley was in every way different from her mother; very stiff, very proud, only moderately intelligent. In February 1704 she married for a second time, John Sheffield, Duke of Buckingham. At the time of their marriage he had recently bought Arlington House and was busily flattening both it and the gardens, with the intention of creating something far more grandiose in their place; exactly the setting his new, vainglorious wife considered her purple blood required. As the bastard daughter of a famous courtesan and granddaughter of a poet, lecher and gallant, she ought to have brought style and vivacity into new Buckingham House, as it would soon be called. Instead she breathed a stultifying formality, at which her husband also excelled. And irony of ironies, this resplendent duke she married, the highest of high Tories, was the great-grandson of Lionel Cranfield, grocer's apprentice and corrupt purchaser of the Ebury Estate some seventy years before.

Out of the six people who had cheated, lied and litigated against each other for the palace site when it first slithered into private hands – Cranfield, Rolfe, Ann Hawker, the two Blakes and Hugh Audley – in the end it was Cranfield who had the last laugh of them all.

What had gone wrong with Lord Arlington's plans for Tata and her son to inherit the palace site, and why had his gracious mansion, its agreeable fountain walks and orchards only survived him for such a short time?

Arlington settled all his property, aside from provision for his wife, in tail male on his daughter and her husband. She succeeded personally to his title and appears to have lived intermittently at Arlington House while her husband was away fighting. When he died of wounds in 1690, their only son, Charles, was seven years old and the property passed into the hands of trustees. Tata subsequently remarried and lived largely on her second husband's property, leaving Arlington House to be let out until her son, now Duke of Grafton, came of age. The first tenant was the Duke of Devonshire, the second John Sheffield, later to be Duke of Buckingham, but at the time holding the title of Earl of Mulgrave.

Devonshire's chief characteristics seem to have been extreme pugnacity allied to arsonist tendencies. Wherever he stayed, his lodgings were liable to burst into flames. Arlington House was no exception, and he was still being pursued for damage caused by a fire during his tenancy there long after the house was pulled down, eventually paying £330 to settle the matter.[4] Grafton's trustees can only have been relieved when Sheffield took over in 1698, and four years later they sold him the freehold, subject to confirmation when Grafton came of age.

John Sheffield was the heir to a family of Lincolnshire and Yorkshire landowners, the only surviving son of the second Earl of Mulgrave, whose mother had been Cranfield's daughter, Elizabeth. He succeeded to his father's title in 1688 at the age of ten, and grew up to be almost a renaissance personality, so multi-faceted were his interests: an amateur poet and dramatist, courageous seaman, a military leader who commanded an expedition to relieve Tangier when it was besieged by Moors; notable lecher, ambitious politician, a fierce and possibly cheating gamester, stately architect and land-scaper; a cruelly witty and dislikeable courtier. For all these talents, it was his luck in being able to marry three times, each time to women who brought handsome additions to his purse, which actually kept his finances afloat.

He also had the foresight to write extensively about himself, using the third person to praise his character, which he considered to be

> . . . of extraordinary sweetness, joined with a lively, penetrating look . . . at the very first sight striking you with an idea of his great understanding, of which he gave the world such various proofs. As for his manners, he was reported to be very haughty and proud, whereas he is really good-natured and tender . . . a little passionate and quick upon people who gave him no occasion.

John Sheffield, Duke of Buckingham, an early frontispiece to his Literary Works, 1729. *Proud aristocrat, reckless gambler, insinuating courtier, he gave his name to the present palace.* (Frontispiece to Buckingham, *Works*, 1729)

A less biased critic described him more succinctly as short, sour, lofty and sallow.[5]

He also possessed an aristocrat's disregard for tact, picking quarrels where he chose. Although appointed a gentleman of Charles II's bedchamber he made no secret of his preference for his brother, James, Duke of York, and while holding Charles's commission as commander of the Tangier expedition, he refused to propose the royal health, saying that if he escaped with his life from His Majesty's rotten ship, then would he cause the king's health to go merrily around. Since the ship was indeed in a shocking condition he had some justification for his disrespect, but the remark naturally found its way back to Charles.

In 1682 he overplayed his hand by appearing to court Princess Anne, James's younger daughter, who was making her debut at Court. Variously described as 'a brisk attempt' and 'only ogling', quite what this wooing did amount to is uncertain. Since Sheffield's reputation as a dangerous womanizer was remarked on even in Charles II's Court, whatever it was alarmed the Yorks, and he was banished from St James's until Anne was safely married. Then Sheffield returned, maliciously to remark that the fits of asthma suffered by Anne's new husband must arise from his need to breathe hard sometimes, or he would be taken up as dead and removed for burial.[6]

Sheffield was appointed Lord Chamberlain when James became king, but the reign was too short and too unpopular for anyone to do well out of it. For a while, Sheffield seems not to have realized the dangers of high office but he did hedge on religion, attending James to mass but avoiding a personal conversion. He remained faithful to James for longer than a strict regard for his own interests demanded, staying on in London while other ministers leaked away to support Dutch William. When James fled but was recaptured in Kent, it was Sheffield who prevailed on the House of Lords to help him escape again, and he who personally intervened when the London mob seemed about to lynch the Spanish ambassador, a service for which he was thanked not only by Spain, but also by the incoming King William.

Temperamentally, Sheffield always remained a Jacobite. He detested William personally and relieved his feelings by attacking him in malevolent poems, thinly disguised as classical narrative. He belonged in the arch-Tory opposition camp, and earned the praise of fellow extremists by his blistering speeches and attempts to exempt peers from paying tax.

Since Sheffield's estates failed to supply him with a sufficient funds to enjoy either tax holidays or extravagance, he began to make peace overtures to William, who was entirely cynical in such matters. If a raucous opposition member's price was reasonable, he paid it to keep him quiet. In 1694 Sheffield became Marquess of Normanby and received a pension of £3,000 a year. He was also readmitted to the Privy Council but his loyalty to William remained entirely financial, and in 1696 he refused to sign even a modified oath of loyalty to the man whose privy councillor he was. William fired him, but maintained his pension in the same spirit as it was accepted: as an investment.[7]

A view around St James's Palace in the time of Queen Anne, redrawn from old prints by F. Waddy in 1873.

Sheffield's fortune changed with the accession of Queen Anne in 1702. He had scraped up sufficient funds to buy the freehold of Arlington House and its surrounding grounds, but would need far more lavish resources than he possessed to build the residence he had in mind, and for which he had already engaged an architect. Only in February 1703, when he married Catherine Sedley's daughter as his third and richest wife, was the construction of what would be called Buckingham House assured. Temperamentally, Catherine Darnley and John Sheffield were well suited; united in their Jacobitism, jointly impressed by her supposedly Stuart blood, rejoicing together in grandeur. So far as two cold hearts could manage the trick of it, they grew to be affectionately attached to each other.

Whether he was married or not, Queen Anne never forgot that Sheffield had been her first and most personable suitor, and his continuing attraction for her suggests that the more extravagant rumours about the extent to which he overstepped the proprieties may have been true. By the time of her accession Anne was growing astonishingly fat, but an old flame of charm and address who had his own interests firmly in view easily overlooked that. She had had a wretched life, married to a well-meaning but drunken and stupid man, and bearing eighteen children, not one of whom reached maturity. Even her throne could be regarded as rightfully belonging to her exiled brother in France, possibly in her own eyes and certainly in the eyes of most high Tories, who now surrounded her.

But when William died, John Sheffield made sure that it was he who brought the news to Anne that she was queen. A prey to so many awkward memories that she felt ill-at-ease and gauche, all she could think of to say was that the day was fine. His reply clinched his fortune, a courtier's flattery which made a rough moment easy and at the same time, grand: 'Your Majesty must allow me to declare that it is the most glorious day I ever saw.'[8]

CHAPTER 17

'A New Palace
Come to Town'

In the general Tory scramble for office following Queen Anne's accession, Sheffield reaped the rewards he expected. He returned to the Privy Council, became Lord Privy Seal and was created Duke of Buckingham, to the great confusion of subsequent browsers through history. The previous dukes had both been called George Villiers, father and son, favourites of earlier Stuart monarchs, and their title had only recently become extinct. Sheffield was actually created Duke of Buckinghamshire precisely to avoid confusion, but in practice no distinction was made. Only the family remained entirely different.

Queen Anne's first ministry soon came to grief when the extremists among them, including the new Duke of Buckingham, threatened to withhold supplies for a war in which a great victory had just been won at Blenheim, unless they were given their way in other matters, such as land tax. The queen, by then dominated by the victorious general's wife and patriotically proud of British success, was incensed by such obstructive and selfish conduct. Although she remained personally friendly towards Buckingham, he was replaced as Privy Seal in 1705 and the Whigs flowed delightedly back into office.

In fact, Buckingham had spent most of his time since Anne's accession either trading on her goodwill while opposing her political wishes, or building Buckingham House. Operations began there in the year of the queen's accession, with the laying out of a formal garden in which the new house would be built. Limes were planted in military ranks which destroyed Arlington's informal walks, and a parterre dug in the latest French fashion, filled with geometrical beds edged by low clipped hedges and gravel paths. Only one small patch remained less formally laid out: the treed mound where the old fort had probably been sited, witness to a puritan past which defied integration into the rational eighteenth century.[1]

The layout of these gardens made clear the duke's intention to build his house on a changed site, for the first time coinciding with that of the present palace. The parterre and avenues of limes pointed directly to the pell-mell walk in St James's Park, no longer a place where games were played but The Mall, a promenade where everyone wanted to be seen. On architectural grounds the choice was sound, but it meant that nearly half the new house would be built inside old Mulberry Garden. Though Buckingham held only the unexpired years of Arlington's ninety-nine year lease there, probably he felt the risk was justified, since at least one of his descendants surely ought to have sufficient address to wheedle the monarch of his day into parting with the freehold.

This calculation must have seemed all the more reasonable in the light of Buckingham's own ability to coax favours out of Queen Anne, and not long after his marriage to Catherine Darnley – which the queen considered made him almost one of the family – Buckingham extracted the most valuable favour of all. In bantering conversation and artfully slipped between compliments, he mentioned a difficulty which had arisen as they pegged out the frontage of his house. The highway straggled past his new frontage there, and being old and English, it curved.[2] It is easy to imagine the thrown up hands, the half-laughing shudder. In the plan for Buckingham House, rectangles ruled, but if Her Majesty would only graciously consent to the slightest of alterations, the awkwardness could be solved. A tree grew in front of the site and beside it was a ditch. (He thought it might mark the old waste boundary and therefore actually belong within his property; or, of course, it might not.) If he could only adjust his frontage just as far as that tree and no further, by this small change his whole design would be perfected.

It must have sounded a very minor matter. It was intended to sound a minor matter, a few yards at most, and Anne apparently gave verbal agreement to it. No documents were issued, the whole affair an informality between friends. What the queen failed to realize was that the boundary had already been advanced as far as audacity would take it by Lord Arlington, and the highway was inconveniently constricted as a result. In Buckingham's view, as in Arlington's before, constricted or not it remained inconveniently close to his house, especially now he had redesigned his new mansion to face the park, and its salons were unprotected by a wall.

As a man who liked wholesale methods of getting his own way, the moment Buckingham won a chance to dispose of this nuisance for good, he made the most of it. The tree disappeared as trees have a habit of doing when they represent the limit to a permission, but so did the St James's Park wall beyond it and a royal entrance lodge which spoiled his view down The Mall. Buckingham then bodily shifted the highway some seventy feet further from his property and into the park, flinging his courtyard forward as a permanent barrier against disturbance. Completing this audacious encroachment were wrought-iron fencing and a pair of magnificent gates, on which were represented the duke's own coronet, coat of arms and insignia. Such a major

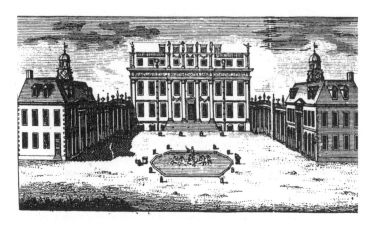

Buckingham House in all its early glory of statues, mottoes and intruded courtyard into St James's Park. The house remained quite modest in size but as the park trees matured into 'avenues of goodly elms and gay flourishing limes', its new setting was superb. (From Buckingham, *Works*, 1729)

change could not happen overnight, and the queen at once protested.[3] After all, the St James's boundary had reached the Tyburn since time immemorial, and the land within it equally indisputably had been royal ever since Henry VIII dispossessed Eton. Anne was fond of the park and had only recently issued draconian instructions designed to preserve it; no hogs or dogs or carts were to be allowed there, no disorderly people or rude boys, and only coaches in the queen's livery might drive down its walks, with the single named exception of the Duke of Buckingham. Under these regulations alone, a brand-new highway bustling with wagons, hogs and rude boys ought to have been shifted back where it belonged at once. Yet time went past while Buckingham hovered attentively beside the queen, and nothing was done. When he chose to exert his charm, it was so much more enjoyable to forget her many troubles in his company than quarrel.

The Buckinghams could simply have set their house further back, which would also have kept any danger from the Tyburn out of its foundations and away from their noses, but as with Arlington, such a thought probably never entered their heads. The purpose of a nobleman's residence was to impress itself on its surroundings, and demolishing that park wall transformed the whole of St James's into a setting for Buckingham House. As the duke himself smugly wrote:

> The Avenues to this House are along St James's Park through rows of goodly Elms on the one hand and gay flourishing Limes on the other; that for coaches, this for walking ... with the Mall reaching to my iron palisade.[4]

Envious contemporaries commented on what they called a new palace come to town, whose situation made it fit for the greatest monarch – which summarized pretty exactly what Buckingham had set out to achieve. As for his duchess, she probably considered St James's Park a part of her own inheritance.

Work on the house did not begin until 1705, a year in which Buckingham demonstrated a lack of gratitude towards the queen as foolhardy as it was bitterly hurtful, when he spoke in a debate on the succession. It was still not too late for her to insist that he withdraw his boundary back where it legally belonged, but while she listened in the House of Lords' gallery, he suggested that it would be as well to secure the throne against the likelihood that she would become senile soon. Her dead children, her own death, the transfer of English loyalties to the Hanoverians; all were discussed in her presence by men well known to her, and she wept for three days afterwards from the cruelty of it all.[5] Yet she never revenged herself. From old and inconvenient St James's Palace ('Bloody cold,' as Dean Swift feelingly described it,[6] a sentiment echoed by generations of courtiers insufficiently important to reach near palace fireplaces) she could watch Buckingham's new house rise like a challenge to her weariness, while his conduct towards her approximated more closely to that of a neglectful husband than a gallant from the past. But bullied wives do not always want to throw off their servitude and Anne was no exception. She was by then so heavy that a block and tackle was sometimes used to lift her, but she remained an old-fashioned good sport. She enjoyed hunting and had a dashing equipage made to fit her which she drove like Jehu, furiously, leaving her attendants scattered in her wake; as late as 1711 she drove for 40 miles cross-country, and in the same year a royal racecourse was laid out on Ascot heath.

She was much less exciting as a conversationalist, and her salons were frequently so empty that her officials whipped in whoever they could catch to make a crowd.[7] In such company Buckingham's facile tongue, his familiar presence and graceful manners, were luxuries the queen cherished; when he condescended to come, she continued to welcome him. Buckingham himself seems not to have retained any softer feelings for her at all. A fastidious man, an amateur poet pickled in pride, he lacked the humanity which might have moderated his disgust for the sick and slatternly woman Queen Anne had become. She snored in company, allowed female favourites to fight like rats in a pit around her person, and conducted too much state business in her underwear. Protocol was haphazard. The queen's religious faith, for instance, made her wish to hear divine service every day, but piety was scrambled anyhow among the gruelling exertions of her toilette. Only one chaplain rebelled, however, and on being banished in mid-service while the queen's intimate garments were put on, shouted that it was blasphemous to whistle the word of God through a keyhole.[8]

Buckingham was so delighted with his new house that he decorated some initial letters and a chapter ending in his published works with vignettes of the garden and buildings. (From Buckingham, *Works*, 1729)

At Buckingham House everything was entirely different. Classical allusion, stately pomp, exact etiquette reigned. The anniversary of the martyrdom of Charles I, whom Duchess Catherine considered to be her grandfather, was sombrely remembered each year, occasions when the duchess wore mourning and received her guests seated on a black-draped throne behind drawn curtains. Both duke and duchess were delighted by their new house, and Buckingham wrote to tell his friends how noble it all was; how enchanting his terrace and spacious each of the principal rooms; how Neptune with Tritons rose out of fountains in the great stone basin at the centre of his courtyard, and the parlour 'measured 33 feet by 39, with a niche 15 feet broad for a Bufette, paved with white marble and placed within an arch'.[9]

Meticulous measurements and descriptions follow of nearly every room. There is a brewhouse, a tank holding fifty tons of water in the pavilion where the upper sort of servants lodge, and he lingers over the tubs in his orangery, the coloured marble slabs flooring a second terrace built at the far end of his grounds from where he can enjoy an uninterrupted view of 'a great part of Surry'. There is even a bathing apartment in one of the greenhouses, which offers a teasing vision of His Grace capering naked among his lilies. But what he loves best of all, Buckingham declares, is his closet of books, also mysteriously placed beyond a greenhouse, although whether as part of the bathing complex is unclear.[10]

As a further feature of the interior of the house, gods and goddesses fairly burst out of the plasterwork; highly fleshed and painted by inferior artists. On the stairway Juno begged assistance from Venus on the ceiling (in the style of Raphael, the duke writes eagerly) and Dido leapt semi-naked from a wall, every spare space being twined around with Tritons. All the rooms seem to have been the same, without a single uncoloured surface to rest the eye.

The exterior of Buckingham House was more restrained, being built of brick embellished with stone and flanked by pavilions topped with cupolas. These latter were much criticized but from illustrations appear delicately proportioned, and allowed the annoyance of cooking smells and danger from fires in the kitchen to be banished from the main building. The house itself looks surprisingly compact after all those lavish measurements. The facade ('wretched', complained one critic) was adorned with four pilasters and statues peered down between the chimneys, representing a ragbag of themes from Apollo to Secrecy, all serenaded by the Four Seasons.[11]

Each frontage was provided with a gilded Latin tag, for which strollers in the park invented translations to make the ladies blush. The one on the most visible east front proclaimed tritely that 'The Household Gods delight in such a situation', but on the north side the moral was less appropriate, urging the beholder to accept obligations circumspectly, but discharge them quickly.

In reality, the duke saw no reason at all to discharge his obligations, and dragged his feet disgracefully over settling accounts for Buckingham House. His architect, William Winde, was nearly ruined by these delays and one day joined his patron on the roof of Buckingham House, where he often went to admire the view. Once there, Winde locked the trapdoor through which they had come and threw the key over the parapet, threatening to throw himself after it unless Buckingham promised on his honour to pay him immediately. 'And what is to become of me, without a key?' asked Buckingham, infallibly grasping at his own comfort first. 'Why, you shall accompany me!' retorted Winde, and made as if to grab him.[12]

Whether to save his dignity or because Winde succeeded in conveying sufficient desperation for Buckingham to believe he might carry out his threat, the duke promised to pay, whereupon the trapdoor was flung open by one of Winde's men waiting below. Such dramatic measures by the architect do not suggest that bricklayers, plasterers or lead-casters did well out of their employment, and perhaps it was as well that they were unlikely to have understood Latin.

Buckingham House was completed by 1708, to general though by no means universal praise. The windows were too many and too large, complained one critic; 'the parts which compose this pile are neither new nor surprising,' wrote another. The decorations were trivial, the side pavilions stuck on for no reason and were miserable things anyway, the statues on the roof mere weights rather than ornaments.[13] Smart society usually finds more pleasure in criticism than praise, and snide words with which to express it. What no one criticized was the site. Buckingham's decision to build centrally to The Mall and project his courtyard into the park was acknowledged as a triumphant *coup de main* which turned an intruder into master and left the queen's St James's Palace stranded to one side, like flotsam on the shore.

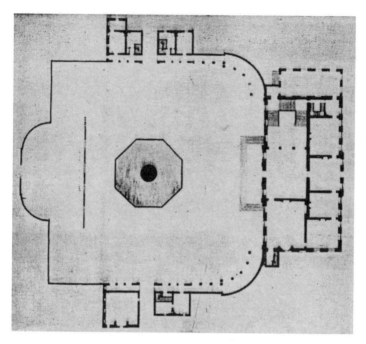

Plan of Buckingham House which demonstrates the relatively modest size of the house, although it surrounds a large courtyard. On this its first floor, the rooms beyond the showy main staircase are mostly surprisingly small. The staircase, decreasing in size as it climbs, is shown on the top right. (From Colen Campbell, *Vitruvius Britannicus*, 1720)

In 1710 the duke briefly held office again, this time as Lord Steward and Lord President of the Council, although he spent most of his time in treasonable correspondence with the Hanoverians. As matters turned out, and much to his surprise, this failed to inspire them with confidence in his trustworthiness, and the new king, George I, removed him from office at the earliest opportunity. Too late, Buckingham realized that only Queen Anne's generous sentimentality had given his selfish talents any value. He died in 1721, after spending most of his final years at Buckingham House; dining with friends and ineffectually discussing Jacobite plots, reading books and writing letters. He also indulged his pride by having his tragedy, *The Death of Brutus* (plagiarized from Shakespeare) performed in the Great Salon there, set to music and adorned by choruses in an attempt to cheer it up. But as Bishop Warburton disagreeably observed, these 'enjoyed the usual fate of ill-adjusted ornaments designed to disguise bad work, and only made the poorness of the piece more conspicuous'.[14]

This watercolour of the garden and terrace at Buckingham House is the only known view of the west front. (The Sheffield Collection, by courtesy of Sir Reginald Sheffield, Bt.)

Among his writings, Buckingham recorded as a compliment to himself that he only took two-thirds of his wife's pension from James II (as well as her personal fortune), and always paid her pin-money promptly unless he happened to be particularly financially embarrassed at the time. Apart from Buckingham House, the main reason for his frequent shortness of cash was his recklessness as a gamester. Several disgruntled opponents complained that he was also a cheat, but if true, it did not prevent him from losing a great deal of money at the tables. On one occasion he pledged part of Buckingham House gardens as surety for a stake, and lost. As usual, he prevaricated over payment and the winner maliciously brought in cattle to graze the flower-beds until his debt was settled. As Winde, the architect, had discovered, only blackmail prised money out of Buckingham.

In spite of his many obnoxious characteristics, the duke's pleasure in his garden, its country air and nightingales, is disarming, as too is the candour with which he admitted he was 'oftener missing a pretty gallery in the old house I pulled down, than pleased with the salon I built in its stead, tho' a thousand times better in all respects'.[15] However, there was no ducal death-bed conversion; sin and retribution were bourgeois concepts and he enjoyed himself all the better for not worrying about them. Before he died, he wrote an inscription to be erected over his tomb, but when the duchess proposed to have it carved in stone the Dean of Westminster indignantly refused, on the unusual grounds (for an inscription) that it was full of lies. In particular it arrogated Christian virtues to a man who at best had been a hypocritical

Romanist at heart, at worst an entire sceptic. A spectacular quarrel followed, but only an expurgated version was eventually put over the tomb.

Buckingham bequeathed his house to his wife on the express condition that she did not marry again; on her death it descended to their only surviving child, Edmund, who, when he succeeded to his father's titles, was only six years old. The duchess never showed any wish to remarry and apart from trips abroad for her son's health she lived at Buckingham House until she died more than twenty years later. Her taste for megalomaniac royal state of the stuffiest kind dominated an unhappy routine there, forcing her enormous retinue to wear court clothes and behave as if she was indeed a queen. In 1723 negotiations were opened on behalf of the Prince of Wales (later George II) for him to lease or purchase Buckingham House, but nothing came of it. Her Grace of Buckingham, it was said, bargained with the haughtiness of a Jacobite and the astuteness of an estate steward, boasting that all His Hanoverian Majesty's revenues could not buy so fine a palace. Eventually she named £60,000 as her price for a property which in reality belonged to her son, an absurd figure intended – and taken – as an insult.[16]

When she died in 1743, Catherine Buckingham remained redoubtable to the last, checking her own funeral trappings to make sure they were of royal quality and making her ladies promise not to sit in her presence even if she lay a long time in a coma. When a clergyman was brought in to see to her soul, her interest in a Christian afterlife remained obstinately confined to etiquette. 'Would respect be shown in heaven to a woman of her birth and breeding?' she asked.

On receiving the unwelcome reply that in heaven no such distinctions were made, she whispered, 'Well, heaven must be after all a strange sort of place'.[17]

CHAPTER 18

Royal Purchase

Only one legitimate son, Edmund, survived the first duke; he seems always to have had indifferent health and his mother quite often took him abroad in the hope of improving it. As a young man he returned to England and entered Queen's College, Oxford, but remained there only eighteen months, coming down in 1733, allegedly because he could not face speaking a public oration as was customary for nobles. It would not be surprising if close experience of the duchess had afflicted an otherwise normal young man with almost paranoid modesty.[1]

Although he spent only a limited time there, Edmund loved Buckingham House, most especially its gardens where he could escape from his mother's mimic court. In reality, escape was an illusion and after he left Oxford Edmund stayed at home only briefly before travelling on to serve as a volunteer in the French Army. Whether he was genuinely fired by martial enthusiasm or could not bear the atmosphere around his mother is uncertain. He was nineteen, and in two years would gain control of his ramshackle estates apart from Buckingham House, which remained in his mother's tenancy for her life.

When Edmund left England, one of James II's natural sons by Arabella Churchill, the Duke of Berwick, was commanding a French army on campaign in Germany, and Edmund joined his staff as aide-de-camp. Shortly afterwards, Berwick had his head blown off by a cannonball and in the casual way of eighteenth-century aristocracy, young Buckingham simply wandered away from the campaign, trailing southwards and feeling increasingly unwell. He died in Rome, possibly from one of its lethal fevers, more probably from tuberculosis. He left a letter to his mother in which he desired her to bury him in Buckingham House gardens, or if that should disturb her enjoyment of them, then 'in the field next to the Garden Terrace'.[2]

The duchess unhesitatingly rejected this request. A body in the garden – or near her terrace – did not suit her ideas at all, nor was there any panache to a funeral held at home. She considered her son's wish to be remembered only by a small monument particularly absurd: nothing less than a mausoleum would do, but that would spoil the view. So, with ostentatious pomp, Edmund was interred beside his father in Westminster Abbey, leaving the Buckingham estates in confusion. The duchess embarked with zest on a prolonged career of litigation over revenues and lands; only Buckingham House remained undeniably in her ownership until she died in 1743, when her husband's illegitimate son, Charles Herbert, inherited.

Charles had been acknowledged and educated by his father but at a decorous distance, in Utrecht. The sole condition attached to his inheritance under his father's will was that he should change his surname to the family one of Sheffield, scarcely a difficulty under the circumstances.[3] Charles must have been in his mid-thirties when his half-brother, Edmund, died, and although he had probably lived in England since he attained his majority, there is no evidence of this. He had been carefully brought up in Holland by an English tutor, but lacked connections in London society and did not inherit his father's titles, all of which became extinct.

Because the duchess contested Charles's rights even after Edmund's death, the Buckingham estates continued to be neglected and mismanaged. There were massive legal bills to pay, and a further delay while Charles established his claim to Buckingham House as well. He lived there from about 1745, 'which he enjoys a fair character in', one contemporary unenthusiastically remarks,[4] but he made little impact on the London scene. He was created baronet by George II, which allowed Sir Charles Sheffield to hope that his offer to buy Mulberry Garden freehold from the Crown would be accepted, or the lease extended.

These hopes were disappointed. The Hanoverian Court remained profitable for its inside operators, but the illegitimate son of a family renowned for its Jacobite sympathies was not among them, especially when he occupied a house the king coveted, and which as Prince of Wales he had been rudely denied by Duchess Catherine.

With half his house built on land which would revert to the crown, at the latest in 1771, Sir Charles Sheffield possessed no leverage at all. Stuart prodigality was out of fashion, which did not mean that the Hanoverians' German following failed to line their pockets. Among George I's domestic staff only the cook was said to have remained honest, begging to be sent home because he was so shocked by robbery in the kitchens. The king refused, advising him to rob like the rest since English revenues were well able to stand it.

The arts of love lacked their historic powers too; a pastime which had for so long been a sure road to profit became a simple waste of time under a monarch who imprisoned his queen and liked his mistresses to be German, ugly and fat. To put it crudely, George I was a tit man. He did not care about cleanliness or looks; what he liked were pneumatically enormous breasts. On this score, the Germans swept unchecked to victory, pouring scorn on English ladies who had no notion how 'to look as great and stately as they can'. The retort that English ladies preferred to show their quality by their breeding and not by sticking out their bosoms, only brought pitying stares.[5]

No bosoms, no pickings. For society beauties accustomed to trade their looks for cash the outlook was bleak, and as Lord Chesterfield austerely wrote:

Charles Sheffield, the duke's illegitimate son, inherited Buckingham House after the death of Edmund, Buckingham's only surviving heir. Charles had to fight the duchess for possession and was ultimately forced to sell the house and gardens to George III. (Courtesy John Sheffield, Esq.)

The standard of His Majesty's taste made all those ladies who aspired to his favour and were near the statutable size strain and swell themselves like the frogs in the fable to rival the bulk and the dignity of the ox. Some succeeded and others burst.[6]

Under George II, corruption returned to more accustomed channels but as described, all overtures for a renewal of the lease on Mulberry Garden or sale of the freehold were rebuffed. The uncertainty began to feel like a time-bomb ticking away under Buckingham House, and ominously, the Crown Surveyor-General used the litigation surrounding Charles Sheffield's inheritance to measure up exactly where the old garden and buildings had been. His plans showed only too clearly that when the leasehold term expired, those missing 4 acres made the whole property untenable, and not just part.[7]

When George III came to the throne in 1760, he was quite as disinclined as his grandfather, George II, had been to treat with Sir Charles Sheffield. The Crown had no motive to change its stance on repossession, nor any intention of doing so. All its officials had to do was wait, and Buckingham House would be at their mercy. In 1761, and very reluctantly, Sheffield reopened negotiations on the basis of selling his interest in the entire site to the king, and a price of £28,000 was eventually agreed, less than half that demanded by the Duchess of Buckingham a quarter of a century earlier. In effect, the king was paying to enter the property ten years before the lease on a small part of it expired, plus an almost contemptuous sum for half the house and over 30 acres of garden.[8]

The agreement was signed on 20 April 1763, and looking back, it is clear that only James I's eccentric whim to wean the English from their idleness with manufactures in silk actually delivered the palace site to his successors. It is also worth remembering that, apart from a brief Tudor and early Stuart presence, George III was the first monarch to own this place we consider uniquely royal, since Edward the Confessor gave it to Queen Edith seven hundred years before.

Yet, when George III bought Buckingham House, he bought bad luck too. Children died there at the same rate as in the slums and none of those earlier, non-royal owners succeeded in passing it on to an heir who was able to retain it. Blake the younger's life became a misery; Goring was lucky to escape execution; Mary Davies sold out to pay her father's debts; Arlington was survived by a single daughter (she rarely lived there after her father's death and her son's trustees sold it off as a white elephant); Buckingham's legitimate sons died; Sir Charles Sheffield had two children, yet could not retain the site.

The lack of heirs among the early owners of the Buckingham Palace site is striking. The Tyburn might be more or less confined but the house remained damp and its surroundings miasmic. One of the worst inundations occurred in November 1751, when Buckingham House was isolated behind a sheet of water stretching from Parliament Square to Constitution Hill, and which must have entered the buildings.[9]

George III's motive for acquiring a property so close to his Palace of St James, apart from seizing an opportunity it would have been churlish to refuse, was a simple desire for privacy. He had been bundled into marriage after exhibiting an indiscreet passion for Lady Sarah Lennox, and wanted a domestic setting of his own. His wife was Charlotte of Mecklenburg-Strelitz, a princess disconcertingly reported as '*sans de beaux traits*'.[10] The king himself was young, highly sexed and considered handsome, kind but very dull. Fortunately, Charlotte's expectations were not great. Even in unexacting Mecklenburg she had been considered ugly and plans were in hand to put her in a protestant convent. A well-behaved girl, when the new King of England's offer of marriage was conveyed to her, she accepted her change of fortune with the same stolid good humour as she had contemplated entry into religious life, and she and the king were married the same evening as she arrived in London, in case he had second thoughts. While his attention remained insultingly riveted on Lady Sarah, the same could not be said for the congregation. Charlotte's bridal gown was fussy and wrapped around by an overmantle of velvet lined with ermine, which dragged down her dress each time she tripped over it, until by the end of the service Horace Walpole gleefully reported that 'the spectators knew as much of her upper half as the King himself'.[11]

Meticulous organization of royal ceremony in Britain is of modern origin. Victoria's coronation was a model of propriety compared to that of her grandparents, George III and Queen Charlotte, when preparations were so miserly that guests to the banquet which followed were forced to assemble in the dark and the Duchess of Northumberland complained that there was not the wherewithal to fill a belly. Tempers were worsened by a wait of several hours while Whitehall was scoured for state chairs and canopies suitable for the king and queen to sit on, and when the royal couple did finally enter, bedlam reigned. Lord Talbot, the Lord Steward, should have ushered in the food on horseback to the accompaniment of trumpets, kettledrums and fiddles, none of them instruments that horses particularly like. Unfortunately, Talbot had decided to train his mount to walk backwards out of the hall afterwards and not turn its rump on the royal pair, a lesson too well learned because the animal, unsettled by the noise and scattering guests as it went, insisted on entering backwards instead. 'A terrible indecorum, but suitable to such Bartholemew Fair doings,'[12] wrote Walpole, who enjoyed farce and indecorum better than anything.

George III was the only virtuous member of an almost uniquely scandalous family, and there can rarely have been a better example of the damage that blinkered virtue can inflict. In an age of excitement, his court was unbelievably pedestrian. Ceremonies were staged without flair, the royal couple normally retired to bed promptly at ten o'clock, and conversation foundered on the king's inability to appreciate that, as a pastime, it assumes some willingness to exchange opinions. Only the simplest reply was not interrupted by a flood of interjected what-what-whats, which soon ceased to be a joke. He was also boringly strait-laced, shocked by such minor levities as the Archbishop of Canterbury's wife giving a ball at Lambeth Palace. He preferred pantomime to drama, liked plain boiled food, and penny-pinching made a dismal court more wretched still. The king squirrelled away cash he should have doled out in tips or gifts, and ministers coming to transact business soon learned to eat elsewhere at their own expense. Even the usual royal passion for hunting alienated those who witnessed it. The king drove his horses and his followers hard, and when they returned, soaked and exhausted at the end of a day, barley water was his idea of suitable refreshment. 'Barley water!' shouted one of these hard-drinking gentlemen, 'Barley water after a hard day's hunting! What use is that? But there it was, standing ready in a jug and fit for a sickroom.'[13]

Queen Charlotte had come to England in high spirits, but was soon crushed by childbearing and her husband's plodding routines. She had no friends in England and the king saw no reason why she should want any, when he felt awkward in company. Charlotte was a stranger who found difficulty expressing herself in English; given time, she might have opened out again into the cheerful, decided personality she had shown herself to be during the journey from Mecklenburg. As it was, the move to Buckingham House cut her off from social chatter ('although there is nothing she so much desires,' wrote Mrs Delany),[14] and the physical hardships of bearing fifteen children in twenty-one years removed her from view for long periods of time. She never had a chance to unbend. Instead, she became an unloving, even cruel, mother and much disliked queen. She rarely complained, but did once bitterly quote the lines:

> They ate, they drank, they slept, what then?
> They slept, they ate, they drank again.

George III bought Buckingham House as a gift for his wife, believing he was being loving and generous, but Horace Walpole was not far wrong when he observed that 'Buckingham House was purchased and bestowed upon her majesty, St James's not seeming a prison strait enough'. Henceforth the king's and queen's lives were segregated from their court, such as it was. They drove across the park for ceremonial occasions, and to this day ambassadors are accredited to St James's and not Buckingham Palace. At the end of whatever function they had attended, they simply drove home. Gates that the Duke of Buckingham had left open to invite company, snapped shut behind them. Everyone else must enter on foot through a side grille and even visiting relatives were lodged at St James's. When the Danish king refused to stay there after reports that the rooms were not fit to house a Christian, George remained adamant. No living-in guests at Buckingham House was the rule, and that was that.

The actual move from St James's was carried out with excitement and good humour. Other royal palaces were raided for furniture, Hampton Court for pictures, and a great many alterations were put in hand. It was probably the happiest time of Queen Charlotte's life. Her first child, the future Prince Regent, had recently been born and the London crowd cheered her as a consequence. Now she had the joy of bustling about almost like an ordinary married woman, discussing colours and hangings and nurseries in her new home, while her husband was as pleased as she by the impending move.

Hotchpotch additions spoiled the symmetry of Buckingham's original plan, as new ideas kept occurring to the king. As one observer wrote:

> the front view is not yet damaged, but so many irregular additions have been made
> on each side as to inspire the spectator with the idea of a country parsonage house,
> to which each incumbent has added something; one a wash-house, another a stable,
> another a hen-roost, till the whole is a mere jumble of patchwork.[15]

More agreeably, in place of Buckingham's book-room beyond the greenhouse, the king added an extensive library including a great octagonal reading room, and there concentrated the various collections scattered through other royal palaces. The library soon received a further magnificent collection purchased to order by the British Consul in Venice, although the king probably found more pleasure in cataloguing his newly acquired collection than reading it. Considerably later, he met Dr Johnson there, who was much impressed by the king's easy manner in such surroundings. Before this meeting, when at

The King's Champion offers a challenge to all-comers at George IV's coronation. During the ceremonies attending his father's coronation bedlam reigned, disagreeably described as 'Bartholemew Fair doings' by Horace Walpole. (Gentleman's Magazine, 1821)

Court, Johnson had nursed a great man's annoyance at not being listened to between the staccato of meaningless royal questions, remarking acidly that it was as well His Majesty answered them all himself. But this occasion was different, and Johnson underwent the familiar metamorphosis of those who have had their egos flattered by royal interest. Lesser mortals could sneer as they wished, but from then on in the doctor's estimation, George III was the finest gentleman he had ever met.[16]

The documents of sale relating to Buckingham House were not completed until April 1763, but the royal couple moved in as soon as the paint was dry in its redecorated salons. The king's apartments were very plain, this being to his taste, and elsewhere dark crimson and blue hangings largely blotted out Buckingham's voluptuous paintings, but the fittings and furniture were generally conceded to be very rich. Splendid cabinets, carpets and curtains had been purchased, with preference firmly given to home producers; among them a woman joiner, Katherine Naish, who specialized in carved beds. Outside, there was still work to do, but when all was finished within, the queen had the agreeable idea of giving a combined house-warming and birthday party to the king. He was, with difficulty, persuaded to return to St James's for two nights while at breakneck speed she masterminded the preparations, in great secrecy for fear he would consider them too extravagant.

On the night of 6 June 1763, a message was formally delivered across the park desiring His Majesty's presence at Buckingham House. When he arrived, the queen ushered him upstairs to a room which faced the gardens and there drew back the curtains from the windows, revealing an entrancing spectacle below. A sham temple had been erected in the garden together with a bridge, the whole tableau illuminated by over four thousand lamps. In front of the temple was a large transparency of the king giving peace to the world while, in contradiction to this pious wish, at his feet were gathered trophies representing Britain's recent conquests in the Seven Years' War. Illuminated birthday mottoes and moral devices were set up around the gardens, an orchestra broke into George's favourite music as soon as he put his head out of the window, and for once a more than adequate feast was laid out on long tables in the garden. As the king watched, a grand firework display began.

George was delighted by his gift, which demonstrated remarkable organizational skills in his wife on the only occasion she was allowed to use them. The meal was enjoyed by everyone, and in garden surroundings the ladies relaxed in stiff-bodiced gowns which allowed bare shoulders, previously anathema at St James's. 'The ladies will catch their deaths,' Walpole wrote with relish, 'And what dreadful discoveries were made, both fat and lean! I recommend to you the idea of Mrs Cavendish when half-stark.'[17]

After this happy occasion, for Queen Charlotte life at Buckingham House would travel downhill for the next fifty-five years.

CHAPTER 19

The Queen's House

By Act of Parliament the king settled Buckingham House on the queen for her life, exchanging it with Somerset House, the former dower house.[1] It was, the Act directed, henceforth to be known as the Queen's House and officially this latest change of name was invariably used. It is not surprising that George III did not care to live in a house known by a subject's name, an unsatisfactory Jacobite subject at that, but the Londoners' nickname of 'Buck House' has outlasted an Act of Parliament, long vacancy and subsequent rebuildings and renamings, to bring an echo of earlier history into modern usage.

Another eighteenth-century fashion carried into the present is to mock George III and his consort, but the reality of their lives was more contradictory. The king worked conscientiously at the business of being a monarch, and his obstinacy had considerable influence on the governments that served him. He may not have read the books he collected, but many bibliophiles are the same. He was intellectually limited but supported a Royal Academy for the Arts and gave it £5,000, a substantial sum for a man who hated to part with money. He was fascinated by clocks and astronomical instruments, liked farming and was acknowledged as a bruising rider. He enjoyed music, drawing, theatricals and architecture; Johann Christian Bach, Dr Herschel, Josiah Wedgewood, Lawrence and Gainsborough all came to the Queen's House and there are numerous stories of his personal courtesy away from critical stares at Court.

The queen was a collector of taste, particularly of porcelain and jewellery. She was a capable manager, physically uncomplaining, and filled the Queen's House with beautifully arranged flowers. She was vigilant over her household, including spartan arrangements for an enlarged range of nurseries built between 1767 and 1770.[2]

The tragedy was that the couple's gifts gave little pleasure either to their possessors or to their subjects. One reason for this seems to have been that nothing dislodged their awkwardness with people, an insensitivity to the feelings of others which alienated courtiers and their own children. For all the royal couple's varied interests there was no dynamism or style within their circle. Wit, learning, innovative curiosity, all struck their sparks elsewhere.

The Queen's House painted by Edward Dayes late in the eighteenth century. The statues and mottoes have vanished, but various side buildings, a library and riding school have been added. (Courtesy of the Trustees of the Victoria and Albert Museum)

A stultifying routine settled early on life at the Queen's House, and wherever the royal couple travelled it rarely varied. The queen presented her husband and the nation with three children every four years and the king disciplined them harshly, in the widely shared belief punishment and humiliation were good for them. Simplicity and absurd formality clashed continually in their lives. Food, conversation and pastimes were of the most basic kind, but no one could pass a room containing a member of the royal family if the door was open, the queen's ladies could never sit in her presence even while she knitted silently for hours, and they were forced to wear a uniform of blue cloth with scarlet collar and brass buttons, hot weather or cold, like so many German band-masters.

The royal princesses only ever responded to their parents and never spoke first even when adult. There was almost never a late night, or a morning which started after six. Ministers invariably stood throughout their interviews, and old William Pitt, when suffering from gout was kept on his feet for two hours, although the king did say afterwards that he hoped he felt no worse for it. It never seems to have occurred to him that an elderly, sick and distinguished public servant might have been invited to sit, and imagination strays back to a very different stickler for decorum at court, Queen Elizabeth, who invariably invited her minister, Lord Burleigh, to pull up a stool when they discussed state business, and visited his bedside when he was dying.

At the Queen's House visitors and attendants must never sneeze ('even if you break a blood vessel to avoid it'), never leave the room for the most pressing call of nature until after the king and queen had done so, never start a conversation, never initiate a new topic if they happened to be addressed. Always, when royalty entered a room, everyone in it must move backwards and away, until they reached a wall. As Fanny Burney remarked, retrograde motion without tripping was the most essential of Court arts. All this in a house bought because the king wished to be away from ceremony, and it was so ridiculous that it appealed irresistibly to gossip writers and lampoonists.

The day began with the queen supervising her younger childrens' baths at six. The king left his room at around seven-thirty and went at once to the queen's salon, where he expected to find her and one of his daughters (in rotation) dressed and waiting to greet him. They then went to the chapel to hear divine service, and after breakfast the king usually rode into Hyde Park and beyond. (In 1798 a pension was awarded out of the privy purse to a man accidentally shot by the royal keepers during a hunt for fox in Kensington Gardens, which gives an odd idea of the sport enjoyed by His Majesty.[4] Purists probably disapproved of shooting foxes more than they did the accident to an onlooker.) On his return the king usually played chess, and was easily pleased if he won. Afterwards came a succession of royal meals: the king dined at two, the queen and princesses at four, while the princes ate in their schoolroom, also at two, and were not allowed anything more until breakfast the following day. At five the king visited his wife and drank a glass of watered wine with her, before settling to work on state papers in his study. This was when ministers were received. The evenings were passed at cards in the queen's drawing room where supper was set out, but only for show: the royal family did not eat supper, which meant no one else could either. This effectively deterred hungry statesmen from lingering, and promptly at ten the royal family went to bed. For more than forty interminable years, until the king became permanently ill, this was the royal day.

A few outside excitements did occasionally intrude. In 1764 several thousand silk-weavers set a fashion by crowding into Queen's House courtyard to petition against the miserable condition to which they had been reduced by French imports. The following year the hatters came and then the peruke-makers, complaining that people had begun to wear their own hair instead of wigs. Since they were not wearing wigs either, scuffles developed with onlookers in the park and some peruke-makers had their hair forcibly cut off, their assailants jeering that now they would have wear wigs even if no one else did.[5]

These events and a surge in robberies made St James's Park less fashionable than before. Maintenance was poor, the frequency of floods increased and undergrowth became so thick that some areas reverted to swamp. Numerous improvement schemes were discussed but nothing was done until 1768, when a great storm blew down so many trees that most of the walks were blocked. Heavy rain overwhelmed the drainage system too, and cellars from Westminster to the Queen's House filled up with stinking water, prompting George Selwyn to remark that the park and the civil list were both in the same condition, with a number of useless but expensive drains in both of them. William Grenville commented that the Queen's House was damned unhealthy.[6]

By 1773 the park was back in some kind of order, when a German traveller described it as 'swarming in the evening and night with people of all ranks, and . . . when the sun shines, the ground sparkles with the pins which have dropped from the ladies's dresses'.[7]

And somehow that last phrase makes the scene come alive. All those pins were witness to the excitement and unreason preceding a promenade in the park, the agony in a hundred bedrooms where spoilt beauties schemed how to outshine the pack, while flustered sempstresses were forced to rip out seams they had sat up half the night to finish. And then frantically pin in new tucks and flounces until there was no more time, and out the ladies swept with sharp pins in their stare as well as in their clothes.

But for all its crowds, St James's decline in exclusivity continued until by 1800 another German crushingly described it as 'a sort of meadow for cows'.[8] This was partly because the works carried out were inadequate and partly because high society decided that Green Park, and later Hyde Park, were more to its taste. During these changes the Queen's House remained the royal family's home, but during one of their absences a Mrs Powys was able to wangle an highly illicit visit

> to what is most difficult to see of all, the Queen's Palace. The hall and staircase are particularly pleasing, the whole of the ground floor is for the king, whose apartments are fitted up rather neatly than profusely. The Queen's apartments are ornamental with curiosities from every nation that can deserve her notice. The most capital pictures, the finest Dresden and other china, cabinets of more minute curiosities. . . . The floors are all inlaid and every room full of roses, carnations, hyacinths, etc dispersed in the prettiest manner imaginable. On her toilet, besides gilt plate, innumerable knick-knacks. Round the dressing room, let into the crimson damask hangings in a manner uncommonly elegant are frames of fine impressions, miniatures etc. It being at that time the coldest weather imaginable, we were amazed to find so large a house so warm, but fires are kept the whole day even in the closets.[9]

George III might hedge himself about with social walls, but security in any modern sense was anathema in eighteenth-century England. Mrs Powys even felt mildly aggrieved that an excursion into the king's private home should take time, influence and bribery to arrange; as a prize for her trouble, she was quite entitled to poke about where she chose.

Political failure set in with the American War of Independence (1775), and for a king who took his coronation oath as seriously as George III, this defeat was a severe emotional loss as well. Then, at the height of the struggle, violent rioting broke out in London. The immediate cause was increased tolerance towards Roman Catholics, but disorder fed on the wretched conditions most Londoners endured, as an outdated urban administration crumbled under the strain of large-scale immigration and booming growth. Members of the House of Lords were assaulted, the Bishop of Lincoln escaped lynching only by dressing as a woman, Newgate Prison was stormed and its prisoners released, magistrates' houses demolished. A large crowd broke into a gin distillery in Holborn and its contents were passed out by the bucketful until carelessness started a blaze which exploded like rocket fuel, incinerating drunks too paralytic to escape and further maddening the survivors. The Bank of England was besieged and more prisons broken into, leading to an entire collapse in the rickety framework of law. Magistrates simply lost their nerve and left the mob to run wild until it tired.

This situation brought out the best in George III. He raged against the cowardice of his ministers and law officers alike, and when it seemed likely that the Queen's House would be attacked he sat up for two nights, waiting to lead its defence. When troops were brought in to bivouac in the gardens and in St James's Park, he talked personally to many, upset that no one seemed to care that they were sleeping on bare ground:

> My boys, my crown cannot purchase you straw tonight, but depend upon it, a sufficiency shall be here tomorrow forenoon. And as a substitute for straw, my servants will instantly serve you a good allowance of wine and spirits.[10]

They cheered him then, one of the most dramatic scenes in the history of the Buckingham Palace site. The buildings beyond Charing Cross were starkly outlined against the glow of fires, and sparks had begun to fly above the rooftops of Mayfair, showing where looters had embarked on a fresh orgy of destruction. Distant yells, and a more threatening deep rumble from a multitude on the move could be distinctly heard by those inside the Queen's House, where the latest rumour was that the wild beasts had been released from the Tower menagerie to gulp down victims in the streets. Scarlet flames from camp-fires flickered over the soldiers' scarlet jackets and touched in the trees beneath an ominous orange sky: to some watchers it must have seemed as if the soldiers, too, were glowing embers thrown out by the mob.

Privately, the king was almost beside himself with rage at the inactivity of his government and roundly told them that if neither ministers nor magistrates knew their duty, he did. If nothing was done, he personally would lead his troops from the Queen's House to clear the streets. Faced with this ultimatum, the cabinet agreed that the king should personally order the Commander-in-Chief, Lord Amherst, to use all necessary force to bring the situation under control; one of the last instances of royal power being used in its over-riding, executive sense.

Amherst's troops did a ruthless job, and on the night of 7 June 1780, the gutters around the Bank of England quite literally ran with blood. Several hundred men, women and children died when they were trapped on the approaches to Blackfriars Bridge; trampled, shot or drowned trying to escape. Looters were fired on at sight and by morning the rubble-strewn streets were empty, except for soldiers.

Fashion ran wild with the Macaronis, when gentlemen and ladies alike risked death by discomfort while outdoing each other in extravagant attire. (From Larwood, *History of the London Parks*, 1881)

As soon as the siege was lifted at the Bank of England, the staff were set to slapping whitewash over blood on its outer walls, and it reopened promptly for business in the morning.

The king was elated, but although he had behaved sensibly while his ministers ran like ferrets down their respective holes, he was no more popular than before. Once the immediate danger was past, military law in London seemed intolerable and the search was on for scapegoats; to George III's astonishment, he and not the mob was blamed for unrestrained massacre, and from feeling uplifted, he became despondent. All this took place alongside terminally bad news from America, and anxiety over his eldest son, the Prince of Wales, who, as Horace Walpole wrote 'had issued from that palace of supposed purity, the Queen's House, as if he had been educated in a night cellar'.[11]

Even before he set up his own establishment in Carlton House, the prince's debts topped £30,000, reaching a quarter of a million inside five years, a fantasy sum for the period. He was also illegally married to Mrs Fitzherbert, about which the king knew nothing, and led the most raffish set in town. The king was appalled by his son's behaviour, and the quarrel between them worsened as equally unsavoury scandals began to surround his brothers. Nor did Queen Charlotte act as peace-maker; perhaps she reckoned that being forced to live among a pack of imprisoned adult daughters more sexually repressed than tabbies in a cage was task enough for any woman.

In truth, the palace site had become little more than a detention camp, an ironic situation when it was the Crown's title to a pleasure garden which enabled George III to purchase it. Now it consumed the spirits of those who lived there, turning Queen Charlotte from a cheerful housewife into an ungenerous, coldly bad-tempered woman, tyrannical to serve and unloving to her family. The boys escaped but took with them the burden of a punitive childhood; the daughters remained trapped in nun-like solitude while cherishing far from nun-like thoughts, until their eldest brother was in a position to insist that if his sisters could find suitors, they should be allowed to marry. By then Elizabeth was forty-eight and Mary fifty, but they still bolted after the first unlovely males they found, and were happier than they had ever been before.[12]

The Turkish Ambassador's Public Entry in 1793, on his way to present his credentials at the Court of St James. His procession is here seen passing the Queen's House, to which guests were rarely invited; also in view are two of the six caparisoned Arab horses presented to the king as a gift from the sultan. The Duke of Buckingham's magnificent railings and gate have vanished – probably because they bore his personal insignia and coat of arms – together with his costly fountain. (Gentleman's Magazine, April 1793)

The last victim was the king. His first serious relapse in health came in 1788, and whether the cause was porphyria or mental collapse, or both, the result was terrifying. He became frenetically active, over-talkative, unable to sleep. Spasms shook his bowels and his limbs, which swelled up painfully. His behaviour was eccentric, even threatening, and worsened under the treatment he received. The details have often been written about, but so far as the palace site is concerned, his illness marked the beginning of a long rundown in use. For the rest of his reign the royal family returned to the Queen's House only intermittently, including for the Prince of Wales's marriage to Catherine of Brunswick, when the prince was so horrified by his bride's appearance that he fell in the nuptial fireplace after drinking himself into a stupor. He was still snoring in the morning; and since Lady Jersey, the prince's mistress, had amused herself by sprinkling epsom salts on Princess Caroline's dinner, with predictable results, the wedding night could only in the most ribald circles be considered a success. In spite of this, Caroline became mysteriously pregnant, which her husband seized on as an excuse to announce that they would never, ever live together in the future.

The Grand Salon was extensively refurbished in 1799, a time when the family were more frequently in residence, but soon afterwards the king again became unwell. The queen continued to hold levées and drawing rooms alone when necessary, and for convenience transferred them from St James's to the Queen's House. Sometimes the king was able to perform public duties such as opening parliament, with only minor eccentricity, at others he could only with tact and time be brought to sign essential papers, although he did not agree that he was unable to transact public business until 1811, when his eldest son became Prince Regent.

His behaviour in his private life was worse: inconsiderate, as restless as a bee in a bottle, capricious and demanding, sometimes losing his grip on reality altogether. He dismissed faithful servants without compensation and frightened the queen by his unbuttoned behaviour. Finally, she refused to see him alone and locked her bedroom door against him, despite all pleas to change her mind. She had had enough, she said, and it is hard to blame her.

The truth was, she no longer loved her husband and probably had not done so for years. She may even have despised him, and now she was frightened and embarrassed by him. She was free for the first time in her life, but also too old to change much beyond the one matter which annoyed her most: her husband's physical presence. For the last years of her life Queen Charlotte only visited London to hold her drawing room receptions, travelling regularly from Windsor to the Queen's House regardless of the weather, and insisting on being paid £10,000 a year for her trouble. The last of these was held on 27 February 1818, when the new United States ambassador, Robert Rush, brought his wife to be presented and wrote home about what he saw, bowled over by the spectacle and not yet tuned in to the furies boiling below its surface.

> Four rooms were allotted to the ceremony. In the second was the Queen. She sat on a velvet chair and cushion, a little raised up. Near her were the princesses and ladies in waiting . . . the Prince Regent and royal family. If the scene in the hall was picturesque, the one upstairs transcended in all ways. The doors of the rooms were all open. You saw in them a thousand ladies all richly dressed . . . I had already seen in England signs enough of opulance and power – now I saw radiating on all sides British beauty.[13]

Six months later, Queen Charlotte was dead, although the king lingered on at Windsor until 1820. The curtains were drawn at the Queen's House, holland covers put over the furniture, the gardens left to grow ragged. The princesses rushed away to find husbands. Queen Charlotte's collection of porcelain and ornaments was auctioned off to pay a few of the Prince Regent's debts. Damp, that curse of the Buckingham Palace site, began to reclaim the buildings, creeping up the walls, rotting rich fabrics, springing inlay. The only properties of any size close by were fever hospitals, and people began to say that some such use was all the Queen's House was fit for any more.

CHAPTER 20

A Monstrous Insult to the Nation

Not long after Queen Charlotte's death, the Prince Regent met a few friends and advisers to discuss the future of Queen's House. He was ambivalent about the place himself. It held disagreeable memories but he considered it the right place for him to live when he became king. Already he visualized The Mall as a triumphal way down which he would drive surrounded by royal pomp, to reach a ceremonial palace such as British kings had never previously owned.

The advice he received was salutary. With strict economy – never the prince's strong point – perhaps £150,000 might be saved from Crown rents over three years, a sum which the Regent instantly declared to be quite insufficient to restore the Queen's House, let alone rebuild it as he wished. His architectural advisers agreed. Five hundred thousand ought to be enough, four hundred and fifty at a pinch, but who wanted to be miserly where building works were concerned?

The short answer was, the government did. In the economic depression and public unrest which followed the end of the Napoleonic Wars, money for a new palace was an extravagance ministers were quite unwilling to argue through a hostile House of Commons. No one could remember when a popular monarch had last sat on the throne and pessimism reigned over the prince's chances of breaking the tradition. Nor did parliamentarians trust him just to refurbish a building which was widely condemned as dowdy and in decay. Ministers had visited Brighton and shuddered to imagine what Prinny might build once his talents were let loose at the end of The Mall. Mock Chinese pagodas that leaked in a storm might (just) be forgiven as a seaside folly, but to wake up one morning and find almost anything growing under scaffolding just beyond St James's, and in multicolours too, was unthinkable.

Since the Prince Regent could not save even the most meagre sum from his revenues and was exceedingly cosy at Carlton House, nothing was done for several years. Only when George III finally died was the question of a suitable royal residence in London revived. So too, though, was the question of cost, several members of parliament going so far as to say that if the new king wanted to rebuild Queen's House, then he should pay for it by selling St James's Palace for development.

But even near-republicans agreed that such a site in the heart of London should not be occupied by a fever hospital, nor left to moulder indefinitely. Three years later a bill came before the House of Commons, to authorize repairs and improvements to the Queen's House. Plans were agreed and the cost estimated at £200,000, which seemed not too outrageous, and the measure passed without overmuch fuss.[1]

The architect was John Nash. He had long been a favourite with the king, their most famous collaborative scheme being the entire new townscape of Regent's Park and Regent Street. But by the time he started work on the Queen's House, Nash was over seventy years old and the king, once the leader of London fashion, had degenerated into a painted, sick and bloated caricature of majesty. Whereas Nash's earlier designs had been admired, that for Buckingham Palace was derided from the outset and he himself confessed that as work proceeded he became disappointed with how it looked: the outer wings he thought too narrow, a dome intended for additional lighting unintentionally showed above the roofline and was promptly nicknamed 'the pimple', the king's after-thoughts confused the symmetry of his facade. They also delayed contractors and contributed to unrest on the site. On one occasion strike pickets had to be dispersed by a detachment from the Coldstream Guards, and Nash was driven close to despair by these apparently endless disputes.

The Prince Regent, later George IV, who rebuilt the palace largely as it is today. His decorations were widely criticized for vulgarity and extravagance, and Cruikshank here cruelly caricatures the descent of Prince Charming into dissolute, sick old age. (Copyright Trustees of the British Museum)

*John Nash by Sir Thomas Lawrence,
whose designs for Buckingham
Palace brought him before a
Select Committee of the House of
Commons and dismissal in disgrace.*
(Reproduced by kind permission
of the Principal, Fellows and
Scholars of Jesus College, Oxford)

However, the king's impatience hustled work on the palace forward even
before the parliamentary bill or estimates were approved, and to try and hurry
things further Nash used timber partitions physically to divide the site in three,
so that separate teams of builders could be employed in competition with
each other. Far from speeding things up, this device confused them further.
Three separate clerks of works squabbled among themselves and often failed
to defer to the overall superintendent, William Nixon, who had been clerk
at the Pavilion in Brighton. There were three sets of day books and accounts,
which a later committee of enquiry could not reconcile, three sources of chaos
and three sets of excuses every time anything went wrong. Most householders
have been surprised at one time or another by how swiftly financial calamity
unfolds once a builder's plan is varied: a new window here, a different pattern
or quality of material there, and the final bill bears little relationship to the
original quote. At Buckingham Palace, once the king's imagination took flight,
the scale of work produced overspends of startling dimensions; raspberry-
coloured pillars, state staircases and suites, statuary and royal escutcheons by
the gross, a triumphal entry arch, all were added to the design. Far from being
too large, the king soon decided the new palace would be too small for the
ceremonial role he now envisaged for it, and Nash needed little encouragement to add another storey to his outer pavilions, hoping that height would
reintroduce some balance to his design.[2]

Another controversy was Nash's 'extensive and peculiar use of ironwork'
in the palace. He had experimented for years with cast-iron girders in bridges
and viaducts, but traditionalists regarded their use as load-bearing members
in a complex building such as Buckingham Palace as unproven and unsafe,
and ridiculed his stress calculations. Nash retorted that if they disbelieved

him, then the unfinished palace should be crammed with soldiers as a practical load-bearing test, a novel idea that the military presumably rejected out of hand. The Commons' Select Committee, on examining the matter, refused to take sides in this particular dispute, but members were not reassured by evidence given by one of the contractors on the site, who remarked that 'the palace itself is of a different construction to any building I ever saw of the same nature, it is so strong it must last for ever, or go all at once'.[3]

By 1828 a number of inquisitions had already begun into Nash's – and indirectly into the king's – conduct, ranging from the Commons' Select Committee to a series of increasingly infuriated minutes between ministers, when, among other things, it was discovered that Nash had acted as his own wholesale supplier for bricks, marble and other goods. Nash argued that this made the contract cheaper and there is little evidence that he made substantial profits out of a thoroughly irregular arrangement, but as costs continued to rise the government's patience ran out. On 13 September 1830 the Prime Minister, the Duke of Wellington, wrote to his Chancellor of the Exchequer recommending that he make 'a hash of Nash'[4] even though the unpalatable fact remained that now so much money had been spent, there remained little alternative but to complete the monstrosity at the end of The Mall.

George IV had died in June 1830, not long after a further furious exchange in which he wrote that during these enquiries Nash had been: 'Infamously used. If those who go through the furnace for me and for my service are not protected, the favour of the sovereign becomes worse than nugatory.' An editorial in *The Times* expressed the same thought more cruelly:

> Mr Nash and Buckingham Palace are again before the public today, and a sorry figure each of them makes. However, we must say that . . . upon the whole there is a great meanness in pouring the stream of vengeance on Nash, now that the prime mover of the folly [the King] is no longer alive to protect him, or to frighten his accusers.

But even if George IV had lived longer, by then Nash was beyond even a monarch's protection.[5]

The matter limped on for months while the architect was too unwell to answer questions, the government fell and Lord Grey's new administration was too preoccupied with the Reform Bill to worry about a mere palace. Eventually Nash was dismissed when the Select Committee found him guilty of 'inexcusable irregularity and great negligence'. This marked a sad end to his career, and Nash retired to the Isle of Wight, where he died in 1835.

Meanwhile, neither public nor political feelings were soothed by the reflection that at a time of widespread distress and disorder, there in the middle of the captial stood a massive, unwanted and unfinished monument to royal vanity and extravagance.

The new king, a younger brother of George IV, was very different to his predecessor. William IV, Sailor (or Silly) Billy, was unpretentious and foul-mouthed, not very bright although occasionally shrewd; in silhouette his head bore remarkable resemblance to an avocado pear. He cherished unhappy memories of the Queen's House, loathed what he saw of his new palace and had no intention of living there. His government might decide that it had little choice but to finish a building on which so much money had already been expended, but the diarist Charles Greville confided that the monarch looked much delighted when the Houses of Parliament burned down in 1834, since His Majesty was at once enabled to offer Buckingham House to the nation as its new parliament building.[6]

Unfortunately, parliamentarians disliked this idea quite as much as William detested the notion of living there himself, but when his offer was declined he soon proposed another scheme, in which the palace would become a barracks for his foot-guards. For several weeks after the fall of the Melbourne ministry in the autumn of 1834, Britain had no government, no prime minister, no Houses of Parliament and no agreement on the future ceremonial centre of the kingdom.

Meanwhile, Buckingham Palace continued to grow in size, in spite of the fact that every party to the enterprise no longer wanted it, nor could see a use for it once completed. The architect who followed Nash was Edward Blore, and he proposed substantial changes to Nash's design. Certainly Blore was more businesslike than his predecessor, but his style was not particularly compatible with Nash's (whom he personally disliked and whose work he belittled) and he, too, was frequently forced to halt operations, mainly to check that the Treasury would pay the next set of bills. By 1835 costs had risen from the original £200,000 authorized by parliament to over £750,000, and for a still unfinished building.[7]

The hotchpotch palace became the latest sour joke of London, and both Earl Grosvenor and the Duke of Northumberland were canvassed as possible purchasers of 'this monstrous insult to the nation, this cumbrous pile, this monument to reckless extravagance'.[8] Satirists gloated when the pimple-like dome had to be dismantled and replaced by servants' attics. Officials tore their hair as reports came in that the kitchen quarters mysteriously flooded whenever it rained. Gossip-mongers sniggered over plasterwork which peeled off the walls as soon as gilders or artists attempted to decorate it. The arched entry (which no one yet realized would be too narrow for the coronation coach) was pronounced horridly ostentatious, and Blore himself considered the lack of architectural connection between it and the rest of the palace a major flaw in design.

A German visitor, von Raumer, wrote scathingly of a visit to the empty building in 1835:

Satirical drawings published to accompany anonymous verses deriding the 'House that N**h built', and which convey with deadly accuracy the confusion on site, military strike-breaking (above) and infuriated bafflement in government circles as the Duke of Wellington and Chancellor Goulburn struggled to decide what to do about an intrusive and useless dome that leaked (below). (Westminster City Archives)

Many objections might be made to the proportion of the exterior, though its extent and colonnade give it a certain grandeur . . . But what shall I say of the interior? I never saw anything that might be pronounced a more total failure in every respect and for my own part I would not live there rent-free. I should vex myself all day long with the fantastic mixture of every style and decoration, the absence of all taste, the total want of measure and proportion.[9]

A spoof letter from a supposed French architect had previously been printed in all seriousness by the press, delightedly scoffing at:

de Buck-and-Ham Palace in de spirit of John Bull, in plum pudding and rosbif taste, for which de English are so famous. It is a great curiosity. In de first place, de pillars are made to represent English vegetable, de leek and de onion; then de friezes are enrished with de leg of mutton and de pork, with vat dey call de garnish, al vary beautiful carved; then on de impediment of de front stand de man-cook with de large English toasting-fork in his hand, ready to put into de pot de vary large plum pudding behind him [the dome] which is a vary fine pudding . . . On de wing of de palace, called de gizzard wing (de other wing is cut off) stand de domestique servant, in neat dress, holding de trays of bisquit and tart. The architect is M. Hash. The English people seem vary much to like dis palace, and do laugh vary much. There is in the front one vary large kitchen range made all of white marble [the Marble Arch] vich I was told would cook von hudred of goose at von time. De palace, ven complete, will be called after famouse English dish, de Toad-in-de-Hole![10]

Creevey, the diarist, was equally scathing, railing against the raspberry-coloured pillars (described by von Raumer as like raw sausages) and describing them as part of 'a wicked and vulgar profusion which . . . made him sick to look at it'.[11]

The finished exterior was similar in ground plan to Buckingham House, but larger. It surrounded the same three sides of courtyard with the open side facing St James's Park, a composition the free-standing arch partially obscured; the present facade of the palace which entirely hides the old courtyard is a later addition. Otherwise, today's palace remains much as it was built then, complete with raspberry-coloured pillars.

With the building still far from finished and perhaps in reaction to so much criticism, King William suddenly declared that since the thing was there, he might as well live in it, and no sooner had he done so than the same impatience that had afflicted his brother, George IV, took over. Planned outbuildings were abandoned, floors completed at breakneck speed, furniture and fittings bundled in. Then, perhaps fortunately, the king died before he could discover that his forebodings about the general inconvenience of his new royal residence were to prove entirely justified.

CHAPTER 21

'Everything Most Filthy and Offensive'

Young Queen Victoria had no such qualms. She succeeded to her uncle's throne in the middle of a June night in 1837, and within days of her accession decided that the sooner she left her childhood home at Kensington, the better.

Her first domestic action after succeeding to the Crown had been to order that her bed should be moved out of her mother's room and into private quarters, but this only highlighted a different dilemma. Queen she might be, but she had no power to dismiss her mother nor her entourage, several of whom she disliked and one, Sir John Conroy, she positively detested. But the new young sovereign had other facets to her character besides the girlishness shown to the world right up to the day of her accession, and she meant to be rid of them just the same. Sufficient space into which unwanted faces could be banished surely existed in the vast chilly rooms of the unfinished palace at the end of The Mall. There, too, she would be rid of her Kensington past, and establish herself as queen for all to see on an unrivalled site at the centre of social and political affairs.[1]

Whether her mother, the Duchess of Kent, was aware of the extent of her daughter's plans is doubtful, but from the day they settled in at Buckingham Palace, if the duchess wished to see her daughter she was forced to ask permission, to which requests only a curt note was sometimes returned, containing the single word, 'Busy'. As for Sir John Conroy, the queen did not allow him anywhere she could prevent him from entering. Whether he had actually been her mother's lover was beside the point – and contemporary opinion was divided on the issue – to Victoria he was anathema. There were plenty of people in fashionable London, including the Duke of Wellington, who believed he had been, and her dignity was injured by malicious gossip.

At first her government was appalled by the queen's insistence that she would occupy Buckingham Palace, come what may, within a month. The practicalities of such a transfer sent Whitehall into a tailspin, and civil servants (via the Prime Minister, Victoria's 'dear, kind, good Lord Melbourne') tried to explain all the reasons why a hasty move into a largely unfurnished marble barn was ill-advised.

Hanoverian impatience brushed aside these arguments. When it was pointed out to her that the floors were as yet uncarpeted and furniture sadly lacking, Victoria replied that she did not care for carpets and there was enough furniture for her. When she looked around, she failed to see what the critics made such a fuss about; marble should be multi-coloured, and royalty expected a great deal of gilding in a palace. The only shortcoming she did cavil at was when she discovered there was no throne. The Treasury had presented the old one to the House of Lords, although whether this was because they expected a republic or the result of miserliness is unknown. Victoria immediately ordered a new one from an upholsterer called Mr Dowbigin, and gave instructions that the bill (not to exceed £1,000) should be sent to the Chancellor of the Exchequer. The Treasury, unwilling as ever to accept the most trifling of defeats, retaliated by insisting that the queen should pay the £12 cost of changing WR to VR on the throne at St James's and removing therefrom the arms of Hanover, to which under Salic Law her uncle the Duke of Cumberland had succeeded.[2]

'I rejoice to go into Buckingham Palace for many reasons,' the queen confided to her journal,[3] at the same time admitting she felt briefly nostalgic for Kensington: 'My rooms are so high, pleasant and cheerful . . . the garden is large and very pretty. Dear Dashy [her dog] was quite happy in it.' The following month and in spite of court mourning, nearly every night there was either a private dinner or a concert, or both. When Thalberg played, whom Victoria described as the most famous pianist in the world, she went into ecstasies over his romantic appearance, as an afterthought adding that he played well too. Cards were a popular pastime, and Victoria ordered no fewer than twelve dozen packs – six with pink backs and six with white – within weeks of moving into the palace. Although sophisticated guests complained of nursery-style games and juvenile conversation, in that first year of her reign Queen Victoria was very far from staid.

What the queen apparently did not care about but could scarcely avoid knowing, since she took pleasure in showing visitors over the palace, including the kitchens, was that the building had become an instant domestic disaster.

Blake, Goring, and probably Lord Arlington too, had placed their kitchens in outhouses, the Duke of Buckingham in side pavilions. Nash put them in the basement.[4] For the period this was not unusual, but there were plenty of people alive who must, surely, have warned him about how wet the palace site could be. Nash himself would have seen St James's Park flooded during his years of working in London as an architect, but he seems not to have considered whether this might make the basement a less than ideal place to put kitchens. To make matters worse, in order to prevent royalty's walks on the terrace from being overlooked by servants, windows were almost entirely lacking. Very little consideration was given to what a kitchen's most basic

The highly defensive contemporary commentary which accompanied this etching of the Queen's Yellow Drawing Room attempted to demonstrate that the palace interior was not nearly as tasteless as outsiders believed. But since the writer then chose to add that the apartments exhibited a harmony of colour which ought not to be confused with 'A German critic's view that the rooms are like clumsy stage scenery transformed into rooms by a wicked magician', it is hard not to feel he defeats his own purpose. (Illustrated London News, 1844)

needs should be, especially in a palace where it was expected to produce several hundred meals each day, including banquets which might comprise as many as seventy-five different dishes. In the absence of windows the huge bank of ranges produced an atmosphere straight from the stokeholds of hell, and the maze of boot-rooms, larders, stores and pantries which even fairly simple nineteenth-century homes required if they were to function at all adequately, were either incomplete or inadequate, or had been deleted from the plans altogether during one of the various bouts of cost-cutting. The stable block, for instance, had suffered in miniature nearly every trial and quarrel that blighted construction of the main palace.

The Master of the Household was soon complaining bitterly that the palace staff had to clean boots and shoes in their own tiny garrets, into which the rain and snow leaked, and small though these servants' rooms were, eight or ten were crammed into each. There was no unified palace water system; many, perhaps most, of the fifty new water-closets did not work. The heating, too, was so inadequate that coal fires needed to be lit in every inhabited room. This meant that dozens more servants must be employed to carry coals and clean grates, and posed the insoluble puzzle of how to keep so many fires burning when, alas, it was discovered that the palace chimneys smoked abominably. Victoria herself had to choose between being kippered or frozen during the winter season; and although she never complained, in the early years of her reign especially, her Court regarded a winter tour of duty at the palace with almost universal trepidation. As Baron Stockmar austerely reported a year later, 'the absence of system, which leaves the Queen's Palace without any responsible authority and in intolerable confusion . . . ensures that order, comfort and economy are manifestly impossible'.[5]

Royal household organization was indeed abysmal. Responsibility was split between the Lord Chamberlain (Lord Conyngham), the Lord Steward, the Master of the Horse and a recently reorganized Office of Woods and Works, among whom only the Lord Steward had a representative actually resident in the palace. Duties were based on medieval principles which corruption and changed circumstance had turned into a farcical shambles: the Lord Steward, for instance, was responsible for providing fuel and laying a fire, the Lord Chamberlain for lighting it. The Lord Chamberlain provided lamps, the Lord Steward cleaned and trimmed them, the Master of the Horse lit some and there were arguments over the rest; the Lord Chamberlain cleaned the inside of windows, the Office of Works the outside. As Stockmar again commented: 'The degree of light to be admitted into the Palace depended proportionately on such well-timed and good understanding as might exist between the Lord Chamberlain's office and that of Woods and Works.' No one was at all suprised when the Lord Chamberlain's idea of discharging his duties was to appoint his mistress as housekeeper at the palace,[6] a task for which she had no qualification beyond easy access to her person when his lordship was on duty.*

In practice the palace staff were left very much to their own devices and became renowned for their rudeness to royal guests. 'There is nobody to observe, correct, or reprimand them . . . they come on and go off duty as they choose, they remain absent even on their days of waiting or they may commit any excess or irregularity without being disciplined,' was Stockmar's later, outraged comment.

---

* Lord Conyngham's mother had been one of George IV's mistresses, when she quite often appeared in company wearing the Crown Jewels.

In November 1838 a boy intruder was apprehended after a chase across the palace lawns, and, when questioned, twelve-year-old Tom Cotton admitted that he had spent a year living inside the palace. He had pilfered a number of objects and opened the queen's own sealed letters, presumably in the hope of finding money. The servants were aware of his existence, since he had often hidden in chimneys and advertised his presence by leaving sooty footprints on the furniture or triumphantly smudged across beds, but apparently no one thought it worthwhile to track him down. His eventual capture seems to have resulted from his own increasing temerity in strolling where he chose, and security continued to be lax.[7] Shortly after the birth of the Princess Royal, in December 1840, the queen's monthly nurse was astonished to discover another boy, Edmund Jones, asleep under the sofa in Her Majesty's own sitting room.[8] He displayed great pride in his achievement, saying that this was his second visit to the palace and he enjoyed sitting on the queen's throne. Although Tom Cotton disappears at once from history, the Home Office investigated Jones, tracking down his family to Derby Street, Westminster, where his father was a jobbing tailor. The boy was committed to the treadmill at the House of Correction in Tothill Street, but broke into the palace again after his release, in March 1841. After another spell on the treadmill he was sent into the navy, where he joined HMS *Warspite* as a ship's boy, only to abscond five months' later. He was recaptured and punished, thereafter remaining on the ship until 1845; he later served on HMS *Inconstant* and HMS *Harlequin*, with conduct noted as good. On 21 October 1847, when no longer a boy, he applied for discharge and can last be traced awaiting a passage back to England from Malta, later that year.

The worst of many shortcomings discovered at the palace was that the kitchen floor was actually the brick roof of that forgotten hazard of the site, a common conduit. Probably this was one of several originally placed to drain the site into the Tyburn; it may have been the Tyburn itself. When this was first put underground, it ran in front of Arlington House, but after the Duke of Buckingham encroached on St James's Park and also on Mulberry Garden, its route was lost beneath his courtyard and side pavilions. With Nash's enlarged plan, the Tyburn became entirely enveloped within the palace buildings, where it still remains, and the old side drains were likewise forgotten. Presumably when Nash's contractors uncovered what looked like an old brick floor, they saved money by incorporating it into the kitchen. Some workers on the site would have known what it really was, because London remained a metropolis of villages and folk memory dies hard in such communities, but provided the clerk of works passed the floor as satisfactory, the contractor was pleased to pull off a successful fraud.

Even in Lord Goring's day the Tyburn had been a noisome sewer he was anxious to bury out of sight. In a London which had grown out of all recognition yet still lacked a comprehensive public drainage system, it must have carried a greater volume than before, much of it raw effluent. What palace officials had assumed to be the relatively minor inconvenience of servants paddling about their work in wet weather, in fact posed a serious threat to the health of the queen and her guests. Sewage and the royal dinner could not be expected to mix forever without calamity.

When the queen left the palace for a few weeks during the first autumn of her reign, an inspection of the building was carried out by Sir Benjamin Stephenson, one of three commissioners of Woods and Works. This revealed unspeakable squalor, including what was in effect a midden carelessly piled against the kitchen walls,[9] made up of discarded and rotting food mixed with rising filth scraped off the floor. Sir Benjamin was scandalized by what he found. 'Everything is most foul and offensive . . . and when (I spoke) to the Housekeeper she said it was nothing to do with her. . . . None of the rooms has been cleaned since the Queen left, nor any windows opened.' The stench was such that in his opinion it made parts of the ground and first floors of the palace uninhabitable.

Astonishingly, very little was done beyond minor redecoration and 'water-washing'. Perhaps it is not surprising that government departments were reluctant to embark on yet more palace expenditure so soon after having brought the last to a scrambling kind of conclusion. Increasingly furious letters flew between the few conscientious officials of the household and civil servants, the latter being as obstructive as only civil servants know how to be when they are determined not to do something which they privately know to be highly desirable, not to say eventually inevitable. Only when the Prince Consort took the matter in hand some three years later, and the queen decided that with a growing family she needed an entire new wing added to the palace, were domestic arrangements thoroughly but, needless to say, grudgingly, reviewed.

In that first autumn of her reign, when Victoria returned to Buckingham Palace, she at once commented on the pretty new furnishing in her rooms, but neither then nor at any other time did she confide to her journal the slightest unease about smells, freezing temperatures or poor service, although almost every detail of her day was faithfully inscribed there. She seems neither to have enquired about the conditions endured by her staff, nor to have realized that idleness and corruption among them were commonplace. The extraordinary fact that the Prince Consort felt able to cut domestic wages in some cases by over 70 per cent may strike the modern mind as Scrooge-like meanness, but since there seems to have been little subsequent difficulty in recruiting a better quality of royal servants, it also suggests some magnificent racketeering during these earlier years. There was, for instance, a particular type of candle which continued to be ordered in quantity every week. When Albert enquired about the reason, since most of the palace was lighted by gas, the excuse offered was that George IV had used them to relieve his catarrh. Since he never lived at the palace and by then had been dead nearly fifteen years, someone had been doing a very lucrative trade out of the palace back door.

But however squalid her palace, Queen Victoria was entirely different in quality and style to any of the Georges or to William IV, who had roamed the streets almost unescorted but was too undignified to fulfil anyone's idea of what a king should be. When she drove out of Buckingham Palace gates on her chaotic, joyous Coronation Day, Victoria had already reigned for nearly a year, and could look back on something of an *annus mirabilis*. By simply being herself she had restored emotional glitter to a monarchy which had lacked this essential ingredient since the days of Charles II, possibly even since Elizabeth I, and one result was to transform Buckingham Palace from a contemptible extravagance into a centrepiece for Empire. Yet unseen corruption in the queen's own home was symbolic too, of the rotten core of degradation within a Victorian achievement which briefly made Britain the richest, most proud and most powerful nation on earth.

CHAPTER 22

The Hard Road to Reform

As the radiance of her coronation faded, Queen Victoria discovered how hard life could be for a sovereign who courted publicity. She made mistakes, and factious gossip in the palace exposed them to a wider audience than before. The queen ate too much. She was often petty. She was dangerously familiar with Lord Melbourne, and prejudiced against anyone whose political ideas did not agree with his. She was headstrong and the quarrels with her mother grew worse, yet she could not live respectably without a chaperone; even Lord Melbourne thought so, and he, too, was finding her increasingly exhausting to deal with.

In February 1839 the queen noted in her diary that she suspected one of her ladies-in-waiting, Lady Flora Hastings, as being '*with child!*' and on no evidence beyond her own dislike, Victoria soon convinced herself that her pet enemy, Conroy, was responsible. When she confided in Melbourne, he advised her to do nothing: his usual advice in nearly every circumstance, and this time certainly right. However, neither the queen nor her ladies felt inclined to follow it and like some nineteenth-century St Trinian's, the palace fairly seethed with schoolgirl whisperings and plots. Lady Flora herself angrily denied the charge, strongly backed by her family, who published some damaging correspondence involving the queen. This increased public sympathy towards Lady Flora, who was virtually forced to submit to a medical examination which proved Victoria's vendetta to be without cause. Lady Flora was not pregnant, and never had been.

Uproar followed. 'The court is plunged in shame and mortification at the exposure', wrote Greville, '. . . and the procedings looked upon by society at large as to the last degree disgusting and disgraceful.'[1]

The queen grudgingly apologized but the scandal rumbled on, a not unfamiliar scenario. Once royalty invites publicity, then publicity hits back. The Tory opposition used Lady Flora's affair to discredit a queen who remained implacably their enemy, and rumours continued to circulate about the queen's spite towards a woman she still secretly considered immoral.

A Chinese bell largely manufactured in silver which was presented to Queen Victoria in 1843. Many courtiers, past and present, have shared the puzzled sentiments exhibited here, when faced by the insoluble problem of what to do with bizarre gifts from foreign governments. (Illustrated London News, January 1844)

The reason for Tory involvement was a coincidental Cabinet crisis, which forced Lord Melbourne to resign from office, and much against her will Victoria sent for Sir Robert Peel, as leader of the Tory opposition. She was in a mood to detest anyone she considered an enemy and at once decided that he was unfeeling and cold. Peel, with his Lancashire accent, manufacturing inheritance and awkward social manner had long been the target of sneers, but he was politically the coming man. Vigorous in debate, impressively capable in government, creative where Melbourne liked to let things roll on, outstandingly intelligent. None of this reached the queen. She wanted to keep Lord Melbourne as her principal minister, and as a way of doing so fastened on Peel's request that if he was to form a government she should express her confidence in him by replacing some of her Whig ladies-in-waiting with Tories. She would not change a single lady, and announced with blithe exaggeration to Melbourne that same day, 'I suppose they would next deprive me of my dresser and my housemaids. They wish to treat me like a girl, but I will show them I am Queen of England.'[2]

A more juvenile stance can scarcely be imagined, and baffled, Peel withdrew to consult the Duke of Wellington, that arbiter of correct behaviour in a crisis. In the upshot, he declined to form an administration which clearly would encounter only hostility from the Crown, and Melbourne's government pursued its rickety way for another two years. A disappointed Tory Party joined the already widespread condemnation of Victoria's feud against Lady Flora, and public anger increased against 'this baby of a queen who sets herself in opposition to the most serious policies and parliamentary requirements of the nation'.[3] Victoria's ignorance of sexual matters gave the whole affair a disconcerting air of prurience, and Lord Holland, a judicious Whig observer, decided that it was ominous to find such stories, true or false, beginning to spread so soon in the court of a virgin queen.[4]

Four months later, Lady Flora Hastings died at Buckingham Palace of cancer of the liver. By then it was widely realized that she was terminally ill and the queen briefly visited her sickbed, but few adjustments were made to the round of entertainments and balls, which, if not usual after the death of a lady-in-waiting, would have been tactful in this case. A further outburst against the queen followed in the press, and she was hissed at Ascot. The honeymoon between Queen Victoria and her people was well and truly over.

As late as October that year stones were flung through the queen's bedroom window while she was at Windsor but gradually matters settled down again, except between Victoria and her mother, a staunch supporter of Lady Flora. Buckingham Palace was not large enough to contain them both, and the queen said frankly that she found it dreadful 'to have the prospect of torment for many years by Mama's living there'. The palace salons witnessed a series of such shattering quarrels during these months that Victoria finally resolved to accept Melbourne's suggestion and marry, if this was the only way to be rid of a chaperone, and in November 1838 she announced her engagement to Prince Albert of Saxe-Coburg-Gotha.[5]

If marriage was primarily designed to remove Mama from Buckingham Palace, when he arrived for scrutiny Queen Victoria fell in love with Albert. It was an emotion her people did not share. Little was known about him except that he was poor and German, but the British felt they had had more than enough of penniless German royalty: the Commons slashed Albert's proposed allowance, the Church hackled up over information that other Coburgs were Catholic, and there were undignified wranglings over what Albert's rank should be after marriage. The queen's uncle, the King of Hanover, flatly refused to dignify a miserable Gotha wedding by sending Hanoverian horses to draw the wedding coach, a traditional gift on such occasions. The cap it all, the Duke of Wellington dug in his booted toes over questions of precedence. 'This wicked, foolish old duke!' the queen scrawled in her journal. 'The confounded Tories, oh! May they be well punished for this outrageous insult! [over the allowance] I cried with rage. . . . Poor, dear Albert, how cruelly they are ill-using that dearest Angel! Monsters! You Tories shall be punished! Revenge! Revenge!'[6] A queen in this mood was scarcely the constitutional sovereign sober jurists described in their textbooks.

Some alterations were made within the palace in readiness for the wedding, and a new long corridor put in to prevent the servants from having to use inhabited rooms as a passageway. As had become traditional with palace alterations, these exceeded their estimate; the explanation that they had to be done in a very hurried manner and 'in a great part by candle-light' being received with equally traditional scepticism. By this time the stenches in the palace had reached such a level that the royal physician, Sir James Clark, was brought in to report on them. His conclusions were damning, but still nothing was done. The queen, however, was delighted with the improvements to her rooms and looked no further. 'It is all so changed,' she wrote, 'fresh painted and gilded . . . the doors altered and beautiful chintz curtains and furniture. It looks like a new house and so pretty.'[7]

Once her subjects were resigned to a royal wedding, they decided to enjoy it. A seasick Prince Albert was cheered on his journey to London and when he drove to Buckingham Palace to take the oath of loyalty as a British subject, onlookers responded well. The marriage took place at St James's, followed by a brilliant reception at Buckingham Palace, and afterwards the young couple said a firm (and final) goodbye to Mama before going on honeymoon to Windsor. In spite of a cloudburst the crowds outside the palace remained enthusiastic, and celebration parties were well patronized. It seemed as if the troubles of the past two years could finally be forgotten.

The prince had expected that life as Queen Victoria's husband would not be easy, but was unprepared for the rigours of living in her palace. His wife never seemed to notice its depressing cold dampness and disregarded fires that could not be lit because the chimneys smoked, or because the servants were quarrelling over who should carry the coals. Her indifference to smells included escaping gas, which her household comptroller considered a hazard of the first magnitude. This did not prevent him from extending its use into his own suite of rooms, while forbidding it in the attics for fear the roof might be blown off. It was installed there nevertheless, in error or so it was said, and he let it stay, saying that on reflection it was probably even more dangerous in the basement, where it was the sole form of illumination.[8]

Soon after his marriage Prince Albert and Baron Stockmar, his secretary, initiated an enquiry into the royal household, with particular reference to defects at Buckingham Palace. New gilding and chintzes had not satisfied the prince that all was well, nor did he consider a major explosion in the basement a desirable way of getting rid of insanitary kitchens. Stockmar wrote the report which followed, detailing so many horrors that his arguments in favour of fundamental reform seemed irrefutable, but by then Albert had been in England long enough to know that wholesale change was unlikely. His wife, though loving, was 'too hasty and precipitate for me to speak of difficulties. She will not hear me out but flies into a rage and overwhelms me with reproaches.'[9] Even a hint of change stirred up trouble, and not only with the queen. Office holders and domestic staff shared a fear of losing their mutual profiteering at the queen's expense, and joined the chorus of dismay.

Above all, Stockmar had become convinced that the ludicrous division of management responsibility must be swept away. This extended not just to lamps or fires but to the palace as a whole, where the Lord Steward managed the upstairs except for the queen's private rooms, which were separately ordered, and the Lord Chamberlain most of the ground floor 'but whether the kitchens, sculleries and pantries remain under his charge is a question no one can reply to'.[10] Staff supervision was similarly fragmented. Housekeepers, pages and housemaids were under the Lord Chamberlain, who, with the sole exception of Lord Conyngham's intimacy with his mistress, in practice had no contact with them. Footmen, grooms, porters and under-butlers were answerable to the Master of the Horse, by whom they were both paid and clothed, a chancy procedure when any underspending stayed in his pocket. The remaining palace servants from cooks to watchmen, cellarers to launderers, were supposed to be managed by the Lord Steward, although arguments kept erupting over fringe activities such as coal-carrying. If a pane of glass was broken, six separate officials, who in their turn answered to four, possibly five, masters must sign authorization to replace it. Consequently these went unmended for months, allowing rain to damage valuable furniture, floors and decorations, not to mention the draughts which must be endured. Meals were congealed by the distances they must be carried, and cooking was a hit and miss matter anyway because vital fittings in the kitchen, once broken, usually stayed broken. The roof and drains leaked, the chimneys continued to smoke.

All the great officers were political appointments and changed when the government did and the only one resident was the Master of the Household, but as the Lord Steward's appointee his authority was ignored by the rest.

The Master of the Household's office ... may be pronounced a nullity, and ... two-thirds of all servants are left without a master. They may commit any excess and ... if smoking, drinking and other irregularities occur in dormitories where footmen sleep ten or twelve in each room, no one can help it. . . . There is no one to attend to the comfort of the Queen's guests ... and no one is prepared to show them to and from their apartments ... or even knows where they are lodged. It frequently happens that visitors are at a loss to find the drawing room or their own bedrooms and wander for an hour helpless and unassisted. There is no one to apply to in such a case and the only remedy is by some means to reach a porter in his lodge.

The boy intruders, Stockmar adds, were a consequence of this total lack of system.

Against formidable opposition, Prince Albert persisted in his view that change was necessary, while Victoria and Peel – to whom she was now reconciled – clung to the notion that antique arrangements designed for quite different circumstances should remain sacrosanct. Victorian self-confidence ripped apart established customs almost everywhere it touched, and Peel himself shook the Church by repealing anti-Catholic laws, antagonized nearly everybody by introducing income tax in peacetime, but the relatively pettyfogging matter of administering royal palaces was different; there he doubted the wisdom of change.

Outwardly, the prince agreed, only to rally his arguments and try again.[11] Years passed. Finally, in 1846, a bargain was struck: the great officers of state remained, but would delegate their authority in the palaces to two inspectors, made directly responsible to the Master of the Household. One of these must always reside at Windsor, the other at Buckingham Palace, where they would possess absolute authority, subject to supervision over the payment of accounts. Albert personally drew up the agreement, adding the valedictory instruction that 'Waste, the canker of all, but especially of all great, establishments, should be made as difficult as possible, at the same time that nothing shall be spared which is essential for the befitting splendour of a Great Monarchy'.[12]

Flushed by this triumph, the prince turned his atttention to the understaff at Buckingham Palace. Wages were reduced wholesale on the not unreasonable grounds that the current recipients pursued their own purposes away from the palace for as long as six months in the year. Practices such as serving wine to a non-existent guard originally appointed to protect George III during his fits of madness were stopped, footmen were forbidden to replace every candle in the palace each day, regardless of whether these had been lit or not. Since trade in such perquisites was the principal reason for seeking positions in the palace, wholesale resignations followed and were instantly accepted. Dishonest and sexually loose behaviour would henceforth be punished, and the maids of honour received a tough new code of conduct which was framed and hung in their bedrooms. A new age had dawned.

Prince Albert had also been busy with alterations to the structure of the palace. A comprehensive if far from ideal system of heating and ventilation was installed during 1843, and the queen enthusiastically agreed to replace a conservatory with a private chapel. Their growing family posed additional problems; by January 1847 the queen had borne five children in less than seven years of marriage, uncomfortably keeping pace with Queen Charlotte's rate of production. Attics were converted into nurseries and a mezzanine inserted to accommodate the additional servants considered necessary, hugger-mugger arrangements which proved particularly unsatisfactory when a workshop directly below added clangings and smells of oil and glue to the other palace inconveniences.

Queen Victoria's costume ball was eagerly depicted by fashion magazines, but much resented by her ministers at a time of high political tension. (Illustrated London News, 1845)

Edward Blore, the architect who had completed Nash's work, was called in again and suggested closing the open side of the palace frontage with a new east wing. This would allow the nurseries to be rearranged and generally provide additional space, a ballroom for instance, since so many more people now expected to attend royal entertainments. As a bonus, the 'absurd' Marble Arch would have to come down, as it would be in the way. Almost as an afterthought, but perhaps prodded by Prince Albert, new drains were decided on and a plan made to bring the kitchens up to ground level.

As always, cost remained a difficulty, and Blore's estimate of £150,000 was a severe blow. To Sir Robert Peel, embroiled in conflict over his new income tax and faced by starvation in Ireland, such a sum represented political suicide. He would see what he could do next year, but for the moment his answer was no.

In the interim and with some lack of tact, the queen held a splendid fancy dress ball at the palace, at which her preoccupied ministers were expected to prance in high-heeled shoes and wigs. The Duke of Wellington appeared as Butcher Cumberland, which perhaps expressed his feelings with fair accuracy.

A Commission was set up in May 1846 to consider the proposals for more building at Buckingham Palace, and a decision taken to sell the Royal Pavilion at Brighton as a gesture and to help defray the cost. On this basis parliament voted £150,000 for the execution of Blore's plans and work on the palace began; the pavilion was only rescued from demolition by Brighton councillors, who raised a loan to buy it for the town.[13]

This was the signal for Buckingham Palace to bounce back as a vociferously disliked building. Closing the courtyard was held to isolate the monarch as if she was a Russian Tsar – and there was no worse insult – but despite a storm of protest Nash's colonnades were filled in and the last remnant of old Buckingham House vanished out of sight behind curlicues stuck on a blank facade. Only towards the end of the work did a more gifted architect, James Pennethorne, come on the scene, who designed a new block to contain the kitchens, domestic offices and ballroom as a pleasing feature instead of a further disaster on the garden side.[14]

On 28 February 1854 the queen and her family stood for the first time on a new balcony placed centrally on the completed east front, which would in the future be the national focus for many great occasions. But in 1854 cholera had come to London, and the bloodstained muddle in the Crimea oppressed the country; this particular ceremony marked the departure of a battalion of Foot Guards to reinforce the British force there. 'A fine morning, the sun shining over the Towers of Westminster Abbey and on an immense crowd,' the queen wrote. 'A touching and beautiful sight; many sorrowing friends were there and one saw the shake in many a hand.'[15]

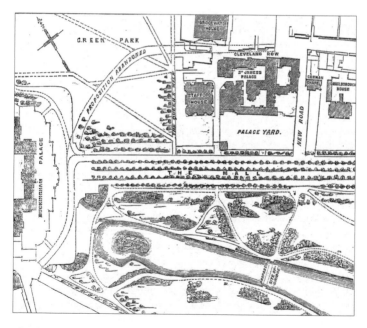

Plan showing the new entrance into the Mall and layout for improvements around Buckingham Palace, 1856. (Illustrated London News, 1856)

No further alterations of importance were carried out during the queen's lifetime and there were, almost inevitably, continuing defects. Blore's stonework did not wear well and constant, irritating sums of money kept needing to be spent on the structure until her grandson, George V, refaced the entire frontage and erased its fussier features. Somehow Buckingham Palace never quite succeeded in outgrowing its unsatisfactory beginnings, a few of which might even be traced back to Blake's first hastily cut corners, such as proximity to traffic. Most grew out of the slipshod work carried out in a state of sniping warfare during the 1820s and early 1830s.

The cold reception given to the changes at her palace reinforced the queen's distaste for long residence in London. Even Windsor was not secluded enough and she bought Osborne on the Isle of Wight, where her household was privately run and free from the tensions which outlasted all reforms at the palace. This was followed in 1848 by her purchase of a lease on the Balmoral Estate, and for months at a time recently enlarged Buckingham Palace was left standing empty, in the charge of a reformed but largely idle staff.

On formal occasions splendour at the palace was greater than before, an almost paralysing decorum extending from the servants to the guest list. Attendance was largely confined to the aristocracy, landed gentry, clergy and the richer professions: hopefuls from commerce were admitted only if their operations were empire-wide. As for retail trade

> the line was drawn and very strictly so ... were a person actually engaged in trade to obtain a presentation, it would be cancelled as soon as the Lord Chamberlain was made aware of the nature of his occupation. The sons of wealthy manufacturers are not precluded if their education and association warrant their participation.[16]

Rot, in every sense of the word, remained at the core of the state. For those who were admitted, court dress was obligatory. If a lady wished to be excused from wearing a low bodice, she had to obtain a doctor's certificate that to do so would injure her health, and then get it accepted by the Lord Chamberlain's department. United States' ambassadors in particular faced political firing squads over the clothing they should wear, after Secretary of State William Marcy ruled[17] that the Republic's ministers abroad must wear only the simple dress of an American citizen. The mid-century US ambassador in London was James Buchanan, a future president, and protracted negotiations with Her Majesty's master of ceremonies ensued. Letters sailed slowly back and forth across the Atlantic, filled with tricky arguments on breeches and gold lace. The ambassador considered the position was complicated by the British sovereign being a lady, and lack of gallantry might lead to a boycott by society; when someone jokingly suggested that he should appear as George Washington, he seems to have considered this fancy dress solution seriously for a while and it is difficult to avoid a sneaking suspicion that Buchanan would actually have liked to dress in gold-laced tails and silk stockings. The knotty question was still unresolved when he received an invitation to the State Opening of Parliament, which he had to decline as court dress was obligatory, a slight maliciously trumpeted by the press.

Finally, after further stern instructions from Marcy in Washington, Buchanan decided that the simple dress of an American citizen could be most favourably interpreted by a black coat and pantaloons, white waistcoat and cravat. A further difficulty occurred when it was pointed out that unless he wore a sword he was likely to be mistaken for a butler, and at the prospect of such a hideous insult to his nation he capitulated, deciding on a note of swagger that a black-hilted, black-sheathed shortsword was manly, after all.[18] In this costume Buchanan attended a levée in February 1855, and smugly enjoyed a sense of distinction among the gaudy throng.

This served as a useful pointer for the future, when radicals such as John Bright, a member of Gladstone's government in 1868, believed it betrayed their ideals to wear silly clothes. The queen was consulted and agreed to receive Bright in black velvet. He next had objections to kneeling when he kissed hands on taking office, and she was satisfied by a low bow. With painful slowness the modern world struggled into life even inside Buckingham Palace.

The middle classes, in spite of their exclusion from it as retailers or manufacturers (and their wives fared even worse, being denied entry even when their husbands qualified as rich, military, or holy), approved of the uplifting moral tone now pervading the palace. Aristocrats might agree with Lord Melbourne that damned morality was sure to ruin everything, and resent a loss of favour if they had the ill luck to be caught in the wrong bedroom,* but they were compelled to behave decorously while at court. Family life was all the rage and tale-tellers ensured the growth of hypocrisy as well.

However, despite improvements, within the palace one aspect of family decorum was not going smoothly: the education of the Prince of Wales. The Hanoverian legacy of discord between monarch and heir continued under Victoria, made worse by relentless pressure on the prince. His wicked inclination to enjoy life was already roundly condemned by the age of four, and every day was divided into hourly or half-hourly periods crammed with instruction to prevent him from developing such a dangerous weakness further – a regime to which the Prince of Wales responded with fits of temper, disobedience and violent destructiveness. When his tutor considered that it would be beneficial for the prince to have some companions of his own age, he was removed from office and lessons were stepped up from five to six days a week. The prince's attacks of rage grew worse, and for all his charm, Edward remained prone to fearful seizures of anger all his life.

* Lord Palmerston was discovered in a lady's room at Windsor while Foreign Secretary, and the Queen's lasting dislike of him dates from this incident.

The new ballroom and south entry to the palace. The stone piers and cast-iron gates are noted as 'decidedly an improvement on the brick piers and lumbering wooden gates of former days', but a familiar moan follows: 'The charge however has been somewhat costly . . . amounting to £2,450.' (Illustrated London News, January 1857)

The queen, too, quite often lost control of herself. Throughout the 1850s she was subject to occasional hysterical fits, usually but by no means always directed against her husband and connected with her frequent pregnancies, which she resented. For this period in her life the image of stiffly dignified Victoria is false, and the atmosphere within the palace was frequently very difficult. Tension eased in the tranquillity of Osborne or Balmoral, and in a very real sense the royal family continued while in London to share the bad luck that the Buckingham Palace site attracted for much of its history.

When the queen flew into one of her furies, Albert usually withdrew to write her sorrowful, soothing letters, which seldom achieved their purpose. Yet they were devoted to each other and the queen's outbursts came close to being a frantic gloss on passion. Albert was everything to her, the most momentary loss of his attention a slight she was unable to endure. Albert's sensibility; the elegance with which he wore shooting clothes, a kilt, the garter robes; the set of his shoulders; the stripes on his trousers – each was a separate, sensual pleasure. Queen Victoria wrote like a romantic novelist about her husband, and then, in 1861, he died.

The Prince Consort's illness was typhoid contracted from the drains, not of rebuilt Buckingham Palace, but re-medievalized Windsor Castle. It was made more severe by insomnia and pathological worry over the Prince of Wales, who was then a young man of twenty dividing his time between Cambridge and the Guards, while enjoying a sexual escapade with an actress. Most parents would have condemned his behaviour without being surprised by it. To Albert and the queen it confirmed their doomsday fears of an heir steeped in wickedness, and Victoria ever afterwards considered her son almost as his father's murderer.

This was only one effect of Albert's death on the queen. She withdrew from public life, and Buckingham Palace was shut up. It became almost Albert's mausoleum, a shrine to memory where nothing was ever touched, and until Victoria's own death the solemn ritual of laying out the Prince Consort's evening clothes was meticulously carried out. For two years the queen lived in complete retirement. There was no Court, and public functions were taken over by other members of the royal family, the queen herself only reappearing at a drawing room in 1868, when she moved it to the discouraging hour of two o'clock. This meant that ladies attending it must dress in feathers and jewels after breakfast and endure shouts of 'Mothballs' from irreverent onlookers as they drove through the streets. No refreshments or toilet facilities were provided at the palace; self control was all, and anyone skimping the slightest detail of attire was ruthlessly turned away.

The nation's relief at the end of the Crimean War was reflected in tremendous celebrations which took place all over the country. Fireworks in Hyde Park are watched by the royal family from the balcony included in the new eastern wing (extreme left) and an appreciative crowd outside the palace gates. This is one of the earliest views of the controversial 'closing of the courtyard', and the now famous balcony; it also shows the more decorative finish to the palace facade, removed in 1912. (Illustrated London News, 1856)

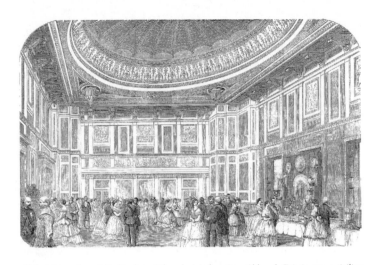

A formal reception at Buckingham Palace during the 1850s. Although Britain was a civilian society this etching and the one following reveal the extent to which Court society was exotically uniformed, continental-style. (Illustrated London News, July 1857)

Public understanding of the queen's grief turned to anger. After all, ordinary people suffered loss and the next day had to keep on earning their living. Monarchy cost money, and it was only reasonable to expect some return on their investment. Privately, the queen's ministers agreed. They were tired of journeying to Balmoral or the Isle of Wight, to sit in darkened rooms while the queen tediously read the papers they had brought. Only meagre hospitality was offered on these excursions and Balmoral in particular was full of bitter draughts. Rumours of an infatuation with John Brown were the last straw, when Radicals were already saying that the only sign of life from the queen was when she rattled her money-box, wanting cash for her relations.

By 1870 agitation for a republic was spreading beyond these radical groups, but it was Disraeli with his flattery and political wiliness who charmed Victoria back to Buckingham Palace. She still spent long months away from London but her interest in affairs revived and she again carried out her ceremonial duties. By the year of her Golden Jubilee, 1887, she had become a world institution, which also had a great deal to do with the growth of British power, for which she became a kind of emblem. Then the rigours of her Court made her presence more awe-inspiring, and the size of her extended family grew into an advantage in foreign policy.

But as with George III, although for different reasons, the conversational arts did not flourish in her presence. At table, this had something to do with the habit of whipping away plates the moment Her Majesty laid down her knife and fork, since guests were anxious not to starve. But there and elsewhere, the queen ruthlessly interrupted if she saw people talking among themselves and demanded to know the topic; if, as often happened, she disapproved of it, a glacial silence followed. Worse still was her idea of entertainment after a meal, when guests were summoned one by one to converse with her, usually an excruciating exchange of trivia; happily, each encounter was exactly timed and victims could count on quick release.

Invitations to State occasions were rigidly controlled, and the most dynamic elements of Victorian society remained largely excluded. (Illustrated London News, June 1855)

Max Beerbohm's cartoon was entitled 'The rare, rather awful visits of Albert Edward, Prince of Wales to Windsor Castle'. Since the prince considered Buckingham Palace 'a Sepulchre', and the queen stayed there as infrequently as she could, his visits to the palace were even more infrequent and the atmosphere equally icy. (Courtesy of the Trustees of the Victoria and Albert Museum)

Staff at Buckingham Palace endured an equally difficult life. It was a crime to move in her presence unless in execution of their duty, they must never look the queen in the face when she gave them an order and instant dismissal followed any involuntary lifting of eyes from the pattern on the floor. The palace remained physically comfortless if not as wretched as in the early years of her reign; work must be completed out of sight at ungodly hours, spells on duty were immensely long and discipline draconian.[19] Their private life was circumscribed, too. The queen believed that she alone should give anyone serving her permission to marry, and frequently withheld it. When her physician, Sir James Reid, defied this rule to become engaged without her knowledge he faced a blast of anger, followed by exclusion from her presence; in his case, she valued his skill as a doctor and eventually agreed to readmit him. She even saw the joke when he promised not to do it again.[20]

Queen Victoria could indeed occasionally unbend, with her grandchildren and Disraeli particularly, to whom in 1880 she sent a valentine card. By the time she died she had simply outlived criticism, as if this tiny black-clad personification of the past could somehow hold back the huge and threatening wave of change, by then visibly piling up on the horizon.

Edward VII was sixty years old when he became king, and he wasted no time when the throne at last was his. He openly called Buckingham Palace the Sepulchre, and tersely ordered officials to clear it out. The Prince Consort's evening clothes were burnt and an army of clerks went through the palace, throwing out junk, cataloguing, heaving mildewed trunks on a bonfire that blazed for days in the garden, offering bizarre treasures to museums. One rediscovered object puzzled all the experts before being identified as Henry VIII's codpiece, prudishly removed from his armour and now restored to it, a sign of a return to heartier times. A cache of statuettes of John Brown, which the queen liked to distribute as gifts, was said to have been personally smashed by the king.[21]

Squads of painters, ventilation experts and telephone engineers were drafted in and, most important of all, plumbers. For the first time bathrooms and hot water became conveniences house-guests could rely on receiving, and lavatories were placed near the public rooms. Ladies no longer needed to refrain from drinking for twenty-four hours before visiting the palace for fear their bladders would burst, nor gentlemen to resolve the same situation by more devious means. Drawing-room receptions ceased to be tests of endurance and were moved into the evening; food and drink were provided and the orchestra ordered never to play church music again. Cars drove through the palace gates for the first time and soon *The Tatler*[22] was complaining that hardly a single carriage with wigged footmen remained in London. The employment of no fewer than thirty-six domestic chaplains was terminated, each previously rewarded by £40 a year for preaching a single sermon. Edward VII's interest in sermons was limited to those occasions when they were impossible to avoid, and he did not under any circumstances expect to pay for them.

However different the Edwardian Court was from its predecessor, the king inherited the Hanoverian passion for precision in manners and dress. Queen Alexandra was sent back to her bedroom when she wore the garter ribbon over the wrong shoulder, her explanation that it interfered with her jewels rejected out of hand, and a famous lawyer who arrived at Buckingham Palace with his sword slung on his right hip instead of his left was curtly ordered to rectify the matter before His Majesty would receive him. This proved easier said than done, since he was an absent-minded man and his staff had thoughtfully sewn it to his underwear. The king remained adamant, and a bedroom was put at his disposal for the fundamental adjustments that were necessary.[23]

Edward's short reign let fresh air into Buckingham Palace. His alterations were utilitarian, his touch lighter, his attitudes cosmopolitan. The world of fashion and pleasure again revolved around his Court, and the king remained personally popular in spite of the many social rancours of the time. Leaders of the new Labour Party were invited to the palace the same as other politicians, subject only to Edward VII's interpretation of proper standards on behaviour. When Kier Hardie told him he ought to call off a visit to the Tsar of Russia, a tyrant who oppressed honest working men, his name was instantly struck off the guest list. On the principle of one-out, all-out, His Majesty was then informed that no Labour Party guests would thereafter visit his palace, and Edward was sufficiently politically aware to restore Hardie to his list and not openly to bear a grudge afterwards.[24]

Sentimentality over Edward the Peacemaker can be overdone, in foreign policy as in domestic affairs, but the task of shifting the monarchy into a new century made some very necessary progress during the ten years of his reign.

CHAPTER 23

Modern Times

Only a series of historical flukes allowed the Buckingham Palace site to emerge into modern times as the ceremonial home of British reigning monarchs; nearly forty acres of prime residential land preserved as private property in the heart of London, containing within it the flaw in title which enabled a king to pick it up cheap.

It could easily have been otherwise. The La Neyte estate to the south, with a parallel early history, languished as semi-swamp and slowly fragmented into hutted slums. Only when intercepting drains finally brought order to London's sewage system and, in the 1840s, when Thomas Cubitt deposited huge quantities of clay there from excavations to form the London docks, did it dry out sufficiently for planned development to start. Poor occupants were ruthlessly turned out and elegant Belgravia took their place; Victoria Street was driven through Tothill slums to Pimlico, leaving no vestige of open space behind.

Some purists considered that the palace site was wretchedly cramped by these developments, although to the east and north it commanded improved processional vistas through freshly landscaped royal parks. Traditionally, English kings moved house when their palaces became too ramshackle to inhabit and Buckingham Palace was considered ripe for disposal in the last days of George III, its buildings described as being 'in woful condition, and . . . to be pulled down'.[1] Then the site was only saved because history had made it too splendid a setting to sell, too central to ignore, and once the costs of rebuilding started to roll up, no one in authority dared admit how much money had been wasted. Unlike its privately owned ancestors, new Buckingham Palace was consistently reviled as architecture and more often shuttered than used, at least until Edward VII came to the throne.

When, in 1910, George V followed his father there, its future was again called into question. The new king was a countryman at heart, not at all social by inclination, soon labelled as boring in company. Really he would have preferred to live in dark, cramped York Cottage on the Sandringham Estate. The old idea of selling the palace site and using the proceeds to renovate Kensington as a more rural town residence for the sovereign was briefly revisited, while Edwardian society speculated glumly about a king who actually preferred living in a cottage. The consensus was that such plebeian values signalled the beginning of the end, which within four years would prove an accurate judgement of the times.

Hedonistic pleasure was shown the palace door and sober virtue came back in fashion, together with reluctant recognition that a monarchy which relied on emotional loyalty for its survival could not afford to vacate the geographical centre of its realm. William Blake's site had finally interlocked with a delicate constitutional balance it would be lunacy to disturb, making Buckingham Palace a cross that British sovereigns simply had to bear, as George V himself was shrewd enough to recognize.[2] The king or queen who relinquished it, risked losing their crown as well.

Politically, it was unthinkable to demolish a building which had cost around £1.5 million of public money almost within living memory, not to mention Edward VII's lavish private renovations and a resurfacing of its eastern facade by Aston Webb in 1912, which successfully erased any vestiges of architectural character from its frontage. Nash's curved and decorated garden elevation survived, but only to grace those fortunate enough to stroll in the palace gardens. More intangibly but even more vitally, when the devastating wars of the twentieth century began only a short time later, the palace for the first time became a focus for mass gatherings of people rather than a Court.

This is not to say that grumbles about cost, archaic rituals and exclusivity ended, or that those monarchs forced to live there liked their palace any better. Queen Alexandra, when she finally and with her customary dilatoriness moved out to Marlborough House after Edward VII's death, described it as 'not *gemütlich*',[3] and it is fair to say that her husband's modernizations made its interior plan even more confusing than before. Passages were cut off by new bathrooms, whole suites of rooms isolated and in practice forgotten, practical convenience as distant as ever. As one critic wrote, 'doors open where you least expect them and lead from a room which can hold two hundred people quite comfortably into the kind of fastidious crevice which might have been designed for one particularly spruce young bachelor'.[4] The atmosphere too remained cold with a lingering smell of damp. It was ludicrously over-decorated and unwelcoming. Queen Mary did her best to humanize a few of the less intimidating rooms, resurrecting delicate regency furniture from forgotten corners and ruthlessly demanding back royal treasures from those who had, rightly or wrongly, squirreled them away. She liked chinoiserie and destested swags of gold dripping from pillars and ceilings, but except for a few scattered havens the sheer acreage of marble and gilding more or less defeated her. Later, she became a feared bargainer for treasures in her own right.

George V's personality as well as his dislike of Buckingham Palace only reinforced its more discouraging characteristics. Like his ancestor,

George III, he was verbose yet uninteresting in conversation, his political acumen and broadmindedness disguised by plodding routines.[5] He worked hard and defended his rights with a tenacity which often surprised his ministers, and through the many crises of his reign – from constitutional uproar to world war – conscientiously performed ceremonial duties which terrified him.[6] The unfortunate result of all this virtue on many of those compelled to be socially involved at the palace was frustrated boredom, and on his heir a traditional, rancorous Hanoverian dislike of his father. Perhaps Max Beerbohm best summed up society's reaction in acid couplets spoken by an imaginary lord- and lady-in-waiting:

HE:　. . . Last evening
I found him with a rural dean
Talking of district visiting:
The King is duller than the Queen.

SHE: At any rate he doesn't sew;
You don't see him embellishing
Yard after yard of calico.
The Queen is duller than the King.[7]

A foretaste of the social tensions of a new century came when a suffragette outwitted tight security at the palace and knelt at the king's feet during a drawing-room reception, shouting out for His Majesty to stop the torturing of women. The king's expression did not change, but he confessed afterwards that he did not know what the world was coming to, and the *Daily Mail*[8] showed a very modern gusto in its headline of 'Wild Woman in the Throne Room'.

Organized protest, the coming of war, banner headlines in the press and increased security; the twentieth century had arrived.

During the First World War, the king was quick to impose strict rationing on meals at the palace. No alcohol was served after April 1915, although few of his subjects chose to follow this particular route to victory. Ministers or ambassadors unlucky enough to eat at the palace were offered a single egg or slice of fish, precisely measured inches of unbuttered bread and lemonade or tea. Abstinence did not save the crown from criticism, however, and because some of this feeling was due to the German titles borne by many members of the royal family, in June 1917 the king decreed a general bonfire of them all. The Germans, he said, were his kinsmen, but he was ashamed of them. Henceforth the British royal family ceased to be Hanoverians and became Windsors; the serene highnesses, Tecks and Battenburgs around them either vanishing altogether as titles, or being Anglicized.

King George VI lies in state under the magnificent roof of Westminster Hall, whose timbers had been winched into place under his ancestor, Richard II, nearly 600 years before. Crown, Church and Parliament symbolically intersect at Westminster, then as now. (Illustrated London News)

After the war, the process of change continued. Garden parties increased in size to include a wider cross-section of the population, innocent parties to divorce were allowed within nodding distance, a few carefully selected actresses received. Socialists in the cabinet were the next shock and here the king proved more statesmanlike than his household officials, who were appalled by such characters as Fred Jowett, who made a political point by arriving to receive his seals of office wearing a cloth cap.[9] From the start, George V made it clear that he treated Labour ministers the same as any others, and he considered their prejudices reasonably. As a result, red-hot socialists came to value the monarchy and to their fury found it impossible to avoid occasionally wearing ridiculous clothes they despised as a gesture towards a monarch they respected.

Queen Elizabeth II rides to her coronation in the same coach and through equally enthusiastic crowds as her great-great-grandmother, Queen Victoria, a hundred and fifteen years earlier. Happily, the ceremony was much better organized. (Illustrated London News)

By the time of his Silver Jubilee in 1935, the king was genuinely surprised to discover how widely popular he had become. In the end, decorum, conscientiousness and family values proved outstandingly durable qualities in a head of state struggling through the treacherous years of change.

Edward VIII was too short a time on the throne to influence Buckingham Palace significantly, although he did install television there as early as 1936, together with a squash court and a few much-needed younger faces among the staff, which also stirred up the faction which rarely simmered far below the surface there.

To George VI was handed the difficult task of making the monarchy respectable again; people had called his father dull but recoiled from unorthodoxy when they met it in his son, and were in a dissatisfied, uncertain mood so far as palaces and Court flunkeys were concerned. As one Labour minister commented, an idler in the palace performing a purely decorative task was paid more than full-time workmen in his constituency, adding ominously, 'As for ladies of the bedchamber I have seen some of them. They would not be ladies in my bedchamber.'[10]

Almost inevitably, nothing was done to simplify Court rituals or staffing. Already the nation's attention was on Hitler, and during the Second World War the palace staff was drastically scaled down anyway. Buckingham Palace was hit nine times by bombs in air raids and twice in one week, when the queen declared she was glad they had been bombed since she could now look the much worse-hit East Enders in the eye. The royal family remained in London, Princess Elizabeth joined the services and the king travelled widely in Britain, and abroad among his troops; his genuine if shy nature was almost an advantage in such circumstances, as was the warmth of his consort, and there was little sense of resentment over privilege or, during the war years, almost non-existent exclusivity.

Like his father, George VI was scrupulous over rations and sharing such hardship as he could. When Mrs Eleanor Roosevelt stayed at Buckingham Palace in 1942, in spite of being given the queen's own bedroom she instantly joined the club of earlier, nineteenth-century palace visitors by finding it intolerably spartan. The windows were boarded up except for minute mica panels in the middle, through which a few rays of light reluctantly filtered. The bitter draughts in her huge royal bedchamber seemed only to be increased by the single, small electric fire allowed there. The food was tepid and tasteless, but served on gold plates which generations of banquet guests had rightly complained were impossible to heat.

Unsurprisingly, the king and queen were both hatching colds. She expected to hatch one soon herself. The only light relief was Winston Churchill, who returned from a telephone call raucously singing 'Roll out the Barrel' when he learned part-way through the meal that the attack at El Alamein was going well. Understandably, she bolted for the American Embassy at the first opportunity.[11]

When victory brought a swift breakup of many established patterns, including a loss of Empire, difficulties returned to a revived Court at Buckingham Palace which changed too little, although open public ciriticism was delayed for a while by affection for the king and queen, the glamour and dedication of a new reign. Reform in any real sense remained elusive. Political change was fairly easily accommodated, even if a seismic shock shuddered through the royal system when the household servants appointed their own shop steward and joined a trade union. But beyond politics as such, it was the scarcely grasped change in modern attitudes which, almost imperceptibly at first, loomed like a lee shore through the murk of tabloid gossip and increasingly visible hypocrisies of class: a growing, cynical and utilitarian approach to the state itself, and all its institutions.

The contrast is, that within such a tempest of change some things remained more unchangeable than before. In previous centuries nothing prevented owners from tearing down well-known landmarks, as the Duke of Buckingham tore down Arlington House and George IV happily demolished the duke's replacement. Royal parks were encroached on. Kings stole a quarter of all the land in England from the Church. The Tyburn was diverted, dried up, changed course, was contained, broke loose, was forgotten and reappeared under the palace floor. Nowadays buildings are listed, heritage consigned to museums, ownerships registered – none of which are bad in themselves but they bring to an end the history of the palace site. It exists, unchanging, and for the first time is open to the public for two months of the year; short of cataclysm it will not be allowed to fall down, or throw out new wings, or have a fort built in the garden.

An end to history for a site is possible, if dull. For the monarchs who inhabit this particular site it is different, and yet they are regarded as heritage too, skewered for merciless vivisection. It is salutary to realize how rarely British kings and queens have actually been popular, and how habitually their families have created public scandals; but it was solid constitutional worth which in the past led ministers wearily to continue defending the Crown from attack, and some affection too.

It takes generations for a great national institution, once rooted, to be grown away from, and we are too close to events to know whether, with the monarchy, this process is now under way. But if monarchy can demonstrate few serious grounds for its continuing existence in modern Britain, there is equally little doubt that it can still work, it is useful, it does add valued glamour to the otherwise drab trade of government.

Here the Buckingham Palace site is again symbolic, a modern paradox; one of the most visible properties in London, whose extent nowadays is largely hidden, a void in most people's topography of the capital. It is there, it looks grand and you drive around it, seeing only trees above spiked walls. The building's size is disguised by Blore and Webb's blank frontage, broken only by a small balcony from which small figures occasionally wave. Nash's elegant rear elevation, the Duke of Buckingham's courtyard and the five-acre lake which still holds drainage water, are all hidden; so is the Tyburn which runs beneath it now, happily in a metal pipe.

But many of the people who fill every acre of this site with such a richly complex inner life, those ghosts who beckon us through the back door of imagination to enjoy their quite different palace which is ours as well, remain surprisingly neighbourly in death.

The villagers of old Eye Cross lie in unmarked graves around where their chapel once stood on an island in the marsh. The monks of Westminster are together still in their abbey, Abbots Litlington and Islip in fine tombs of their own. Also in the Abbey are Edward the Confessor, Geoffrey de Mandeville and his wife, Athelys. Edward I is only yards from the monks who helped to steal his treasure. Next to him lie Henry III and his saucy consort; a few paces away, Queen Elizabeth and James I. A great many laymen are there too: George Goring; the Duke of Buckingham and his tragic son, also his mother-in-law, that witty whore, Catherine Sedley. Her vain daughter lies wrapped in the royal pomp she chose for her burial; Lionel Cranfield under an elegant effigy in a side-aisle; and between the abbey and St Margaret's, Alexander Davies.

Others are missing. Queen Edith and William Rolfe were buried not very far apart, in Wiltshire. William the Conqueror's bones lie in Caen. Harry the Eighth, George III and Victoria are unlikely bedfellows at Windsor. The remains of Hugh Audley and William Blake are in Temple Church. Mary Davies lies alone in Cheshire, Lord Arlington with his wife in Suffolk. The Witch of Eye became cinders long ago in Smithfield and was trodden into the dirt.

All of them share with us a thousand-year memory of one place, where forest was once divided from swampy levels by a narrow, steep-banked stream.

Opening Dates and Times for the Royal Palaces

BUCKINGHAM PALACE

Palace: normally open August, September and early October, times and days to be advertised. Advance booking advisable.

Royal Mews, Buckingham Palace: January to late March, Wed only 12.00–16.00. Late March to late September, Tues, Wed, Thurs 12.00–16.00. Early October to mid-December, Wed only 12.00–16.00. Closed mid-December to early January. Check precise dates if close to the time of your visit.

The Queen's Gallery (art exhibitions): early March until just before Christmas, Tues to Sat 10.00–17.00; Sun 14.00–17.00; Bank Holiday 10.00–17.00.

Changing of the Guard: normally on alternate days at 11.30.

ST JAMES'S PALACE

Largely closed to the public.

WHITEHALL PALACE

The Banqueting Hall in Whitehall is the only surviving part of the palace, which burnt down in 1698. Mon to Sat 10.00–17.00, closed Christmas and New Year.

KENSINGTON PALACE

Mon to Sat 9.00–17.00; Sun 11.00–17.00.

WINDSOR CASTLE

Parts of the castle are open daily 10.00–16.00.

St George's Chapel: open as for castle and for worship on Sundays.

Changing of the Guard: every day between May and early August at 11.00 outside the Guardroom in the Lower Ward; alternate days the rest of the year.

The Queen's Gifts and Royal Carriages: display of presents from all over the world, and of royal transport. Same hours as the castle.

Notes

PROLOGUE

1. Queen Victoria's Journal, 27 June–2 July 1838.
2. Lytton Strachey and Roger Fulford (ed.). *Charles Greville, The Greville Memoirs 1814–1860*, (8 vols, London, Macmillan, 1938).
3. Queen Victoria's Journal.
4. Earl of Stanhope, *Notes of Conversations with the Duke of Wellington 1831–1851* (Oxford University Press, 1931). Earl of Albemarle, *Fifty Years of My Life* (London, 1877).
5. In 1763.
6. Arthur Stanley, *Twenty Years at Court* (London, 1888).
7. Queen Victoria's Journal.
8. Pencil note on copy of Coronation Service, Royal Library, Windsor.
9. Cecil Woodham Smith, *Queen Victoria*, (London, Hamish Hamilton, 1972), Vol. I.
10. M.W. Chapman (ed.), *Harriet Martineau, Autobiography and Letters* (London, 1877).

1. A FRONTIER OF EMPIRE

1. Felix Barker and Peter Jackson, *London, 2000 Years of a City and its People*, (London, Cassell, 1974), p. 3. There is a discussion on early Roman approaches to London by Peter Marsden in *Roman London* (Thames & Hudson, 1980). A Feb. 1995 Channel 4 'Timeteam' investigation produced further evidence of a gravel bank and crossing point to Thorney Island.
2. Dio Cassius, *Roman History*, Book LX, Suetonius, *Lives of the First Twelve Caesars*. See also Stopford Frere, *Britannia* (Routledge, 1987); R.J. Adam, *Conquest of England* (London, Hodder, 1968).
3. N.J. Barton, *Lost Rivers of London* (London, Phoenix House, 1962).

2. QUEEN WITH HANDBAG

1. William of Malmesbury, *Gesta Regum Anglorum* (ed. W. Stubbs, Rolls Series 1887–9) refers to a *monasteriolum* housing an insignificant dozen monks; the *Vita Edwardi Regis* (anon, but see Ch. 4, n. 6 below) to a small community struggling to provide its daily bread.

2. Bede, *Ecclesiastical History of the English People* (trs. Judith McClure and Roger Collins, World Classics, OUP), p. 74, where the translators have replaced the evocative word 'mart' with 'emporium', which sounds oddly Victorian.

3. Recorded in Domesday Book as held of Queen Edith by William the Chamberlain at the time of Conquest, 1066.

4. The best-known chronicles are *Vita Edwardi Regis*, written by a monk in Edith's employ and later extensively rewritten and falsified (see Ch. 4, no. 6); the *Anglo-Saxon Chronicle* and William of Malmesbury. All have to be carefully gleaned for direct and indirect information. Frank Barlow, *Edward the Confessor* (London, Methuen, 1970) is invaluable for the period immediately before the Conquest.

5. Frank Barlow (ed.), *Vita Edwardi Regis* (Nelson's Medieval Texts, 1962), p. 14.

6. Ibid. Probably a later addition.

7. William of Malmesbury.

8. J. Stevenson (ed.), *Chronicon Monasterii de Abingdon*, Rolls Series 1858.

9. *William of Poitiers* (Classiques de la France, 1952), pp. 166–8.

10. Barlow, *Vita Edwardi Regis*, pp. 53–4.

11. *William of Poitiers*, pp. 166–8.

3. THE CONQUEROR AND HIS PLUTOCRAT

1. *Anglo-Saxon Chronicle*, (ed. D. Whitelock with D.C. Douglas and S.I. Tucker, *English Historical Documents*, Oxford, OUP, 1961), Vol. I, Year 1066. *Carmen de Hastingae Proelio*, attrib. to Guy, Bishop of Amiens (ed. F. Michel, *Chroniques anglo-normandes*, Vol. III, pp. 1–40).

2. Michel, *Carmen*.

3. Prevost and Delisle (eds.), *Ordericus Vitalis, Historia Ecclesiastica* (Paris, 1838–55).

4. William of Malmesbury records her as saying she was '*de perpetua integritate*'; Vol. I, p. 239.

5. Michel, *Carmen*.

6. W.J. Corbett, 'Development of the Duchy of Normandy' in *Cambridge Mediaeval History*, V (Cambridge, CUP, 1964).

7. Davis (ed.), *Regesta Regum Anglo-Normannorum*, (Oxford, OUP, 1968), Vol. III, p. 273. See also Judith Green, *Anglo-Norman Sheriffs* (London, 1923).

8. *Anglo-Saxon Chronicle*.

9. Called Aeleneve Wateman (Waterman?) '*De hac terro Goisfridus de Mannervilus erat saisitus quando ivit transmare in servitum Regis*'. (Domesday Book).

10. Where he was recorded as receiving land subject to a previous English owner's obligations to Barking Abbey, which he extinguished – illegally but with impunity.

11. K.R. Potter (ed.) *Gesta Stephani* (Nelson's Medieval Texts, 1955).

12. Westminster Abbey, Liber Niger, f. 56. The grant is undated but Eia was listed as owned by de Mandeville in Domesday Book (1086), and the grant was confirmed by William the Conqueror, who died in Sept. 1087. Its date must therefore be 1086/7.

13. Darby and Terrett (eds.), *Domesday Geography of South East England* (Cambridge, CUP, 1972). A seventeenth-century map in the possession of the Grosvenor Estates still shows traces of these small closes, and the stone cross at Eye was specifically mentioned as a landmark in 23Hen VIII c21 (Sept. 1531).

4. FASHION AND FORGERY

1. M. Rule (ed.), *Eadmer, Vita Sancta Anselmi*, Rolls Series 1884. A.J. Macdonald, *Life of Archbishop Lanfranc* (Oxford, OUP, 1944).
2. J. Armitage Robinson, 'The Letters of Osbert de Clare' in Williamson (ed.), *Osbert de Clare* (Oxford, OUP, 1929); C. Brooke, *London, The Shaping of a City 800–1216* (Secker, 1975); Anstruther, *Scriptores Monastici*, 109–203, Cotton MS. See also *Ordericus Vitalis* XVII, and DNB.
3. Edward Carpenter (ed.), *A House of Kings, the Official History of Westminster Abbey* (Westminster Abbey Bookshop, 1966).
4. In *English Historical Review* LXXVI (July 1961) Scholtz pointed to St Denis, Paris, as the place from which consultants were hired.
5. These forgeries and Osbert's hand in them are detected in P. Chaplais, 'The Original Charters of Herbert and Gervase, Abbots of Westminster (1121–1157)', in *A Medieval Miscellany for Doris Mary Stenton*, ed. P.M. Barnes and C.F. Slade, Pipe Rolls Society, New Series, Vol. xxxvi, 1961. See also Bishop and Chaplais, *Facsimiles of English Royal Writs to 1100* (Oxford, OUP, 1957).
6. Osbert either compiled or totally overhauled the *Vita Edwardi* (see Ch. 2, n. 4) with the aim of sanctifying Edward the Confessor, which makes a balanced evaluation of his reign even more difficult today.
7. Bishop and Chaplais, *Facsimiles* Barker discusses the topographical outlines of Osbert's charter in *Lost Rivers*.
8. DNB.
9. R.W. Southern, 'The Canterbury Forgeries' in *English Historical Review* LXIII, April 1958.

5. BURGLARY

1. A translation by H.E. Butler of *Fitzstephen's Description* was attached to Sir Frank Stenton's *Norman London* (1934); reprinted and revised in G. Barraclough (ed.), *Social Life in Early England* (London, Routledge, 1960).
2. J.T. Appleby (ed.), *Chronicle of Richard of Devizes* (Nelson's Medieval Texts, 1963).
3. A windmill probably existed at Clerkenwell Nunnery as early as 1144, which makes it possible that Fitzstephen was describing wind rather than water or muscle-power: William J. Keeley, *Harvesting the Air* (Univ. of Calif. Press, 1987).
4. Barker, *Lost Rivers*.
5. Ibid.
6. Carpenter, *House of Kings*.

7. Brown and Hopkins, 'Seven Centuries of Building Wages' in Carus-Wilson (ed.), *Essays reprinted for the Economic History Society* (London, Arnold, 1962),Vol. II.

8. Westminster Abbey Library, EdII, 'Grant from Alice and Muriel daughters of Ysabel widow of Walter de Wylton, to Nicholas de Porta and Edith his wife of land in Longditch Street Westminster at a yearly rent of one Rose, witness, John of Eia'.

9. In 1334 the assessment was cut in half, from £10 13s 7d to £4 12s 6d, which continued into the fifteenth century. PRO E179/141/ 6–7 (1334); the medieval status of Westminster is extensively discussed in G. Rosser, *Medieval Westminster* (Oxford, OUP, 1989).

10. I am indebted to Prof. Tout for his unravelling of relevant documents in 'A Medieval Burglary', a lecture given in the John Rylands Library, 1915, and reprinted in *Collected Papers of T.F. Tout* (Manchester UP, 1934),Vol. III.

6. TRIUMPH OUT OF DISASTER

1. Henry Lucas, 'The Great European Famine of 1315–17' in *Speculum* (*The Journal of Medieval Studies*, Medieval Academy of America), Spring 1920 and reprinted in Carus-Wilson, *Essays for the Economic History Society,* Vol. II.

2. John Trokelowe, monk of St Albans, wrote a historical chronicle for the years 1307–23 (during part of which he was himself in prison). H.G. Riley (ed.), Rolls Series 1866, in Vol. IV of *Chronica Monasterii S. Albani.*

3. Estimates projected from those given in Lucas, 'Famine'.

4. Abstract of charters in 'A Cartulary of Westminster Abbey in the possession of Samuel Bentley Esq. 1836', College of Arms.

5. Ministers' accounts PRO bundle 919, 12–24.

6. Ibid. 919, 14–17. See also W. Loftie Rutton, 'The Manor of Eia next Westminster' in *Archaelogica* (Society of Antiquaries, London), Jan. 1910.

7. WAM 16251. (Westminster Abbey Muniments)

8. Cotton MS Claud. A VIII f. 69; Dugdale (ed.), *Monasticon Anglicanum* (London, 1817–30), quoted DNB; Liber Niger f. 85b; WAM 9470.1. Litlington was probably connected with the great family of Le Despenser whether illegitimately or otherwise, whose arms he displayed, and possibly even to the king, Edward III. The monastic habit of giving up birth names on entry and taking a simple geographical identification makes certainty impossible – he probably came from Littlington, Middx, where the abbey had estates. In later life he named his parents as Hugh and Joan, and established a mass in their memory every 26 September in Great Malvern Priory. On a personal level, he was clearly a falconry fanatic, a sport favoured by marshy land like Eye, on one occasion offering a huge 2s. reward for finding a lost falcon (and rewarding the actual finder with 3s. 4d.); in 1367 he paid 6d. to have a wax falcon moulded, to be offered as prayer for a sick falcon's recovery.

9. Ashwell, Herts. The inscriptions in Latin say: *MCter penta miseranda ferox violenta/MCCL/superest plebs pessima testis; In fine ije/ventis validus/MCCC/oc anno Maurus in orbe tonat LXI; primula pestis i Mter CCC fuit L minus uno.'*

10. R.S. Sylvester (ed.), *The Complete Works of Thomas More* (Yale UP, 1963), Vol. II. (And see Ch. 8, n. 8).

11. Westminster Court Rolls October 1377; Abbey Court Rolls, WAM 50699–782 (1364–1514).

12. Exclusion from Pardon of William Peche: Rot. Parl (Rec Com) iii, p. 111.

7. THE WITCH OF EYE

1. William Langland, *Richard the Redeless*.

2. PRO KB 9/176/73; quoted in Rosser, *Westminster*.

3. J.S. Davis (ed.), *English Chronicle* (Camden Soc., 1856), p. 59.

4. J.O. Halliwell (ed.) *Chronicle of Henry VI* (Camden Soc., 1839), cap 7.

5. Davis, *Chronicle*, p. 58; Halliwell, *Chronicle*; J.S. Stevenson (ed.), *William of Worcester*, Rolls Series 1861–4.

6. H. Ellis (ed.), *Fabyan, New Chronicle of England and France* (1811).

7. *Chronicles of London*, Vitellius A XVI 1440–1.

8. Ibid.

9. Ibid., p. 129; Stevenson, *William of Worcester*, p. 460; Cotton MS Cleopatra C(iv); 'Lament of the Duchess of Gloucester', Rawlinson MS fifteenth- and sixteenth-century Songs. See also K.H. Vickers, *Humphrey, Duke of Gloucester* (Constable, 1972).

10. 'Was taken Margarie Gourdemaine, a witch of Eye beside Westminster, whose sorcerie and witchcraft Dame Eleanor Cobham had long time used and by her medicines and drinkes enforced the Duke of Gloucester to love her and after to wed her, wherefore and for cause of relapse, the same witch was brent at Smythfield ye 27 October 1441.' *Chronicles*, Vitellius. WAM 26947B (1393/4) records dealings with 'A farmer of Kine named Jourdemayn', who must have been a relative, and quite likely was Margarie's father or grandfather – if so, a pig farmer in his own right would have been modestly prosperous.

8. ROYAL RETURN

1. WAM 6623, 6624; 32183.

2. Westminster Abbey accounts 1420–85; Abbey Lease Books i–iv (1485–1550). A letter dated 25 March 1467 is addressed directly to 'John Noreys, ffermour at Eybury'. WAM 26984–98 for accompts as bailiff.

3. Vestry Accounts for the Parish of St Margaret, quoted DNB.

4. Carpenter, *House of Kings*, notes the abbey's steward accounting in 1501 for entertaining the king: 'a barrel of strong ale 2s, wine and strawberries 3s. 8d', and 'a potel of wyne to souse ffysche wt (4d)'. Also recorded are 'ii marybons for ii podyngis for the Kyng, 2d.' WAM 24622–49. Henry VII's domestic treasurer's accounts note the annual despatch of wine from the royal cellars.

5. Islip granted a 32-year lease of Eybury to Richard Whasshe at Michalmas 1518, at an annual rent of £21, Abbey Lease Books.

6. Including Geoffrey Chaucer's old lodging. Stow (Annales) writes: 'The chappel of oure laidie and also a taverne neere adioyning called the White

Rose were taken down, on whiche plot on 24 januarie (1502/3) the first stone of our Lady Chappel was laid by the hands of Joh: Islip abbot.'

7. Complaint of Westminster Manor Court, 1533.
8. Incredibly, when Cardinal Wolsey tried to administer an oath to Islip whereby he would swear that those in sanctuary would not commit treason while there, Islip refused. It would, he said, negate the whole principle of sanctuary. Carpenter, *House of Kings*.
9. Dugdale (ed.), *Monasticon Anglicanum* i, p. 217.
10. Rosser, *Westminster*, is a mine of information on this and other subjects in the period.
11. WAM 17117–8.
12. '*Libros galici gestus*'. Quoted in Rosser, *Westminster*.
13. Cal. Pat. Rolls 1345–5, p. 544.
14. PRO E368/123, m49. A. Gasquet, *The Black Death of 1348–9* (London, Methuen, 1893). P. Ziegler, *The Black Death* (London, Penguin, 1982).
15. The lack of supervision and continuing dispute with Westminster Abbey over title enabled the Crown to assume rights there over the years, particularly during the many disasters of the fourteenth-century.
16. PRO E41/216; E41/238. See also Stow, *A Survey of London and Westminster* (ed. Kingsford, Everyman edition, 1955). The transfer to Henry VIII from Eton College reads: 'Indenture made 5 September 23Hen VIII between the King and Roger Lipton, Provost of Eton College, covenanting that the King shall have the site etc of the house of St James-in-the-Field with 185 1/2 acres between Charing Cross and Aye Hill. . . .'

9. ENTRY OF THE SPECULATORS

1. 28Hen VIII 49.
2. J. Armitage Robinson (ed.), *Flete's History of Westminster Abbey* (Cambridge, CUP, 1909, original written in the fifteenth century); Carpenter, *House of Kings*.
3. Stow, *Survey of London*, p. 402.
4. St Martin-in-the-Fields, sixteenth-century Vestry Minutes.
5. Pat. Roll 1033 9ElizI.
6. J. MacMaster, *Short History of St Martin-in-the-Fields* (London, 1861), quotes from documents apparently since lost.
7. A son, John, was christened in Kensington, 1608. He was deep in property disputes by 1611 (Ch. 11, n. 20); see also M. Prestwich, *Cranfield and the Politics of Profit* (Oxford, OUP, 1966), p. 479.
8. Cranfield papers i, 17–26, Historical Manuscripts Comm.
9. C.T. Gatty, *Mary Davies and the Manor of Ebury* (2 vols., London, Cassell, 1921), Vol. I.
10. A variety of sources fill in parts of the puzzle of Rolfe's life and background, his business and kin relationships with Blake: Hon. Soc. of Inner Temple registers; British Library, Sloane MSS 1044 f. 261; Gwilt, *Thomas and Henry Smith of London* pp. 24–9, 69; Somerset and Dorset Notes and Queries, x 310; Wiltshire Record Office, wills and herald visitation 1625, justice sessions

1580–1 and 1592, coroners' returns 1768, 1781, 1788; Decree Rolls PRO C78/371/1, 373/2, 429/8, 433/12. 465/7, 489/20; Privy Council Registers PC2/45/293, 335, and 341; transactions of the House of Lords 3628 (Jan 1642/3); Journal of the House of Lords VII 9, 14, 23 Feb 1642/3, 24 April 1645; Humble petition of William Blake to the House of Lords, Main papers f. 110; leaflet history of Enford in Wiltshire by the late Revd Lawrence; VCH Wiltshire, Enford entry; Prestwich, *Cranfield*.

11. Wiltshire RO, Herald visitation 1625 signed, Thomas Hawker.

12. Humble Petition of Anne Blake (née Hawker) to the House of Lords, 21 Jan. 1642/3.

13. A. Friis, *Alderman Cockayne's Project* (Copenhagen and Oxford, OUP, 1927); B.E. Supple, *Commercial Crisis and Change 1600–42* (Cambridge, CUP, 1959).

14. Prestwich, *Cranfield*. Sackville MSS 4453–9, 4580. Friis, *Alderman Cockayne*, quotes from a note made of this debate by Sir Julius Caesar, 12 and 14 Jan. 1616.

15. BL, Sloane MSS 1044 f. 261; for Pembroke connection see VCH Wiltshire V.

16. Gwilt, *Thomas and Henry Smith*, although he mistakes the name of Rolfe's first wife, letter to the author from History of Parliament Project, University of London, April 1992.

17. VCH Wiltshire I, p. 119.

18. Kensington Parish Register, 2 Nov. 1630, where Blake is described as 'a religious and charitable good friend to the parish'. If this seems surprising in view of his business dealings, it would not be difficult to find modern examples of private virtue allied to political or commercial trickery.

19. Anne Blake's petition.

20. On 10 March 1638 Sir Henry Vane paid Audley £30 for an acre of land 'in or neare a place called the Gravell Pitts at the Cawsey way head, leading to the Windmill within the parish of St Martin in the Fields . . .'. This may have referred to the old Abbot's causeway since Audley's accounts described it as 'part of ye Neate lands.' On another deed it is described as in Ebury, and appears most likely placed as convenient horse grazing somewhere in the wet roughetts south of Blake House (Grosvenor London Docs. 49). As late as 1658 petitioners to the Privy Council are still complaining about the Westminster–Tothill–Ebury roadway, which is 'made up of many thousands of barrows of earth.'

21. The latest as recently as May 1625.

22. Prestwich, *Cranfield*.

10. ANNE HAWKER OF HEYTESBURY

1.   Robert Ashton (ed.), *James I by his Contemporaries* (Cambridge, CUP, 1969). J. Larwood, *The Story of the London Parks* (2 vols., London, 1881), Vol. II.

2.   Circular to Sheriffs, Deputy Lieutenants etc, Harl MS 703 p. 140.

3.   £935 expended 'for embanking a piece of ground and planting mulberries near the palace of Westminster', Cal SP 1603–10, p. 562.

4. Howe's continuation of Stow's *A Survey of London and Westminster* says that Stallenge had succeeded in producing 'a fine silk for all uses', while experimenting on his own account.

5. PRO Exchequer Records, 15 May 1611: 'To William Stallenge, Esquire the sum of £258.2.5d without account, impress, or other charges to be set upon him . . . for any part thereof'.

6. Anne Blake's petition.

7. Ibid.

8. Ibid., '. . . That the better to draw on the said Match, Rolfe affirmed he would do great Matters for the said William Blake, being his next kinsman; and that Wm Blake [Snr] should settle his lands, valued at Seven Hundred Pounds per annum or the Office called the Fine Office, on his said son's choice'.

9. Anne Blake's petition. William Blake's counter-petition.

10. Complaint to benchers of Inner Temple, Jan. 1624/5.

11. Two children survived to be baptised during this time: 'Oct 20 1626 William so. of Wm Blake the younger and Anne, his wyef'; and 'July 5 1629 Marye da of Wm Blake the younger and Ame [sic] his wyef'; both on Kensington Parish Register, as is the death of William the younger's brother, John, on 21 May 1627 [christened 1608].

12. Hale House had been sold by William Weddell to William Blake in 1612 for £80, to be resold by Blake the younger to William Methwold, 1630. It stood on the site of the Natural History Museum and was demolished in 1854. Better known by its later name of Cromwell House when in the eighteenth century it became equipped with the unlikely myth that Oliver Cromwell had once hidden in a niche by its fireplace. It is possible Oliver's son briefly lived there, and in any event the present Cromwell Road is probably named after it.

11. CORRUPTION

1. Gatty, *Mary Davies*, Vol. I, p. 45. A surprising grant was made to Knyvett and Doubleday in 1609 'of the office of keeping plate in the Tower and the coining of money there and elsewhere'. Quite what was behind that I cannot find out.

2. The anonymous author of *Anglorum Speculum*, 1606, refers to Doubleday as 'a Man of great Stature, Valour, Gravity and Activity'.

3. This particular series of complex deals was unravelled by Prestwich, *Cranfield*.

4. Sackville MSS (v) 1625–6. Prestwich, *Cranfield*.

5. Sackville MSS, in a letter to Cranfield, dated 30 July 1625, Blake wrote, 'There dieth every day in London at the least 500 or 600 persons. I leave it to your lordship's consideration if this be a time for despatch of such business'.

6. Isaac D'Israeli, *Curiosities of Literature* (1791), Vol. II.

7. Sackville MSS (v), Cranfield to Catchmay, 5 July 1625.

8. Ibid. Catchmay to Cranfield, 7 July 1625.

9.   Prestwich, *Cranfield*; Gatty, *Mary Davies*, Vol. I, p. 100.
10. Cal. of Inner Temple Vol. II records show the three highest additional assessments on benchers at this time to be: £10 Hugh Audley 'for Wards and Livery'; £10 William Blague 'for office of Chirographer'; £6 13s. 4d. William Rolfe 'for office of Clerk to the Warrant'.
11. And of Hampshire in 1630. Also see n. 18 below.
12. Anne Blake's petition reads in part '. . . his [Blake senior's] son [was] over-awed by Fear of his Father and won by Flattery of Rolfe'.
13. Ibid. '. . . by underhand Agreement between him and Sir William Blake, the said Manor [Heytesbury] was designed partly to pay Rolfe's debts and engagements and his [Blake's] own, and partly for surety for Sir William Blake's [house]; and pretending only to be but a Trustee, by that Pretence his Name was inserted as a Joint Purchaser of the said Manor with Sir William Blake.'
14. William Blake (the younger's) undated counter-petition to the House of Lords, 1642/3.
15. Ibid.
16. Ibid.
17. Journals of the House of Lords, VIII 67: 'If this Cause be not shewed to this House by Monday come Sevennight, then the Cause between Rolfe and Blake is to be dismissed this House.'
18. Privy Council Registers PRO PC2/45/293,335,341.
19. Kensington parish register, 17 April 1666, records the christening of William, son of William and Anne Blake. This may be William the Younger and Anne Hawker's grandson, if their son William by coincidence married another Anne; no marriage recorded in Kensington, and if the father is their son, he would by then have been 40 years old.
20. Rolfe was specially admitted to Inner Temple at the rquest of Edmund Prideaux on 23 June 1617, and Blake is recorded as involved in property development with Prideaux in 1611, when a dispute flared over rights to light.

12. A COURT OF ROGUES

1   DNB; Sir Walter Scott (ed.), *The Secret History of James I*, (2 vols., London, 1811), Vol. I, p. 399, describes him as a 'Master of Games and fooleries'.
2.   Robert Ashton, *The Crown and the Money Market* (Oxford, OUP, 1960). William Hyman, *Court Patronage and Corruption* (London, Unwin, 1991).
3.   Earl of Clarendon, *History of the Great Rebellion* (Folio Society edn., Oxford, OUP, 1967).
4.   Ashton, *The Crown*; D. Starkey (ed.), *The English Court from the Wars of the Roses to the Civil War* (Harlow, Longman, 1987).
5.   Naval costs computed at £47,403 in 1640 by Professor Dietz in *English Public Finance 1558–1640* (American Hist. Assoc. 1964). Goring's income from tobacco monopoly alone was approx. £29,000, sugar brought him a further £4,000 (Ashton, *The Crown*), plus innumerable other positions and perks.

6.   Notes on a plan of Ebury Manor, BM, Add MS 38104. One contradiction exists to the sequence of events described above, 1623–33: a complaint to the Privy Council on 13 March 1629 'Concerning a building intended to be erected neare his majestie's Mulberry Garden by Sir William Black [sic]'. From the first-hand evidence of Anne Hawker's petition to the House of Lords, it is clear that Blake was already in deep financial trouble by 1629 and probably ill: he died the following year. The Grosvenor Papers say that he 'inclosed and built up in this half acre . . . a faire house', in 1623 (Gatty *Mary Davies*, Vol. I, p. 101), and 1629 makes no sense with other events, since Audley was in control of Ebury Manor from 1626. I would suggest that the petitioners were in fact concerned about a likelihood that Blake would shortly be forced to sell, and the purchaser – already rumoured to be Goring – would build a far grander house which would fundamentally alter the agricultural/horticultural character of the area. If corrrect, this supposition further downgrades Blake House to a farmhouse-style building. In 1633 Goring did build 'another pile of building joining south to Sir William Blake's' (BM, Add MS 38104).

7.   PRO Works (vi) no 121 calculates £12,000 on embellishments to the house alone.

8.   Note on a plan of Ebury Manor, BM, Add MS 38104.

9.   Larwood, *London Parks*, Vol. II.

10. Seventeenth-century map belonging to the Grosvenor Estate, copied with modern street plan laid on, Gatty, *Mary Davies*, endpaper to Vol. II.

11. Details unravelled by Gatty, *Mary Davies*, Vol. I.

12. PRO Exchequer Papers, Grant to Lord Aston 4 July 1628. Aston's name as tenant of Mulberry Garden first appears in the St Martin-in-the-Fields' Rate Book, 1627.

13. In 1660 Goring petitioned Charles II for a grant of Mulberry Garden 'according to a former grant thereof prepared by Sir John Barnes, attorney general, and signed by the late King but interrupted in passing the Great seal by the Distraction of the ensuing times'. Cal. SP, Treasury, 1660–7.

14. Privy Seal Grant, 29 July 1640.

15. Gatty, *Mary Davies*, Vol. I, p. 102.

16. N. Brett-James, *The Fortification of London* (London Topographical Society, 1927). City Records, Journals of the Court of Common Council, 40, f. 52.

17. City Records, Letter Book, QQ f. 99b, 10 Jan. 1643/4.

18. Cal. SP, Venice, 1642/3 p. 252, et seq.

19. William Lithgow, *The Present Surveigh of London and England's State* (1643). On the copy of his pamphlet in the British Library a contemporary hand has scribbled his comment on the author as 'a Schotch man and a Lyar', but on forts at least Lithgow appears to know what he is talking about.

20. Journals of Common Council, 44, ff. 56, 59, 61; Cal. SP Dom. 1645–6, 380–1; City Letter Book, QQ 145–8, 162, 189–90, 215, 339. On 9 Jan. 1647 the House of Commons ordered 'that the Petition of Hugh Awdley and Robert Harvy be referred to the Consideration of the Committee of the Revenue, to give the Petitioners Satisfaction for Goreing House during that Time which the French Ambassador enjoy'd it'.

21. William Lenthall, Speaker of the Long Parliament, is chiefly celebrated for his reply to Charles I when the king entered the House to arrest five members by force: 'May it please Your Majesty, I have neither eyes to see nor tongue to speak in this place but as the House shall direct me.' After this high point he trimmed unscrupulously, and died in possession of a large estate, forgiven by Charles II.

22. Matthew Carter, Goring's Quartermaster, wrote an account of the campaign: '*A most True and Exact Relation of that Unfortunate and Honourable Expedition of Kent, Essex and Colchester, 1650.*'

23. Carter, '*A most True and Exact Relation*'. 'Lenthall is said to have received some favour [from Goring] while in youth.'

24. Acts & Ordinances of the Interregnum, i, 1008.

25. Maitland, *History of London* (1756), p. 1365, remarks on the remains of 'three forts . . . one at the lower end of Bruton Street, another at Oliver's Mount, [Mount Street, Mayfair] and the third at Tibourne Lane, Hide Park Road'. In 1746 one fort was noted as 'complete to this day', in the Duke of Bedford's garden, Southampton House (note on BM K20, 16). Revetted trenches were retained as a natural feature there until 1800, when they disappeared under Russell Square; these can be clearly seen in an anonymous drawing of Southampton House held by the London Museum.

26. Conveyance by Trustees of Mary Davies of Goring House to Lord Arlington, 1677, following passage of a private act in 1675 enabling them to do so. (See Ch. 14, n. 6.)

13. 'A RASCALLY WHORING SORT OF PLACE'

1. When Charles I complimented Dean Williams on his courage, he received an acid retort: 'I am a true Welshman and they are observed never to run away until their generals first forsake them.' This, and a letter from Captain Slingsby to Sir John Pennington (SP Dom 1641) quoted in E.T. Bradley, *Annals of Westminster Abbey* (London, 1891).

2. Pepys, 23 Sept. 1660.

3. Gatty, *Mary Davies*, Vol. I, p. 104.

4. DNB, quoting from Wood, *Athenae Oxoniensis*, iii, p. 902.

5. Goring never paid more than his original deposit of £520 and the agreement to sell therefore lapsed in law, as Audley quite probably calculated it would.

6. Cal. SP. Dom. 1656, 262. Davies was pursued by money-lenders who had advanced cash to George Goring, and this comment appears in his reply to their claim, 1663.

7. Chancery Decree, 28 April 1662.

8. Note on Inner Temple Annual Register.

9. Precisely the tactic he followed with Goring, when he felt obliged to convey fields to him while a courtier in high and useful position, see n. 5 above. The full title of the anonymous tract was '*The Way to be Rich, According to the Practices of the Great Audley*', pub. 1662 and reprinted in D'Israeli, *Curiosities*.

10.   '*The Way to be Rich*'.
11.   Cal. SP, Treasury Books, 1660–7, p. 83.
12.   John Evelyn, *Diary*, (ed. E.S. de Beer, Oxford, OUP, 1955), 10 May 1654.
13.   Pepys, 20 May 1668. He visited again in August, in spite of – perhaps
      because of – his bad opinion.
14.   Etheridge, *She Would if She Could*, Act III, Sc I & 2. Shadwell, in *The
      Humorists*, also makes one of his characters say , 'Aye, I was there [in
      Mulberry Garden] and the garden was very full, Madam, of gentlemen
      and ladies that made love together till twelve o'clock of the night . . .'
15.   *Gentleman's Magazine*, 1745, p. 99.
16.   On the road from Windsor, in 1663.
17.   Crown Lease Book p. 1542; Grosvenor London Documents, no. 85.

14. MARRIAGE MARKET

1.   Anyone subsequently writing about Mary Davies is enormously indebted to
      Gatty, *Mary Davies*, although I have treated some of his theses with caution.
2.   Note on an early map in possession of the Grosvenor Estates; House of
      Commons' Journal VIII, p. 483.
3.   Gatty, *Mary Davies*, Vol. I. Alexander created a trust in favour of his
      children but died leaving a sole surviving daughter, Mary, to inherit.
      Under this settlement his widow should have inherited £100 a year only,
      plus their lodging which he probably did not own.
4.   Anon. pamphlet entitled 'London Triumphs', 1677, Guildhall Library.
5.   In 1667, when he went to see Charles II lay the first stone of the new
      Royal Exchange, and Davies was one of the sheriffs.
6.   From the Bill introduced to the House of Commons, 28 April 1675, 'For
      vesting lands of Alex. Davies, Gentleman, deceased, in trustees for payment
      of his debts'. It received the Royal Assent on 22 November.
7.   Document of Release, signed by Thomas Grosvenor, 1 Oct. 1677, Archive
      of Grosvenor Estates.

15. THE FIRST GRANDEE

1.   John Sheffield, Duke of Buckingham, 'Memoir of Arlington' in *Complete
      Works* (2 vols., London, 1740), Vol. II (see Ch. 16, n. 5). Wood, *Athenae*;
      DNB; V. Barbour, '*Arlington*', prize essay reprinted by the American
      Historical Association, 1913.
2.   Bishop Burnet, *History of My Own Time* (ed. 1833), Vol. I, p. 182 et seq.
3.   *Memoires of the Comte de Gramont*, 1713 (trs. Peter Quennell, London, 1930).
4.   Carte MSS in Bodleian Library, intelligence letter 15 Jan. 1666 to Sir
      Philip Frowde.
5.   Pepys, 12 July 1666 (and 10 July 1660 for Nan Hartlibb's sister's wedding visit).
6.   Evelyn (*Diary*) describes Arlington's 'one expensive vice' of building to
      the very limits of his fortune (9 Sept. 1678). In fact, Arlington possessed
      most of the expensive vices with the exception of libertinism, but few
      swallowed cash quite so quickly as lavish building works.

7. 3 July 1673, '. . . Lady Arlington carried us up to her new dressing room, where there was . . . silver jars and vases and other so rich furniture as I had seldom seen'.

8. Anonymous tract 'England's Appeal from the Private Cabal at White Hall to the Great Council of the Nation etc', 1671, reprinted in State Tracts.

9. George Villiers, Duke of Buckingham (not Sheffield) *Works* (2 vols., London, 1775), Vol. II.

10. Evelyn, *Diary*, 1 Aug. 1672.

11. Ibid., 21 Sept. 1671. In 1698 most of the Palace of Whitehall burned down, and was subsequently abandoned; as a result government offices spread like a stain across its ruins.

12. Evelyn's Diary, 10 Dec. 1675.

13. Ruvigny to Pomponne, 21 Nov. 1675, Archive Aff. Etrangéres (Angleterre) 117, f. 92, (Paris), quoted Barbour, '*Arlington*'.

14. Evelyn, *Diary*, 6 Sept. 1676.

15. Lord Bristol's Diary, 7 Feb. 1723.

16. John Verney to Sir Robert Verney, 29 Sept. 1679, Verney Papers at Claydon.

17. MSS of Marquess of Ormonde VI, 23 March 1681, Colonel Edward Cooke to Ormonde, quoted Barbour, '*Arlington*'.

18. Larwood, *London Parks,* Vol. II; Evelyn, *Diary*, 19 Sept. 1667 noted 'In the afternoon I saw a wrestling match for £1,000 in St James's Park before His Majesty, a world of lords and other spectators, twixt the Western and Northern men . . . the Western men won and great sums were wagered'. Pepys, in April 1661, wrote, 'To St James's Park where I saw the Duke of York play at pell mell, the first time I ever saw the sport;' and on 15 Dec. 'To the duke [of York] who would go to the park to slide upon his skaits, which I did not like, tho' he slides very well'.

19. Conveyance, 22 Oct 1681, Grosvenor Estates; Copy plan, Crace Collection, Portfolio 10, no. 30, British Library.

20. A new sewer was levied for and built in 1662 to further drain St James's Park into old Tyburn, which can only have increased the nuisance.

21. N. Brett-James, *The Growth of Stuart London* (London and Middlesex Archaeological Society, 1935).

22. MSS of the Duke of Rutland, Lady Chaworth to the Earl of Rutland, 6 Nov. 1683.

23. North, *Examen*, p. 29, quoted Barbour, '*Arlington*'.

24. Character of Lord Arlington, Buckingham, *Works*. Dryden was also a good if somewhat sycophantic friend of Arlington and wrote some sickly verses which nevertheless interestingly describe the mixed rustic/sophisticated setting of Arlington House:

> . . . Here falling statesmen Fortune's changes feel,
> And prove the turns of her revolving wheel . . .
> Here watch the fearful deer their tender fawns,
> Stray through the wood or browse the verdant lawns,
> Here from the marshy glade the wild duck springs . . .
> A thousand graces bless th' inchanted ground
> And throw promiscuous beauties all around . . .'

16. BUCKINGHAM

1. Allan Fea, *James II and his Wives* (London, Methuen, 1908).
2. Wolseley, *Life of the Duke of Marlborough* (London, 1894), Vol. I, p. 189.
3. Fea, *James II*.
4. N. Luttrell (ed.), *A Brief Historicall Relation . . . 1678–1714* (6 vols, Oxford, OUP, 1657), Vol. IV: 'July 1 1707, Saturday last the Dukes of Devon and Bucks had a tryal in the exchequer. The latter sued the former for damages occassion'd by a fire some time since in Arlington House, and the jury gave the Duke of Buckingham £330.'
5. Sheffield, 'Character', in *Collected Works*, Vol. II, p. 236. The less biased critic was John Macky, *Memoirs* (London, 1733), with characters of the courtiers of Great Britain (with MS notes by Dean Swift).
6. Harleian MS V p. 246.
7. Macky, *Memoirs*: S. Baxter, *William III* (Harlow, Longman, 1966) and David Ogg, *England in the Reigns of James II and William III* (Oxford, OUP, 1957); DNB (Buckingham); J.H. Plumb, *Growth of Political Stability in England* (London, Macmillan, 1967).
8. Abel Boyer *History of the Reign of Queen Anne, Digested into annals* (London, 1703, et seq).

17. 'A NEW PALACE COME TO TOWN'

1. In an etched view of the London Hospital published in 1753, a massive mound is shown to the right of the picture, probably the crumbling remains of Whitechapel Fort, which gives some idea of just how large these works were.
2. A previously unpublished letter from Vanbrugh to the Duke of Newcastle was printed by *Country Life*, 21 Nov. 1951, which comments, among other things, on 'the vexations suffered by my lord of Normanby [i.e. Buckingham]' over properly establishing the site of his new house.
3. 23 Aug. 1703, 'The Queen notes that the Duke of Buckingham hath gone further into the Park then he had leave from the Queen to do'. The Surveyor-General was asked to report, but no further action followed. RA, Windsor.
4. Buckingham, *Works*.
5. Boyer, *Queen Anne*.
6. Dean Swift, *Journal to Stella* (ed. and collected in one volume by George Aitken, London, Methuen, 1901).
7. Ibid.
8. E.S. Turner, *The Court of St James's* (London, Michael Joseph, 1959).
9. Letter to the Duke of Shrewsbury in Buckingham, *Works*.
10. Ibid. Interestingly, he says he often sat there looking out at 'a Wildernesse full of blackbirds and nightingales', which, in an otherwise formal layout, could represent the planted-up roughnesses connected with the old fort.
11. E. Hatton, *A New View of London* (London, 1708), an architectural and discursive survey. Reprinted and enlarged in 1788.

12.   Anecdote re. Winde quoted in W.B.S. Taylor, *Fine Arts in Great Britain* (London, 1920), reprinted in Clifford Smith, *Buckingham Palace* (Country Life, 1931). The duke did eventually pay many of his bills. Buckingham's own manuscript accounts survive in the library of London University; titled 'The intire Expence about my House', in which he details the huge cost of such a project, although not necessarily when each individual was actually paid. The fountain in the courtyard cost £1,497 10s., possibly the equivalent of annual pay for sixty labourers on his property. Brickwork cost £7,000, digging a drainage canal in the garden, £1,000. As a special payment, Arlington's daughter Tata received £107 10s. for her orange trees in tubs.

13.   Colin Campbell, *Vitruvius Britannicus*, (London, 1717), Vol. I.

14.   Revd Francis Kilvert (ed.), *A Selection from Unpublished papers of William Warburton, Bishop of Gloucester* (London, 1841).

15.   Letter to the Duke of Shrewsbury in Villiers, *Works*, Vol. II.

16.   Letter from the Duchess of Buckingham to Mrs Howard (later the Countess of Suffolk), Suffolk Papers, Vol. I, p. 117.

17.   Warburton (ed.), *Memoirs and Letters, Horace Walpole* (London, 1852). A draft of Buckingham's epitaph appeared in *The Times* on the day after his death and excited considerable comment, whereupon a Dr Strange, friend of the Dean of Westminster (Atterbury) wrote to him 13 March 1721 'Were I dean I fancy I should never let it be put up'. Quoted in S. Beeching, *Atterbury* (London, Putnam, 1929).

18. ROYAL PURCHASE

1.   Letter from Revd Allen, Vice Principal of Magdalen College, Oxford, quoted in *Biographa Britannica* (London, 1763), Vol. VI, pt I.

2.   Codicil to his will, 1734. There is a mysterious plaque in Westminster Abbey cloisters which reads: 'To the memory of Magdalen Walsh, one of the daughters of Robert Walsh of Walsh Mountains, Ireland. She, with her sister Margaret Daly were the only co-heiresses of Edmund Sheffield, late Duke of Buckingham and Normanby. Born in Ireland 1684, died in London 1747.' How they connected and what they inherited, I have not discovered.

3.   *Biographa Britannica*, (London, 1763), Vol. VI, pt I.

4.   Ibid.; also Horace Walpole, *Memoirs of the Last Ten Years of the Reign of George II* (ed. Lord Holland, London, 1847), and Horace Walpole, *Memoirs of the Reign of George III* (ed. G.R.F. Barker, London, 1894), Vol. I.

5.   Mary, Countess Cowper's Diary, 1714–20 (London, 1864).

6.   Lord Chesterfield, *Letters* (collected by Jo Justamond, London, 1777), with 'A supplement to his Lordship's Letters with Characters of Eminent Personages of His Own Time written by the late Lord Chesterfield and never before published'.

7.   Royal Library Windsor: 'Buckingham Palace, History and Plans of the Grounds . . . Being extracts from the Surveys, Entries and Records of the Surveyor-General's office etc, relative to the Freehold and Leasehold Estates purchased by His Majesty of Sir Charles Sheffield, Bt, in the year 1762.'

8. Signed by the Earl of Bute and Philip Carteret Webb, in trust for the King: Agreement to Purchase in Royal Archives (RA) Windsor.

9. Larwood, *London Parks*, Vol. II, p. 421. Another flood occurred in Sept. 1768 when a storm uprooted trees and the Thames burst its banks; in Dec. the same year the old drains under the park collapsed under the pressure of water and the entire area was again unundated.

10. Schulenburg, letter to George III quoted in Pain, *George III at Home* (Eyre Methuen, 1975). For Queen Charlotte see Papendiek, *Court and Private Life of the Time of Queen Charlotte* (ed. Broughton, 2 vols, London, 1886), Vols. I and II; also *George III: His Court and Family* (an anonymous description, London, 1820).

11. Walpole, *Memoirs* (ed. Barker).

12. Ibid. Pain, *George III*.

13. J. Huish, *Memoirs of George III* (London, 1861), p. 350. J.H. Jesse, *Memoirs of the Life and Reign of George III* (3 vols, London, 1867), Vols. I, II and III.

14. Lady Llanover (ed.), *Autobiography and Correspondence of Mary Granville Delany* (London, 1861).

15. PRO Abstracts of Accounts, George III, detail many of the alterations; Northouck (architect) 1773, quoted by Clifford Smith, *Buckingham Palace*. The Duke of Buckingham's gates (which bore his arms) were replaced by unpretentious railings and his fountain disappeared; the frontage appears to have been re-bricked and simplified.

16. J. Boswell, *Life of Johnson* (Everyman Edition), Vol. I, pp. 334–9.

17. Walpole, *Memoirs* (ed. Barker).

19. THE QUEEN'S HOUSE

1. 15Geo III c33. 'His Majesty, desirous that better and more suitable accommodation should be made for the Queen in case she survives him . . . makes provision for settling the same palace upon Her Majesty . . .' (Part of the king's message to parliament, 12 April 1775).

2. Grenville, when Prime Minister, is said to have refused the king £20,000 which would have enabled him to purchase further land to increase the privacy of Buckingham Palace. This land is now Grosvenor Place and adjoining streets with overlooking tower blocks.

3. Mrs D'Arblay, *Diary and Correspondence of Fanny Burney* (ed. G.F. Barrett, 6 vols., London, 1904). Huish, *George III*, records a major disturbance in 1787 when the king discovered a louse on his dinner plate and ordered all the cooks' heads to be shaved, which precipitated a strike and 'great and impudent boldness of language' in the kitchens.

4. Wolford (ed.), *London Old and New* (London, 1873).

5. Larwood, *London Parks*, Vol. II, p. 438.

6. Ibid., p. 442.

7. Altenburg, *Bemerkungen eines Reisenden durch England im Briefe* (1775), Vol. II, p. 416.

8. Larwood, *London Parks*, Vol. II, p. 488. Queen Charlotte also kept her pet zebra there; fortunately King James's crocodiles had long since vanished.

9.   Diary of Mrs Lybbe Powys, 23 March 1767.

10.   The best account of the Gordon Riots is by Christopher Hibbert, *King Mob* (Harlow, Longmans, 1955).

11.   Barker, *Walpole*; Roger Fulford, *The Royal Dukes* (London, Collins, 1973), is a detailed and entertaining study of George III's children, especially his sons.

12.   Charles Greville wrote in his memoirs (1938 edition, p. 271) '. . . the princesses are secluded from the world and with their passions boiling over'. One probably had an illegitimate child in the palace. Elizabeth eventually married the Landgrave of Hesse-Homburg, of whom the Duke of Buckingham and Chandos wrote that he was 'the ugliest hound with a snout buried in hair that I ever saw'.

13.   H. Rush, *Memorandum of a Residence at the Court of London* (New York, 1833).

20. A MONSTROUS INSULT TO THE NATION

1.   C.D.Yonge, *Life and Administration of the 2nd Earl of Liverpool* (London, 1868), p. 402; Commons' Journals for 1825. On 11 Nov. 1829 the *Evening Standard* stated that 'It is positively determined that St James's palace shall be pulled down as soon as Buckingham Palace is completed and ready for the King. To forward the new palace such workmen as can, proceed by candlelight, and are engaged until ten o'clock nightly. The site of St James's palace will be partly used as a roadway.' But newspapers are not always accurate, and evidence of an official scheme is lacking.

2.   The various stages in Nash's work (which confused even the architect himself, and his patron) are unravelled in H.M. Colvin (ed.), *History of the King's Works* (HMSO, 1973),Vol.VI.

3.   DNB for Nash's earlier career; Parliamentary Select Commission of Enquiry 1831; Colvin, *King's Works*. A foundation of Nash's career as royal architect was probably the fact he married one of the Prince Regent's cast-off mistresses.

4.   Goulburn MSS, Surrey Record Office; Treasury Minute 15 Oct. 1830 quoted in Colvin, *King's Works*.

5.   Colvin, *King's Works*.

6.   Broughton, *Recollections of Long Life* (London, 1911), says he remembered William IV saying to the Speaker, 'Mind, I mean Buckingham palace as a permanent gift! Mind that!'

7.   Colvin, *King's Works*, p. 281.

8.   T. Gore (ed.), *A Selection of the Letters and papers of Thomas Creevey* (London, Murray, 1948).

9.   Letter to a friend, 20 June 1835, quoted in B. Graeme, *A Century of Buckingham Palace* (London, Hutchinson, 1937).

10.   Printed in Huish, *George III* – who appears to take it deadpan seriously.

11.   Gore, *Thomas Creevey*. Even after such a fundamental rebuild, some interior measurements remain those of old Buckingham House, e.g. the Grand Hall and Marble Hall. Seventeenth-century carved festoons above overmantles in the Marble Hall may just possibly be survivors from the 'pretty gallery' in old Arlington House; John Harris et al. *Buckingham Palace* (Nelson, 1968), pp. 42–3.

21. 'EVERYTHING MOST FILTHY AND OFFENSIVE'

1. Viscount Esher, *The Girlhood of Queen Victoria, Selection from her Letters and Diaries, 1832–40* (London, Murray, 1912), Vol. VI.
2. 'Her Majesty's new Throne', *Morning Post*, 27 July 1837.
3. Queen Victoria's Journal, 13 July 1837 et seq.
4. Blore had reported them as damp, and proposed raising the floor by two feet, but nothing seems to have been done.
5. Details taken from Sir Benjamin Stephenson's report to the Commissioners of Woods & Works, RA Windsor; See also Melbourne Papers, Duncannon to Melbourne 6 Sept. 1838, RA; Report of Conyngham to Melbourne, Sept. 1838, RA. Baron Stockmar, *Memoirs*, (London, 1872), also his report to the Prince Consort: 'Observations on the Present State of the Royal Household', Sept. 1841, RA.
6. Memo by Lord Anson, 24 Oct. 1841, RA Y 54/89.
7. Melbourne Papers, Murray to the queen, 4 Dec. 1838, describing Cotton's examination, RA.
8. Melbourne Papers, RA; *The Times*, 4 Dec. 1840; Cecil Woodham Smith traces Jones's later movements in *Queen Victoria*, Vol. I. (PRO, Admiralty Rec.).
9. Duncannon to Melbourne, 6 Sept. 1838, RA: 'The smell was most offensive and as it appeared to proceed from the basement kitchen offices, Sir Benjamin (Stephenson) proceeded there . . . where he found the remains of garden stuff and everything else the most filthy and offensive and evidently had not been touched. . . .'

22. THE HARD ROAD TO REFORM

1. Charles Greville (London, 1887), Vol. IV, p. 132. Greville's position as Clerk to the Privy Council from 1821 to 1857 gave him a unique insight into personalities.
2. Greville, Vol. IV, p. 200.
3. Ibid.
4. Lord Holland to Greville, 20 May 1839.
5. Queen Victoria's Journal, 15–18 April 1839.
6. Ibid., 19 Dec. 1839; 27–31 Jan., and 2–6 Feb. 1840.
7. Ibid., 10 Jan. 1840.
8. Melbourne Papers, RA, Report by Hogg (Clerk of Works at Buckingham Palace) 25 Oct. 1838; Murray's memos, 12 May, 29 Nov., 1 Dec. 1838.
9. RA Add U2/5: The Prince Consort to Stockmar 18 Jan. 1842.
10. Stockmar, 'Observations'. Prince Albert told Sir Robert Peel in 1845 that the 'palace is admitted by everyone to be a disgrace to the Sovereign and the Nation'; (from Mrs Hugh Wyndham (ed.), *Lady Lyttletons's Correspondence* (London, 1912), p. 354.
11. A proposal that the palace should house the National Gallery and a new royal residence be built at Kensington was briefly canvassed but soon discarded.

12. Minute of Regulations for the Royal Households at Buckingham Palace and Windsor Castle, Lord Chamberlain's Office, 18 June 1846; Sir T. Martin, *Life of the Prince Consort* (London, 1880), Vol. I, p. 160.

13. Not before the Prince Consort had thriftily insisted on removing the best chimney-pieces to the new wing being built at Buckingham Palace, where they still are.

14. Clifford Smith, *Buckingham Palace,* considers him the best architect to have worked at the palace.

15. Queen Victoria's Journal, 28 Feb. 1854.

16. *The Manners and Rules of Good Society*, by a Member of the Aristocracy, published in the 1880s, sets out exactly who was and was not entitled to attend Court, what they were expected to do there and how they should act if they discovered a tradesman or manufacturer had illicitly sneaked an invitation (inform the Lord Chancellor's staff instantly, so that the offender could be unceremoniously ejected).

17. *Dress Circular*, 1854.

18. G.T. Curtis, *Life of James Buchanan* (New York, 1900).

19. Sir Frederick Ponsonby, *Recollections of Three Reigns* (Eyre & Spottiswoode, 1951); Baron von Eckhardstein, *Ten Years at the Court of St James* (London, Butterworth, 1921); Princess Marie Louise, *My Memories of Six Reigns* (London, Evans, 1956).

20. Sir Felix Leman, *Autobiography* (London, 1927).

21. Turner, *St James's*.

22. July 1902.

23. Sir Leonard Cust, *King Edward VII and his Court*, (London, John Murray, 1938).

24. Emrys Hughes, *Life of Kier Hardie*, (London, 1956).

23. MODERN TIMES

1. Colvin, *King's Works*.

2. See Ch. 22, n. 11. Viscount Esher, in his introduction to *The Girlhood of Queen Victoria*, indicates that no one realized more clearly than the king that his personal inclination was unrealistic. Esher was a rather weird eminence grise who hovered closely behind the throne.

3. Letter from Queen Alexandra to Edward, Prince of Wales, 10 Dec. 1910 quoted in Pope Hennessy, *Queen Mary* (London, Allen & Unwin, 1959).

4. Harris et al., *Buckingham Palace*, from the introductory essay by John Russell.

5. Again like George III, almost every action of his day was ruled by preconceived times and distances, from exercise in the palace gardens to exact hours spent working on despatch boxes. Detailed daily barometric observations prefixed even the diary account of his coronation: '22 June 1911. Overcast and cloudy with some showers and a strongish cool breeze, but better for the people than great heat.'

6. The opening of parliament continued to be an ordeal he described as 'terrible' as late in his reign as 1928, quoted in Kenneth Rose, *King George V*, (London, Weidenfeld & Nicolson, 1983).

7. From his satirical *Ballade Tragique* in S.N. Behrman *Conversations with Max* (London, Hamish Hamilton, 1956) and quoted in Rose, *George V*.

8. 5 June 1914.

9. Fenner Brockway, *Socialism over Sixty Years, Life of Lord Jowett of Bradford* (London, Allen & Unwin, 1946).

10. Mr J.J. Jones.

11. Eleanor Roosevelt, *On My Own* (New York, Harper & Row, 1958), quoted in Christopher Hibbert, *The Court of St James's* (London, Weidenfeld & Nicolson, 1970).

Select Bibliography

In trying to trace the history of one famous building, its land and occupants through two thousand years, my selection of personalities has inevitably been idiosyncratic, the sources I consulted many and variable in reliability and value. Most are listed in the notes and references, and those given below are titles which I found of most use, particularly entertaining, interesting or accessible; a few possess all of these agreeable characteristics. (Places of publication are given only if outside London.)

EARLY TIMES AND GENERAL DEVELOPMENT

Marsden, Peter. *Roman London*, Thames & Hudson, 1980
Cottrell, Leonard. *The Great Invasion*, Evans, 1960
Frere, Sheppard. *Britannia*, Routledge, 1987
Barlow, Frank. *Edward the Confessor*, Eyre Methuen, 1970
—— (ed.). *Vita Edwardi Regis*, Nelson's Medieval Texts, 1962
Douglas, David C. *William the Conqueror*, Eyre & Spottiswoode, 1964
Rutton, William Loftie. 'Manor of Eaia', *Archaeologica*, January 1910
Slocombe, George. *Sons of the Conqueror*, Hutchinson, 1960
Bishop, T.A.M. and Chaplais, P. *Facsimiles of English Royal Writs*, Oxford, OUP, 1957
Barton, N.J. *Lost Rivers of London*, Phoenix House, 1962
Brooke, Christopher. *London AD 800–1216, Shaping of a City*, Secker, 1975
Harrison, H. *London Growing*, Hutchinson, 1965
Chaplais, P. 'The Original Charters of Herbert and Gervase, Abbots of Westminster 1121–1157, in *A Medieval Miscellany for Doris Mary Stenton*, ed. P.M. Barnes and C.F. Slade, Pipe Rolls Society, New Series, Vol. xxxvi, 1961
Rosser, G. *Medieval Westminster*, Oxford, OUP, 1989
Carpenter, E. (ed.). *A House of Kings, the Official History of Westminster Abbey*, Westminster Abbey Bookshop, 1966
Armitage Robinson, J. (ed.). *Flete's History of Westminster Abbey*, 1909
Barker, Felix and Jackson, Peter. *London, 2000 Years of a City and its People*, Cassell, 1974
Victoria County Histories of London and Wiltshire
Larwood, J. *The Story of the London Parks*, 2 vols., 1881
Chancellor, E.B. *The West End Yesterday and Today*, Architectural Press, 1926
Besant, Sir Walter. *London*, 8 vols., 1898–1908

Turner, E.S. *The Court of St James's*, Michael Joseph, 1959

Hibbert, Christopher. *The Court of St James's*, Weidenfeld & Nicolson, 1979

Graves, C. *Palace Extraordinary* [St James's], Cassell, 1963

MEDIEVAL AND EARLY MODERN

Tout, T.F. 'A Medieval Burglary', lecture in *Bulletin of the John Rylands Library*, 1915, reprinted in his *Collected Papers*, Vol. III, Manchester University Press, 1934.

Coleman, D.C. (ed.). *Trade, Government and Industry in Pre-industrial England*, Macmillan, 1976

Vickers, K.H. *Humphrey, Duke of Gloucester*, Constable, 1972

Ashton, R. *The Crown and the Money Market*, Oxford, OUP, 1960

Willson, D.H. *James VI and I*, Jonathan Cape, 1963

Ashton, R. (ed.), *James I by his Contemporaries*, Cambridge, CUP, 1969

Askrigg, G.P.V. *Jacobean Pageant*, Harvard UP, 1962

Prestwich, M. *Cranfield and the Politics of Profit*, Oxford, OUP, 1976

Friis, A. *Alderman Cockayne's Project*, Oxford, OUP, 1927

Hyman, W. *Court Patronage and Corruption*, Unwin, 1991

Gatty, C.T. *Mary Davies and the Manor of Ebury*, 2 vols., Cassell, 1921

Brett-James, N. *The Fortification of London 1642/3*, London Topographical Society, 1927

Barbour, V. '*Arlington*', prize essay reprinted by the American Historical Association (apparently distributed but not printed by OUP in England in 1914)

Starkey, D. (ed.). *The English Court from the Wars of the Roses to the Civil War*, Harlow, Longman, 1987

Fea, A. *James II and his Wives*, Methuen, 1908

HANOVERIAN AND MODERN

Lloyd, Alan. *The Wickedest Age [George III]*, Newton Abbot, David & Charles, 1971

Walpole, Horace. *Memoirs of the Last Ten Years of the Reign of George II*, ed. Lord Holland, 1847

——. *Memoirs of the Reign of George III*, ed. G.F.R. Barker, 1894

Pain, N. *George III at Home*, Eyre Methuen, 1975

Fulford, Roger. *The Royal Dukes*, Collins, 1973

——. *The Prince Consort*, Collins, 1949

Woodham Smith, C. *Queen Victoria*, vol. I, Hamish Hamilton, 1972

Longford, Elizabeth. *Victoria RI*, Weidenfeld & Nicolson, 1964

Ponsonby, Sir Frederick. *Recollections of Three Reigns*, Eyre & Spottiswoode, 1951

Princess Marie Louise. *My Memories of Six Reigns*, Evans, 1956

Cust, Sir Lionel. *Edward VII and his Court*, John Murray, 1930

Rose, Kenneth. *King George V*, Weidenfeld & Nicolson, 1983

Colvin, H.M. (ed.). *History of the King's Works*, vol. VI, HMSO, 1973

Clifford Smith, H. *Buckingham Palace*, Country Life, 1931

Graeme, B. *A Century of Buckingham Palace 1837–1937,* Hutchinson, 1937

Harris, John, et al. *Buckingham Palace*, Nelson, 1968

Index

Page numbers given in italic refer to illustrations.
References are indexed only where they supply new information.